DOMINATION

DOMINATION

The Fall of the Roman Empire
and the Rise of Christianity

PROFESSOR
ALICE ROBERTS

SIMON &
SCHUSTER

London · New York · Amsterdam/Antwerp · Sydney/Melbourne · Toronto · New Delhi

First published in Great Britain by Simon & Schuster UK Ltd, 2025

Copyright © Alice Roberts, 2025

The right of Alice Roberts to be identified as the author of this work has been asserted in accordance with the Copyright, Designs and Patents Act, 1988.

1 3 5 7 9 10 8 6 4 2

Simon & Schuster UK Ltd, 1st Floor
222 Gray's Inn Road, London WC1X 8HB

www.simonandschuster.co.uk
www.simonandschuster.com.au
www.simonandschuster.co.in

Simon & Schuster Australia, Sydney
Simon & Schuster India, New Delhi

The authorised representative in the EEA is Simon & Schuster Netherlands BV, Herculesplein 96, 3584 AA Utrecht, Netherlands. info@simonandschuster.nl

The author and publishers have made all reasonable efforts to contact copyright-holders for permission, and apologise for any omissions or errors in the form of credits given. Corrections may be made to future printings.

Simon & Schuster strongly believes in freedom of expression and stands against censorship in all its forms. For more information, visit BooksBelong.com.

A CIP catalogue record for this book is available from the British Library

Hardback ISBN: 978-1-3985-1008-1
Trade Paperback ISBN: 978-1-3985-1009-8
eBook ISBN: 978-1-3985-1010-4

Typeset in Perpetua by M Rules
Printed and Bound in the UK using 100% Renewable Electricity at CPI Group (UK) Ltd

MIX
Paper | Supporting
responsible forestry
FSC
www.fsc.org   FSC® C013604

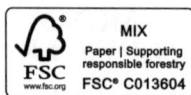

'Archaeology is in an unequalled position to help shape revised views of the written data and thus to write new histories . . .'

GUY HALSALL (2010)

CONTENTS

III

The Heart of Empire

IV

The Business of Empire

V
Ruler of All

A QUESTION IN A CLIFF

Some twenty years ago, I found myself hanging on a rope, looking at the face of a red sandstone cliff. Pale, broken bones were sticking out of the earth near the top of the cliff. Part of a clifftop cemetery, these bones had been eroding out over time, tumbling onto the beach below, where they were discovered by walkers. I was part of a small team mounting a rescue operation to recover some of these remains and find out more about this small, forgotten cemetery on the coast of South Wales. One of the graves further back from the cliff edge was covered by a stone slab on which a cross had been roughly hewn. It was old, maybe seventh century. Some other cemeteries in Pembrokeshire, containing long cists – stone-lined graves like this – are even earlier, going back to the fifth century.

I became fascinated in burial archaeology; in questions about the relationship between archaeology and history; about whether we can trace the spread of ideas and beliefs through changes in material culture, especially during a time in Britain that is so deeply shrouded in mystery. That cross-inscribed stone got me thinking. How did Christianity reach the west? How did this religion travel so far from the land where it started, far away in the Middle East? How did it become so powerful, so quickly – how did it supersede other belief systems and rise to domination over such a vast stretch of territory?

And then I caught myself – because talking about 'it', as though this religion had some agency of its own, is too abstract. I realised that what I really wanted to understand was *who* had spread this religion. *Who, how* and *why.* What did people have to gain from joining this religious movement? If I could answer that, I'd get closer to understanding how and why Christianity was so successful.

As I started to dig into these questions, I knew that I wanted to look for evidence from many different sources. I set out prospecting for archaeological clues – hard, physical evidence. But I knew that there would be plenty of clues in the written histories too, perhaps even some that had been overlooked; hidden by a veil of mysticism, obscured by myth, worn by the passage of time.

And so I embarked on an investigative journey, which would take me from a secluded valley in South Wales to the shores of Brittany, to the heart of the Roman Empire in a time of political turmoil; in the footsteps of the apostle Paul, to the ancient city of Corinth; to fourth-century Alexandria on the Nile Delta, to Constantinople and back to the disintegrating Roman Empire in the west. And I was astonished by the answers I found. I was also surprised by how many people had been looking at this question in various different scholarly fields, while barriers between these disciplines seemed to have prevented the exchange of ideas, making it difficult to reach a holistic, integrated answer. (Some people are clearly trying to join up the conversation, but there also seems to be some resistance.)

Christianity was many things to many people, of course, as we shall see, but I ended with a surprising idea about what the

Church actually *was*, which shed a light on how it had become so successful in such a short time. What I hadn't anticipated when I set out was that quite so many myths would be uncovered, exposed and pierced in the course of my enquiry: myths of humble origins, asceticism, pacifism – and the popular narrative that Christianity was ever about questioning the *status quo*, or challenging 'the establishment'.

Come along with me, then, as I delve into this archaeology and history – and lift the veil on secrets that have been hidden in plain sight.

A NOTE ON PAGANS

'Paganism' is a tricky word. It seems to be a derogatory term used by Christians, since the fourth century, for anyone who wasn't a Christian. In pre-Christian Latin, *paganus* meant 'rustic', 'countryside dweller' – someone unsophisticated. But it also had a military connotation as 'civilian', perhaps capturing the idea of someone who was not a 'soldier of Christ'. Christians also used other less pejorative Latin terms for non-Christians, including *gentes, nationes, ethnici* and sometimes *Graeci* (Greeks). The Greek *Hellenes* (Greeks, Hellenes) was used by Paul to refer to non-Jewish people, but is also used elsewhere in the Bible for Greek-speaking Jews. All these markers of in-groups and out-groups are complicated, and meanings change over time. Today, we're perhaps most familiar with the term 'pagan' and occasionally 'gentile' today for people who were non-Christian, and then also 'pagan' for ancient non-Christian beliefs and religion – lumping all of that huge cultural diversity under one label.

Some historians replace paganism with 'polytheism', but this still sets up a hard dichotomy between Jewish and Christian monotheism on the one hand, and Greco-Roman polytheism on the other. However, some followers of traditional religions – such as those who saw Apollo or Sol Invictus (often assimilated together) as the one, supreme god – were effectively monotheists, or at least henotheists (believing one god to be superior to all the others).

Eusebius of Caesarea is one writer who attempted to define all the religions that existed in the ancient world. In his *Praeparatio Evangelica*, written between 313 and 324 CE, he wrote about the religions of the Greeks and barbarians, in the cities and the countryside, and how myths and rituals had developed and spread through contact between different cultures; he saw them as all having something in common, as branches of the same tree. He was rehearsing an idea that earlier writers had articulated. But what he didn't do was recognise Judaism, and its offspring Christianity, as branches of that tree; Eusebius wanted to set these two religions apart, and to lump all the others together as one thing, 'paganism', even if he didn't use that word.

Historians and theologians through time have tended to follow the same taxonomic instinct as Eusebius – categorising Judaism and Christianity as something *completely* different from all the other religions around at the time. This is to ignore the evolution of those religions out of polytheistic traditions (so brilliantly expounded in *Anatomy of God* by the historian of religion Francesca Stavrakopolou) while also glossing over the many elements that Christianity borrowed, not just from other religions, but also from Greek philosophy. Writers in antiquity were also divided – some stressing the separateness of Christianity from traditional Greco-Roman philosophy and religion; others emphasising a continuity with antique intellectual traditions.

Now I'm in a bind, as I want to look at the expansion of

Christianity from a political perspective, and so it's useful to have an understandable word that sums up 'the rest', and in modern discourse 'paganism' is that word. So I'm getting my excuses in here, as to why I'm persisting in using the term. But at the same time, I want to emphasise that it's really just a convenient label. We shouldn't take it to mean that there are no similarities or links between Christianity and 'pagan' beliefs and practices. To do that would be to fall into a dangerous trap where Christianity springs into existence in a moment of divine creation, rather than evolving out of the Jewish tradition and then absorbing many different influences — including Greek philosophy and broader Roman culture. It's possible to push the uniqueness of Christianity to a point where you end up with a very myopic or blinkered view, where any ideas and practices that emerged within a Christian framework or setting are seen as entirely *de novo* inventions. (Some theologians and historians have been guilty of doing this in the past, treating concepts of morality and charity as uniquely Christian, for instance.) Those blinkers also discourage us from looking at wider political, social and other more personal reasons for human behaviour; instead, reducing everything to theology and personal religious beliefs.

People are complex, human societies are complex, and over the course of my investigation, I found many and varied reasons to explain the success of Christianity. But by the end, I would be very sure that the main reasons were not to be found in the pages of the Bible, but in a powerful alliance born of complex — and very human — incentives.

LAND OF SAINTS

'Both the laity and clergy in Ireland, Scotland and
Wales held in such veneration portable bells . . .
that they were much more afraid of swearing
falsely by them than the gospels; because from
some hidden and miraculous power with which
they are gifted, and the vengeance of the saint
to whom they are particularly pleasing, their
despisers and transgressors are severely punished.'

GERALD OF WALES (C. 1146–1223 CE)

The Lost Monastery

I arrived in Llantwit Major on a beautiful summer day, though there was an unusual chill in the air. Driving along progressively narrower lanes looping around St Illtud's medieval church, I eventually found myself turning through a gate into a sloping field, fringed with ash trees that seemed to have miraculously escaped dieback, and elders bearing creamy white flowers. Rooks were chatting loudly in the trees; a wood pigeon cooed. On the lower half of the field, archaeologists had stripped away the turf and were digging down into dark sediments. The remains of tumbledown walls were appearing deep in the earth.

I'd come to see Tim Young, an archaeologist from Cardiff University with a special interest in metallurgy. But what he was hoping to find here wasn't metal – but a monastery. Because there's a story about Llantwit Major – a story that claims it was the site of a very early, and extremely important, medieval monastery. The problem is, there are no traces of it today. Some have suggested that it's little more than a myth, a historical illusion. Archaeology, though, is about the remains of material culture – cold, hard evidence, buried in the ground. Tim was there at Llantwit, with colleagues and a cohort of enthusiastic students, ready to dig into the mystery and search for elusive physical traces of the fabled monastery – if indeed such traces existed. If they did, and he was able to find them, he'd have found the earliest monastery in Wales; perhaps even the earliest monastery in Britain.

The archaeologists had uncovered one wall thought to be of Norman age (five centuries too late for the early medieval period), but it ran over and through earlier walls – could these be part of the lost monastery? Charred wheat found in the last season's dig had been radiocarbon dated to the late sixth/early seventh century. But Tim was really hoping to find even earlier archaeology, from the fifth century – when Britain officially ceased to be part of the Roman Empire and slid into what has been called the Dark Ages. The historical sources are very sparse for this period of British history, making archaeological evidence even more precious. But we do know that it was broadly an era of political turmoil, as the western half of the Roman Empire fragmented into smaller kingdoms. It was also a time of religious transformation, even here, on what had been the extreme north-western edge of the Empire; the ends of the earth. Christianity was spreading and embedding itself in the landscape. And that's what Tim was hoping to trace in these fields below the much later church: some of the earliest traces of that eastern religion, many miles from its birthplace, here in Britain.

Tim opened his hand to show me something he'd found. It was a small lump of clay; I found it hard to believe that it could be a significant clue, but Tim's expertise in ancient metallurgy now came to the fore. This little piece of clay had come from a layer of blackened, charcoal-rich sediment, full of metal-working residues. It was baked hard as stone, and curved to fit *something* on its inner surface. Tim believed that it could, possibly, have once coated a bell. He'd seen this sort of thing before.

Bells feature in early texts from the insular or Celtic Church; they were used to mark time, to call monks to prayer and to punctuate the liturgy. And, as Tim told me, many actual bells still exist – as physical artefacts. Most of these are still held within their churches, where they may have been kept safe by a succession of bell-keepers. Very rarely, they are found in archaeological digs. There are around fifty from Ireland, twelve from Scotland, and a couple from early medieval sites in England. Only one has been found in Wales, but historical sources refer to them being made there: the Welsh saint Gildas was reputed to have made bells for himself, as well as for St Bridget and St Caradoc.

These religious bells were made from sheet iron, folded and riveted, and then finished – brazed – with bronze. Some are inscribed with crosses. They're very similar to other iron bells that were used at the time for a whole range of domestic and agricultural purposes, some of which were also brazed.

In the winter of 2004–2005, archaeologists were digging at a site near Clonfad, in central Ireland, checking for archaeological remains before a new road was constructed. The route of the road had been adjusted to avoid a ruined church and graveyard, but the archaeologists quickly realised that they were digging within the wider enclosure of an abandoned, early medieval monastery. And this site was totally dominated by evidence for iron-working – the archaeologists uncovered nearly 2 tonnes of iron-working debris. (It's an important reminder that monasteries in Britain and Ireland were often sites of industrial metalworking, as well as agricultural estates and trade hubs, and they were often very large compared with high-status secular sites.) Along with the iron-working debris at Clonfad, the archaeologists found fifty-two baked clay fragments. Those pieces of clay were important clues – they preserved the shape of the objects they'd once encased: handbells. Some even bore the impressions of rivets. And they proved crucial to working out how the bells were brazed; Tim Young himself carried out experiments in order to understand the process.

It seems that an iron bell would have been made in the usual way, then wrapped in cloth and finally shrouded in clay, leaving the rim exposed. Then copper ingots were placed on the rim of the upturned bell, which was then put into a brazing hearth. As the cloth burned away, the copper would melt and flow over the surface of the bell, filling the gap between the bell and its clay shroud. When it cooled, the fired clay could be broken off – leaving the newly brazen bell. The thin coat of copper would transform the mundane iron bell into something beautiful, lustrous with divinity, rust-proof – and apparently even sounding better too. The brazen bells would be blessed; later medicval laws differentiated between 'baptised' and 'unbaptised' bells.

So far, there's one other site with evidence of brazen-bell-making like this in Ireland; while many monasteries would have had metalworking happening on site, this creation of brazed bells was a specialist process, requiring expert smithing knowledge and skills. Had Tim just found another brazed-bell-manufacturing site, here in Wales? That fragment of baked clay was too small to be sure, for now – but I hoped Tim's excavation might eventually uncover more. That could strengthen the case for an early ecclesiastical site herc.

I left the trenched field, its dark earth keeping its secrets for now, and crossed the road into the churchyard of St Illtud's. The church sprawled across its whole length. It had been extended several times, growing as long as a cathedral – as long as St David's, the vicar proudly informed me. The latest renovation had involved the transformation of the Galilee chapel at its western end into a gallery to house five great stones which had been hauled inside, out of the churchyard. The move had been controversial; some had wanted the stones left where they belonged, outside, but the patterns on the stones that had survived for centuries were wearing away, and it would be sad to see them disappear now.

Two stones – one short, one tall – may have formed part of

a doorway. Two were like flattened obelisks, or tombstones with sloping sides. One, set in the centre, was a familiar design of Celtic cross – a wheel cross – its circular head reunited with its body. It was covered in intricate patterns: snaking key-patterning and intertwined Celtic lattices. Crosses like this turn up all over Wales, Ireland and Scotland, as a staple of insular art. It's unclear how the design emerged; some have suggested it developed out of a pagan sun symbol. Or that it was designed that way deliberately to appeal to pagans as a new religion took hold. Patterns engraved on Welsh crosses tend to be less elaborate than other examples, but they do often include inscriptions. This cross was no exception – its base was inscribed with a dedication:

hanc crucem Houelt preparavit pro anima Res Patris eius

'This cross Houelt [Hywel] prepared for
the soul of his father Res [Rhys]'

The tall slab to the right of the cross was covered in what looked like a dense pattern at first glance – right across the face that had been determined as its front, standing here in this new gallery. But the writing – cursive Latin – was much more like handwriting than a regular, capital-lettered, Roman inscription. There were no gaps between the words, but with some help, I could match up the inscription with a transcript – and its translation.

*In nomine d[e]i summi incipit crux salutaris quae
preparavit Samsonis apatis pro anima sua et pro
anima Iuthahelo Rex et Artmali et Tecai*

'In the name of God most high begins the cross of
Salvation prepared by [Abbot] Samson for his soul and the
soul of King Iuthahelo [Idwal] and Artmal and Tecai'

Strange names, some of them – almost lost in the shadows of
the Dark Ages. But they can be cross-referenced with literary
references. Samson is a familiar biblical name, and a common
enough name for abbots, it seems, but there is a particular Samson
mentioned in an eighth-century grant, along with a king called
Iudhail, presumed to be a variant spelling of Iuthahelo. A very similar name, Juthael, appears in the royal genealogy of the western
region of Brittany known as Domnonia. These stones, inscribed
with the names of abbots and kings, bear witness to Llantwit
Major having been a very important place indeed – a place with
royal connections. And in fact the court of the pre-Norman kings
of Glamorgan lay just 4 miles to the north, at Llysworney.

The tall stone standing to the left of the wheel cross had also
once been the base of a cross. It was covered in faded patterns
on its front surface, and round the back, I found a crudely inscribed cross followed by just a few letters: *ILTI* . . . the end of
the word had fractured away.

When I got home, I tracked down more information about
this cross and its inscription – in a late-eighteenth-century
journal article, dusted off and digitised in that vast virtual
library of the internet. I noticed the author of that article had
recorded a longer version of the inscription: *ILTU* TI; a couple
more letters had clearly fallen away since that record had been
made. Stylistically, this cross must have been carved in the
tenth century – but the name is that of someone who's thought
to have lived at least *four centuries earlier* – the very saint Llantwit
is named after: Illtud.

Llantwit Major is the anglicised version of the Welsh, Llanilltud Fawr, loosely translating as 'the great church of Illtud'. While some have suggested that this place was just named after the cult of Illtud, long after he'd died, medieval documentary sources claim a more tangible connection between the man and the place: that he had founded or at least run the monastery here. And if that's true, that makes him a very significant figure in the early history of Christianity in Britain. The medieval literature is tricky – history mixed up with myth. But it must surely contain some clues. It was time for me to dive into the hagiographies – the medieval biographies of saints – and Illtud is mentioned in several.

The Life of a Saint

Illtud's own hagiography, the *Vita Sancti Iltuti*, or *Life of Saint Illtud,* was written in the twelfth century, six hundred years after Illtud is thought to have lived. It would have been based on earlier sources, certainly, but veers determinedly into the realms of myth, even connecting Illtud with perhaps the most famous British legend of all.

It tells us that he was born in Brittany, the son of a Breton noble descended from dispossessed British nobility – 'Bicanus was distinguished, a most famous soldier, illustrious by ancestry and through military prowess' – and a British princess called Rieingulid. After a good education in the 'seven arts', Illtud became a soldier, but was still renowned throughout Gaul for his philosophical discourse. Then, we're told, he travelled to Britain to see his famous cousin – none other than the legendary (and certainly not historical) King Arthur. After spending a period of time at King Arthur's court, the *Life* recounts, Illtud went on to become master of the soldiers at another court, that of Poulentus, king of Glamorgan.

The *Life* then describes how, following a narrow escape from disaster on a hunting expedition (when all of the rest of the royal household was swallowed up by the earth), Illtud had a dream in which an angel told him to ditch his military career – and his wife – and become a cleric. The requirement for celibacy here seems to reflect the cultural milieu of the writer rather than that of Illtud's time; by the twelfth century, Lateran Councils had declared that priests must be unmarried. Although celibacy had been promoted in monastic settings for centuries, there had been no general rules about clerics marrying before this. In fact, some monasteries were run by dynasties, with abbots' sons inheriting their fathers' positions. But, as it's related in the *Life,* Illtud behaved as he would have been expected to had he wanted to be a cleric in the twelfth century (when this hagiography was written): he pushed his wife away, saying, 'Thou shalt not cling to me further.' Having escaped that obligation, he then went off and found a suitable place to live and build himself an oratory or chapel: a lovely fertile valley called Hodnant; and the bishop of Llandaff made him an abbot. And so the monastery of Llanilltud was founded.

The *Life of Saint Illtud* contains a few miracles: that escape from being swallowed up by the earth; a story about Illtud forcing the sea back in order to enlarge the meadows for the monastery's cattle; a magical delivery of corn from Llanilltud's stores over to Brittany to relieve a famine; and a miracle to satisfy Illtud's own hunger, during an episode when he was hiding from his followers in a cave, on a sort of three-year-long sabbatical, where an angel conveniently delivered fresh bread and fish to him, every nine hours. These are all biblically inspired miracles – with similar versions appearing in many saints' stories. But there's another, more unusual, miracle detailed in the *Life*; a minor but distinctive, magical episode – and it features a bell. Illtud apparently took a shining to a sweet-sounding brass bell that a traveller was delivering to (the saint-to-be) David. When the bell reached David, it wouldn't ring – so David decided it was meant for Illtud, and sent it back to him. (With the tantalising suggestion that brazen bells may have been made at Llantwit Major, it's hard not to hope that there's a distant ring of truth to this one.) Finally, the *Life of Saint Illtud* recounts how Illtud returned to his homeland of Brittany, and died at the monastery of Dol.

While the *Life of Saint Illtud* is an entertaining read, it's probably not particularly useful as a source of historical facts. Not only was it written many centuries after the events it claims to record, it was compiled at a time when the Welsh dioceses were being reorganised – and pilgrimage sites were also being created and promoted. (Tim Young calls the *Life,* 'The Rough Guide to Llantwit' – it describes key spots in the landscape, for pilgrims to visit.) Pilgrimage was a big money-making exercise for the Church, and the need to promote the importance of Llanilltud was perhaps more pressing than historical accuracy. The monastery had much to gain if its founder could be claimed to have descended from royalty – and of course connected with King Arthur himself – as well as being a saint.

On the one hand, we are very fortunate that the Christian tradition was a literary one, that we have surviving documents like the *Life of Saint Illtud,* because otherwise we'd be left looking at that name inscribed on the back of a medieval stone and wondering who on earth Illtud was, and why someone saw fit to memorialise him in this way. But on the other hand, these histories, preserved by generations of monks, nuns and priests, scribbling in their scriptoria, laying their oak-gall ink on calfskin vellum, present us with an extremely skewed view of the past and its people, even when we get past the myths. It's important to remember that those histories were politically relevant at the time they were being written – they were not only *about* the Church, but *for* the Church. All these sources will be biased – some more than others. And perhaps unsurprisingly, historians tend to treat this particular *Life of Saint Illtud* with a very healthy dose of scepticism – it's heavily mythologised and probably largely fictional.

Luckily, there are mentions of Illtud in hagiographies of some other saints. The earliest of these sources is very early indeed: the first *Vita Sancti Samsonis* or *Life of Saint Samson*, written by a Breton monk, is thought to date to around 700 CE (and may have been based on even earlier sources). Interestingly, it's much more down-to-earth than the later *Life of Saint Illtud*, containing far fewer miracles. Illtud also gets a mention in the *Life of Paul Aurelian*, written in the ninth century, the *Life of Cadoc,* written in the eleventh, and the *Life of Gildas,* written in the twelfth. (It's also possible he gets a mention in an even earlier source too – Gildas himself, who's thought to have lived in the sixth century, wrote a polemic in which he criticised the king of Gwynedd, Maglocunus or Maelgwn, saying, 'But warnings are certainly not wanting to thee, since thou hadst had as instructor the most refined teacher of almost the whole of Britain' – that instructor, though unnamed, could have been Illtud.) Apart from those hagiographies, Illtud is also mentioned in Welsh lists of the genealogies of saints. Together, these various sources indicate that he was a real person, and, triangulating from other people mentioned, point to him having been alive from the late fifth into the early sixth century.

But unfortunately there's not much else that the various sources concur on, when it comes to the details of Illtud's life. Even the most basic biographic details are often found to be contradictory. The *Life of Saint Illtud* says that he was from Brittany, and eventually returned there, to the monastery of Dol, where he died. But in the *Life of Samson,* Illtud is Welsh, and is said to have died in his own monastery in South Wales. Given that Samson's hagiography was written so much earlier – five hundred years or so before the *Life of Saint Illtud* – it's considered more authentic and reliable. It seems very unlikely that Illtud died in Brittany, and, in fact, there's no suggestion in any other documentary source that he even visited Brittany at all. (While there are places in Brittany that are definitely named after Illtud, with more than twenty Breton churches dedicated to him, this doesn't necessarily tell us he was ever *there*; it could have been the cult rather than the man himself that travelled, perhaps because he was known and revered as the teacher of Samson and Paul Aurelian, two of the founder-saints of Brittany.) There are other contradictions in the sources, including over which clergyman appointed Illtud as an abbot, and where his monastery was sited. For instance, the *Life of Paul Aurelian*, written by a Breton monk, places Illtud's monastery on Caldey Island, 80 miles away from Llantwit Major, off the coast of West Wales. It's all a bit of a mess.

There are just a few points where the sources are in agreement. Illtud's character and reputation as a scholar are unimpeachable. In the *Life of Paul Aurelian*, Illtud is described as 'a man of noble birth and great learning'. The *Life of Samson* records that saint being taken by his parents to 'the school of the famous master of the Britons, named Illtud'. The passage continues: 'Illtud was truly the most accomplished of all of the

Britons in all of the Scriptures – Old and New Testaments – and in all kinds of science, and geometry, rhetoric, grammar, arithmetic, and all kinds of philosophy.' (It's interesting that this *Life of Samson* gives Illtud such a thorough introduction, suggesting he wouldn't have been familiar to readers, perhaps.) This education wasn't free – the *Life of Samson* tells us that his parents followed the custom of donating gifts to Llanilltud. (His parents were clearly very wealthy; they'd visited another holy man when they were having difficulty conceiving, and gifted him three silver ingots – each as big as Samson's mother – in order to improve their fertility.)

Distilling everything down, the only really reliable facts that we can glean about Illtud from all these sources are the rough dates of when he was alive – and that he was an abbot and famous teacher at Llanilltud, the monastery named after him, and perhaps founded by him. As for the rest, maybe Illtud really was a soldier for a time; maybe he really was descended from royalty; but we may have to accept we'll never know the details. But all these sources, especially that very early *Life of Samson*, do tell us something important about the wider context, about what Christianity in Wales was *like* in the middle of the first millennium.

It's hard to know when Christianity 'officially' reached South Wales – as an organised religion. It could have been established there from the early fifth century, or even back in the fourth, when Britannia was still part of the Roman Empire. The *Life of Samson* contains the earliest reference to a bishop in Wales: Samson is consecrated as a bishop by an existing bishop, Dubricius (Dyfrig in Welsh), around 521. It's assumed that this bishop Dubricius presided over a Welsh see or bishopric, but the details of his life are lost in myth, with later legends adding to the fable, even claiming that he crowned (the legendary) King Arthur. Still, the fact that a seventh-century source records one bishop anointing another in 521 reveals not only the presence of Christians in Wales by that time, but of an organised, established form of Christianity.

The *Life of Samson* also tells us that Illtud was a follower of a certain St Germanus, who was bishop of Autissiodorum (modern Auxerre, in central France) in the first half of the fifth century. But here we must question the historical accuracy of the *Life of Samson*, as the dates don't work. Germanus of Auxerre was dead by the year 448, while Illtud is thought to have been born around 460, and didn't found his monastery until the early sixth century. It's been suggested that the writer of the *Life of Samson* was getting mixed up with *another* Germanus; one who was bishop of Paris in the sixth century. Despite this muddle over names, then, this still suggests a connection between churches in Wales and central Gaul.

And, in fact, the hagiographies suggest an even stronger connection existed between the early Church in Wales and the far north-western corner of Gaul. The writer of the *Life of Samson* was himself a monk in Brittany (apparently tasked with writing this biography by a Cornish bishop, with the very excellent name Tigernomalus). Samson, apparently coming from South Wales himself, was educated at Llanilltud, and then reputedly went on to found various monasteries, including one at Dol in Brittany, where he became both abbot and bishop. He's considered to be one of the seven founding saints of Brittany, to this day.

So, while Illtud himself remains something of a shadowy figure, all these stories about him – and Samson – open up a window on early Christianity in north-west Europe.

Here are four observations:

First: there seems to be a very strong link between Christian and Roman traditions. We can see that quite clearly in the curriculum on offer at Illtud's monastery-school. The *Life of Samson* says that Illtud was an expert in 'all kinds of science, and geometry, rhetoric, grammar, arithmetic, and all kinds of philosophy' – as well as the Scriptures, the implication being that you could learn all of that at his monastery. It looks very much like a standard classical, Roman education with added lessons on Christian scripture. Cicero described the subjects that were taught in Roman schools back in the first century BCE: literature, rhetoric, philosophy, mathematics, music, geometry and astronomy. When Illtud is described in his own hagiography as being trained in the 'seven arts', those would have been similar subjects – a solid Roman-style education, which would go on to be the mainstay of medieval schooling.

Second: there's a resoundingly clear link between religious and secular power in these hagiographies – between kings and princes, abbots and bishops. The details may be somewhat hazy, but we're being told that all these important people in the early Church were all part of the nobility, all drawn from the elite echelons of post-Roman society. Even if we have doubts about the historical veracity of the *Life of Saint Illtud*, there are so many royal connections it's hard to ignore that milieu, at least. The more dependable *Life of Samson* tells us that he was high-born too: '. . .the parents of this married couple [Samson's parents] were court officials of the kings of their respective provinces' and that '[Samson] was nobly reared, following the noble custom of his ancestors'. Important to that 'rearing' was a good education, just as the sons of the nobility had received for centuries, back in the glory days of the Roman Empire. Illtud's monastery-school was a training college for the elite, including would-be clerics (and royalty, if Illtud was indeed 'the refined teacher' of Maelgwn, mentioned by Gildas), many of whom would later be remembered as saints. Some of them may have been truly, deeply pious, devout and prayerful; some may have been motivated more by naked self-interest and ambition. But there's one thing we can be sure of: they were all from noble families – they were all part of the social elite. And training the children of the elite, in that classical-plus-Christian education, would have provided a monastery with an income stream, on top of its agricultural wealth.

Third: Christianity certainly doesn't look like a recently introduced phenomenon in South Wales when Illtud was alive, presiding over his monastery in the late fifth or early sixth century. Instead, it appears to have already been operating as a highly organised, well-resourced, embedded and established organisation.

And the fourth observation we can make is that this organisation was very well networked, with connections from Wales to ecclesiastical centres in Cornwall, Ireland, Gaul – and, especially, Brittany.

Even if Illtud himself was not a Breton, or buried at Dol, we're still seeing plenty of evidence of important links between Wales and Brittany in the hagiographies. It felt like an important lead. If I wanted to understand how – and why – Christianity had become quite so embedded in Wales by the middle of the first millennium, I might find more clues across the Channel. I needed to go on a voyage.

And Brittany is absolutely stacked full of saints.

Saints Everywhere

Place names are like archaeological clues, hidden in the land-scape – preserved memories. Take a road trip around Brittany, or just peruse a map, and you see that it is liberally sprinkled with saints' names. Some of them are really obvious – they have 'Saint' in them: Saint-Malo, Saint-Cado, Saint-Brieuc, Saint-Coulomb, Saint-Gildas-de-Rhuys – the list goes on and on. But there are even more: any place name beginning with *Plou-* will be followed by a saint's name; the same with *Lan-*. Very few of these saints are recognised as such by the Catholic Church today – they are local saints, and they belong to an earlier strand of Christianity. And these saintly Breton place names are also distinctly, well, un-French.

Just as the map of Brittany is dominated by saints' names, so is its early written history – most of it coming down to us in the form of hagiographies, those 'Lives of Saints'. It's the same in Wales, Cornwall and Ireland. There are around a thousand Irish saints mentioned in medieval sources, though some may be doubled up. St Patrick (who sounds much less Irish and much more *Roman* in the original – *Patricius*) alone has dozens of places named after him. In Cornwall, there are around 140 sites with saints' names. There are over 500 Welsh saints mentioned in the annals and 346 of those are associated with specific places. And in Brittany, around 700 early medieval saints are recorded, with literally hundreds of place names containing saints. What's fascinating is that there's also quite a lot of overlap between these regions – particularly between Wales, Cornwall and Brittany – with the same saint's name (with varying spellings) appearing in different places.

This may not come as too much of a surprise. We might

expect to find cultural similarities in these areas; after all, they have a long, shared heritage, with closely related languages whose origins go right back into prehistory, before the Romans arrived in north-west Europe. Those languages are described as 'Celtic' (although this is a label applied by later linguists; no one in antiquity would have used that word to describe their languages, but they would surely have recognised the similarities between them). The Celtic language family includes two main branches: the Goidelic languages, which are Irish, Scottish Gaelic and Manx, and the Brythonic or Brittonic languages: Welsh, Cornish and Breton. Latin was spoken alongside those languages in Roman times and beyond, with plenty of Latin loanwords ending up absorbed into Celtic languages. Some of the same saints turn up in each of these areas, but the formulation of the place names is similar too, with similar prefixes – coming ultimately from Celtic or Latin roots – found in Wales, Cornwall and Brittany.

Like Brittany, Cornwall also has a lot of places simply named 'Saint whoever'. This type of toponym is rare in Wales (and England), although fairly common across the rest of France. Sometimes the 'saint' bit gets dropped and the place is named very simply after the saint – like Siz, for St Sixtus, in Brittany, and Mullion, from *Eglosmeylyon* in Cornwall.

The Latin *martyrium* – for the shrine or burial place of a martyr – appears as *merthyr* in Wales, *merther* in Cornwall and *merzher* in Brittany. The Latin for 'church', *ecclesia*, becomes *eglwys* in Welsh, *eglos* in Cornish and *iliz* in Breton, while the Breton place name ending -*loc* comes from Latin *locus*, '[sacred] place'. Then there's the prefix *plou-*, which is extremely common in Brittany. It comes from Latin *plebes*, 'people', and came to mean 'parish' – in other words, a whole community and a parcel of land. The cognate or equivalent Welsh and Cornish words – *plwyf* and *plu* respectively – are much rarer as place names.

The *Lan-* names of Brittany and Cornwall come from a Common Celtic root **landa,* originally meaning 'cleared space', but later taking on the meaning of 'church'; in Wales it becomes *llan-,* as in Llanilltud, and so many others. These names are everywhere – there are around a hundred scattered across Cornwall, 930 in Brittany and 870 in Wales. Again, these seem to map onto parishes, broadly speaking, but whereas the Welsh *Llan-* and Cornish *Lan-* names seem to be reserved for relatively important churches, operating at a parish level or above, the Breton *Lan-* names include much smaller, sub-parochial churches.

Now, I love diving into place names and looking for connections. I'm an anatomist after all, which is all about the naming of parts. But this exercise really does help us to reach back through the centuries and to look at how Christianity was becoming embedded in the landscape and society of north-western Europe, between 1,500 and 1,000 years ago. We're seeing connections between Wales, Cornwall and Brittany in these similar place names; people were clearly travelling around these regions, taking ideas with them. But we can also learn something about patterns of settlement too.

The *Plou-* names of Brittany have been a subject of much historical debate. Along with the *Lan-* names, they're thought to be early, having become attached to the landscape by the seventh century. But just who were these people, these *plebes*? Some have suggested that the name may have originally referred to a group of migrant British soldiers and their dependants arriving into Brittany and settling down, developing into 'clans' run by hereditary leaders. Others have suggested that these communities started with a religious focus. A third suggestion combines the idea of migrants with that of religious identity, hypothesising that these *plebes* may have originally defined and separated themselves on a cultural and religious basis, before being absorbed into, or absorbing, the wider population around them in Brittany.

Combining place names with information from land charters and facts dredged out of hagiographies, we learn something about wider political organisation at the time – how power was distributed across the landscape in the middle of the first millennium. In Cornwall and Wales, there's a clear hierarchy – which fits with a broader picture across Britain and Ireland, and the European continent. There's an obvious link – reflected in the literary and physical evidence – between high-status secular and ecclesiastical sites. At the top of the pile, in larger settlements, are cathedrals and basilicas, often with royal connections, and their own bishops; then there are important rural churches (baptismal churches in France, Anglo-Saxon minsters, Welsh 'mother-churches'); then monasteries, with large rural estates; all the way down to small chapels and hermitages.

The picture in Brittany is different – flatter, with less of an obvious, nested hierarchy. There were very few episcopal centres – Vannes, and possibly Dol and Alet – and only one large monastery, at Landévennec on the west coast. Below that level there were very few high-status Breton churches – just a *lot* of smaller churches in villages, with all those *Plou-* names. This reflects a more scattered settlement pattern, typical of a semi-pastoral economy, but also the fact that there seems to have been very little in the way of large-scale landowning in early medieval Brittany. Instead, land was distributed among numerous smallholders – and the Church administration simply reflected that pattern. And while the few bishops and abbots may have officially been in charge of all these smaller establishments, the community in each *Plou-* setting may have been practically autonomous. But still – what we're seeing across Wales, Cornwall and Brittany is that political organisation *was* religious. The Church wasn't separate in the way we might think of it today; it was completely embedded in the political landscape.

Place names also hint at shifting power over time, as well, with different branches of the Church – completely enmeshed with wider, secular political power – vying for hegemony. In Brittany, *Plou-* names and *Lan-* names, usually combined with local Breton saints, tend to be early. To me, this suggests that Christianity, which arrived as an imported idea, quickly became a 'home-grown' phenomenon. After the ninth century, we see more *Loc-* names appearing; many of them combined not with local saints, but with Christ, Mary and Michael. This timeline seems to fit very neatly with western churches – churches that had been part of an earlier Celtic or insular tradition, doing Christianity their own way – being brought into line with the Roman Church, with local saints being sidelined.

Cornish *Lan-* names appear to be relatively early too, from the seventh century onwards. Records show that some of these old names were later replaced, perhaps when Cornwall was brought under the sway of the powerful Anglo-Saxon kingdom of Wessex, in the ninth century. In contrast, *Llan-* names in Wales continued to be introduced all the way up to the twelfth century, reflecting the persistence of the Welsh language, certainly, but also perhaps the strength and autonomy of the Welsh Church.

Heading back to the early medieval period, before all these power struggles within the Church, the place names are already helping us glimpse the way that society was organised, the way that land was divided up – and the fact that the Church was very much part and parcel of all of that. We're seeing strong links between religious and secular power – links that go back a long way. These clues in the landscape complement what we learn from the hagiographies, including that very early *Life of Saint Samson*. There, we read about some noble men who assumed powerful roles in the Church, as abbots and bishops, becoming automatically transformed into saints on their deaths, while others became secular rulers – kings, princes, counts and 'judges'. And these two branches of power supported each other. Samson, for example, was gifted the land for his monasteries from the Frankish king, and, with a second monastery at Pental on the lower Seine, in Francia, his power and reputation were ensured both there and in Brittany.

But we're also seeing that fifth- and sixth-century Brittany does seem to be a little different from the rest of Francia, and from Britain. Not only were bishops thin on the ground, early medieval kings seem conspicuous in their absence here. So it looks as though both religious and secular power structures in Brittany were relatively decentralised and less hierarchical. It also seems that the organisation of the Church was generally a bit looser in Brittany: charters record some landholdings passing in and out of ecclesiastical ownership, for instance. This loose organisation and control may have meant that the Breton Church depended quite heavily on support from Britain – from Cornwall and Wales, in particular – for training clerics or even supplying clergy. And that's exactly what we saw with Samson, of course, who probably came from South Wales, and was educated at Llanilltud, before travelling to Brittany to found the monastery at Dol.

Charters and place names provide us with important evidence, revealing how the Church was quite literally gaining ground as a landowner in the early medieval period and how much it was enmeshed with secular power – but here again I find myself referring to 'it'. These place names are important in another way – they remind us that *people* are central to this story. They enshrine the names of influential people in the early Church – the very people who became known as saints, whose names echo down to us through the centuries, like the ringing of a distant bell.

What's in a Name

When a personal name appears in more than one place name, it's tempting to infer that we're glimpsing an itinerant saint moving around the landscape – perhaps even one of the first people to bring Christianity to that region. Wherever they pause on their travels, they get a mention in a place name, like a pin stuck in the map. But unfortunately, and somewhat predictably, it's not that simple.

First, we have to be sure that a place name really does refer to a person. There's no hard-and-fast rule, and some ecclesiastical place names relate to aspects of the landscape, not people at all. Those might be obvious, like Llandaff/Llandaf in South Wales, which is the 'church on the River Taff'. But sometimes confusion over a place name seems to have led to the invention of a saint where there was never one to start with. Saint-Logod in Brittany may have originally have been *san-logod*, the 'valley of mice', for instance.

Around a quarter of all the hundreds of *Plou-* names in Brittany are not personal names, but other nouns or adjectives, often relating to the landscape. The rest are people's names. A third of these are unique – not known from any other sources as saints, so they don't help us in tracing connections or journeys. (It could be that these people simply weren't that famous beyond the local area; they may not even have held official positions in the Church; perhaps local leaders or founders of settlements were honoured in this way.)

Setting aside the more geographical *Plou-* names, as well as the personal names that aren't mentioned anywhere else, we're left with around half of the total. These relate to people who are either commemorated at other named sites, or mentioned in historical sources, such as hagiographies, so we know a bit more about them and their cults.

There were clearly no official rules about who could become a saint – that would come along much later. (In the west, you didn't need sign-off from the Pope to be sanctified, before the twelfth century.) We can see that some of these early saints were considered to be very holy, soon after their deaths, with reports of miracles accumulating posthumously; others seemed to take time to acquire a saintly reputation. In this way, founders of settlements or local leaders could potentially morph into saints over time – a kind of 'saintly grade inflation'. Rather like the Roman-style education on offer at Llanilltud, this also seems to be a reflection of, an extension of, Roman culture. (It could also have been a feature of Iron Age societies in Britain and Gaul too, but we know much less about those.) Emperors had always been deified on their deaths; the sanctification of local leaders such as bishops broadened that trend. This created a host of venerable ancestors for a religion that was meant to be about one supreme god, and also provided strong local links for a religion that originally emerged some five thousand kilometres away from Brittany.

With saints who pop up in more than one place, or are mentioned in literary sources as well as honoured in place names, we might hope to be able to trace their movements around the Atlantic archipelago. But it's still more complex than it looks at first sight. Sometimes there are good, near-contemporary sources that describe those journeys – for people like the Irish monk Columbanus and the Welsh monk Samson (of Dol), for instance, whose hagiographies are both thought to have been written within a century of their deaths. But careful historical analysis suggests that hagiographers may have invented some voyages retrospectively, posthumously – perhaps even in an effort to explain why a particular saint's name appeared in numerous places. This means the written history can't be entirely trusted as an independent source of information. In some ways, it's better if the saint's name *isn't* included in a place name because then we can be sure that the hagiographer wasn't trying to provide an explanation for that. (And it does actually seem quite rare for a major ecclesiastical centre to have been named after a founding or influential cleric: Luxeuil remained Luxeuil after the Irish monk Columbanus set up his school there; Dol stayed as Dol after Samson founded his monastery there.)

There's a further complication – and unfortunately a final nail in the coffin for the idea that we can track the voyages of saints by looking for those 'pins in the map'. In fact, it's much more likely that what we're actually seeing recorded in place names is not the journey of a saint himself at all, but the spread of that saint's *cult* after he'd died – to places he may never have visited in life.

The reasons, the drivers, for the dissemination of a saint's cult were manifold. Those reasons *could* link back to places visited by the sainted individual, but there are plenty of other possibilities. A cult could also be imposed on churches that fell under the jurisdiction of a successful higher-level church, already linked to the saint. Churches could become associated with a particular saint's cult after acquiring a relic of that saint (although the trade in body parts seems to be a somewhat later development in the Celtic-speaking world; objects like gospels and altars, and of course bells, were more popular). A group of refugees could take their favourite saint's cult with them to a new home. Families of saints – often noble or royal, as we've seen – could work hard to promote the cult of their relative. Ireland is unique for the survival of early genealogies of saints, revealing family connections between ecclesiastical centres. But it's likely that the same pattern was happening everywhere; noble families would have invested heavily in making sure their saintly members were remembered and revered. And ultimately, some saints would just have been more attractive or relatable than others; their cults more likely to be picked up and spread, just like a successful meme. Culture is always complex, and in many cases, many different factors – from Church organisation to relics; from elite familial interests to cultural appeal – are likely to have played a role in spreading a saint's cult.

We may be a little disappointed; it seems that place names are more likely to reflect the dissemination of a cult, rather than the movement of a saint themselves during their lifetime. But mapping place names and saints' cults across different regions still reveals important links between the religious communities of the Atlantic archipelago. Of the better-known saints recorded in those Breton *Plou-* and *Lan-* names, around a third are Welsh or Cornish. The strongest link is that between Wales and Brittany (but we should bear in mind that some Cornish connections are likely to have been lost as Cornwall became anglicised, with earlier place names being wiped from its landscape).

It can be hard to know which direction these cults were travelling in, but it seems to be generally accepted that the Welsh links represent an influence extending from Wales to Brittany. That's a really abstract way of saying that the Welsh Church was spreading into Brittany, and *that's* a really abstract way of saying that *people* were coming from Wales to Brittany. Perhaps they were sent by the great Welsh monasteries – perhaps at the behest of Welsh kings – to establish communities in Brittany. There are three Welsh saints in particular who get repeated mentions around Brittany: Cadog, Teilo and our old friend, Illtud, who's memorialised in Kerilut, Lanildut and Ploerdut. These saints were all associated with leading sixth-century Welsh monasteries – and the Breton place names probably reflect the spread of their cults, rather than personal visits from the saints themselves. The fact that some of these places are *Plou-* names – such as Ploerdut – suggests early contact between Wales and Brittany, but these saints' cults are also likely to have been reinforced by ongoing contact. Irish cults – of Patrick, Brendan and Brigit – also seem to have arrived early in Brittany, possibly via Britain or Gaul.

Place names show saints' cults spreading northwards across the Channel too – from Brittany to Cornwall in particular; this may have happened somewhat later, in the ninth and tenth centuries, when Bretons were fleeing from Viking attacks, taking their saints with them. The Anglo-Saxon king Aethelstan also helped to reinforce the links between Brittany and churches in the south-west, gifting Breton relics to Exeter. And even more Breton saints' cults are thought to have been introduced to Cornwall after the Norman conquest of England. Gunwalloe and Cury on the Lizard Peninsula are named after the Breton saints Winwalloe and Corentin respectively – just a couple of examples of the many saints' names shared between Brittany and Cornwall.

In case it sounds like scholars are now completely dismissing the idea that people who would become known as saints were travelling around north-west Europe in the fifth and sixth centuries, this isn't the case at all. When it comes to the hagiographies, some are more trustworthy than others, especially those written closer to the time of the person they are describing. While we may doubt that Illtud strayed far during his lifetime, for instance, we can be more sure that Samson did. And these journeys were crucially important to the viability of the Celtic Church – in all these places separated by the sea, but linked by voyages.

Voyages of the Saints

Scholars of early Christianity in what became known as the insular or 'Celtic Church' have often stressed what they saw as its unique qualities. A penchant for peregrinating, as well as a particular enthusiasm for monastic asceticism, have been held up as defining features.

In the early twentieth century, historians and theologians seemed quite sure that the reason for all the saintly voyages was a pious, missionary instinct, driving men who had dedicated their lives to God to travel between Scotland, Ireland, Wales,

Cornwall and Brittany, forging a Christian identity in what would (much later) become known as the Celtic Church, an identity that was staunchly set against the hierarchical 'Roman' Church that held sway in Western Europe. (This retrospective labelling of the Celtic Church probably overplays the unity of the western churches as well as their antagonism to Rome.)

The prevailing view was that holy men in the post-Roman era had travelled around those 'Celtic' regions, bringing Christianity to some areas for the first time; in others, correcting a reversion to paganism. Indeed, the hagiographies often described the voyages of these saints in missionary terms – as though conversion of pagans was the primary objective. But it's not hard to find reason to doubt this narrative. You don't even have to read between the lines to note that Christianity was already *there* in many places – established, embedded. As we observed with the story of Illtud and his monastery, it seems that Christianity was already well established in southern Wales and Brittany by the late fifth century. So those peregrinating saints weren't spreading the word of their god for the first time, they were just spreading *their version* of it – crucially, a version that benefited their own social status, and that of future generations of their families.

In many ways, Samson was the archetypal voyaging saint – his travels probably influenced similar tales in other, later hagiographies. His very early, seventh-century *Vita* is thought to be more dependable than many later hagiographies, due to its near-contemporaneous authorship, and it describes his journeys in some detail. The author of the *Vita Sancti Samsonis* is at pains to stress that he'd put together his account having seen earlier documents about Samson that had been curated by a Cornish cleric. He writes that his words are not 'are not put together from wild speculations of my own, or from confused and unauthorized rumours'.

Samson was born into a noble family in Demetia (another name for Dyfed, part of modern Pembrokeshire, in south-west Wales), the son of Ammon – 'a man of royal stock' – and Anna. (Samson, Ammon and Anna are all biblical names.) He was baptised by Illtud and later went to study with the abbot at his monastery, where he proved to be a very able pupil, and was ordained as a deacon by Illtud. He moved away from Llanilltud to a monastery on an island – thought to be Caldey Island – close to his family home of Dyfed, in other words, and just off the coast of what's now Tenby (medieval Dinbych – 'small fortress', making me wonder if there's an even earlier Roman story to be dug out, there. The settlement is first mentioned in a tenth-century poem, with reference to a royal court or *llys* on St Catherine's Island; Roman coins were discovered under the chapel on the island in the nineteenth century). After meeting two learned Irish men, returning home from Rome, Samson travelled back to Ireland with them, where he spent a few years working various miracles, including restoring sight to the blind, healing lepers and exorcising demons (all very biblical). He sailed home to his island monastery, where his father and uncle were now also priests, and sent his uncle off to Ireland to be an abbot in a monastery there.

But Samson's own voyages weren't over – he had a vision where an angel commanded him to leave his family and travel to Armorica (Brittany). The archbishop, Dyrfig, sent him off, saying, 'May you be a strong man; go and fight on the battle-field. May the prayers of Britain lead you from here with joy and zeal.' He sailed off in a ship, taking some monks with him, stopping off on the way to convert a few pagans in Cornwall.

Arriving at the port of Dol in Brittany, he cured a couple of people suffering with leprosy and demonic possession and then founded a monastery. He quickly involved himself in local politics; a foreign count called Commor had recently seized Brittany, killing the previous Breton king, and sending that king's son, Iudwal, to the Merovingian king Childebert. Samson went to Childebert to ask him to release Iudwal – which he eventually did. Then Samson and Iudwal went on a small voyage to the Channel Islands, assembled an army and returned to Brittany, where Iudwal killed Commor and became duke of Brittany.

Despite the description of travels, the *Vita Sancti Samsonis* is quite myopic. It describes Samson travelling from one ecclesiastical or royal centre to another, with fairly detailed descriptions of monastic life. But apart from a confrontation with a witch, a huge serpent, and the idolatrous pagans in Cornwall, Samson rarely meets anyone outside the Church who isn't a member of royalty.

When we realise the saintly voyages usually seem to have been undertaken at the request of a king, abbot, bishop or pope – and are enmeshed with high politics – they start to make much more sense. Itinerant clerics were necessary to maintain connections between the insular churches – and between churches and secular rulers – to form alliances, secure favourable treatment and share resources. They're described as travelling widely – between Ireland, Scotland, Wales, Cornwall, Brittany and beyond. The travelling clerics appeared to expect hospitality from elite establishments wherever they went. And they clearly had the resources to make long journeys, presumably making use of well-trodden (or well-sailed) existing trading networks. Samson is very sensibly described as boarding ships to sail to his various destinations (unlike later tales of other saints, such as Brendan 'the navigator', which describe perilous voyages in unfeasibly small coracles – impressively miraculous, if a little foolish).

For elite clerics, the ones we hear most about, their peregrinations often started with their education, as they travelled to study with eminent leaders at famous schools. In preceding centuries, this was what the sons of wealthy Roman families had always done – studying grammar then going away to be educated by famous rhetoricians (in Latin in the west, Greek in the east) – but it was now happening under the aegis of Christianity. And as we learn from the biography of Samson, who made his way to Llanilltud for his training, he could expect a thoroughly Roman education, with a bit of Christianity bolted on. And then his travelling continued; again, this was prefigured in the way that Roman elites had always functioned – after a solid education, the sons of the wealthy and powerful would travel around the provinces (and to Rome itself) passing from one high office to another, fulfilling administrative duties, ambassadorial roles and occasionally getting involved in a battle.

As historian Caroline Brett and her colleagues point out, the peregrinations in this 'Age of Saints' were not unique to the Celtic fringes of Europe – this was happening everywhere as elite families sought to consolidate their power after the fragmentation of the western Roman Empire. As the son of a prince, you could expect an elite education, and then a series of appointments that might culminate in being made a bishop. You might also be granted some land from a king (who may indeed be a relation) and set up your own lucrative franchise there – a monastery. That monastery would generate income for itself, and potentially for the king who granted the land in the first place. If you were clever or lucky or both, that monastery could also grow into a cult centre and a college where other rich sons could be brought and schooled, helping to grow the brand of both Christianity and *you* – you were destined, after all, to become a saint.

The 'missionary instinct' represented nothing more than the traditional way of life for elite families – or at least, their sons. In those politically unstable late Roman and post-Roman centuries, elites were scrambling to consolidate their power – and it seems the Church was offering the potential to do just that. Rather than something unusual then, the voyages of the Celtic saints start to look more like business as usual.

But in the hands of the later hagiographers, these voyages were transformed from something that could have been a fairly mundane feature in the life of an ambitious post-Roman aristocrat to something mythical, other-worldly and emblematic of sainthood. The journeys were embellished and embroidered until they acquired a mythical quality, studded with marine monsters, islands full of angels, and stone coffins that could sail themselves across the sea. To be a saint was to be a voyager.

But there are many other themes and symbols that recur in the hagiographies – that seem important to that saintly identity. Celtic saints are often refreshed with miraculous food; staffs are pushed into the ground and start sprouting into trees; and they are lauded for their asceticism and reclusive habits. Sprouting staffs and angelically provided dinners are clearly the stuff of legend (and carry scriptural resonance as prominent biblical motifs). Ideas of an ascetic life and the saint-as-hermit seem to be more rooted in the real world, or at least more *possible*. And yet it seems like there may be some sleight of hand here. We're talking about very wealthy, well-connected people, after all.

But a study of much more recent celebrities might just help us understand this apparent dissonance, making those medieval saints much more relatable.

The Myth of Asceticism

The discovery of angelic islands, successful voyages in unfeasibly small boats, God-given meals and sprouting staffs are miracles that demonstrate saints being in receipt of divine favour, as well as being somehow magical or other-worldly. Such things do not happen to ordinary, unsaintly people. But the self-denial and seeking out of splendid isolation is something different; it says something about their characters: their capacity to accept suffering in some way, to abstain from luxuries and indulgence, to separate themselves from society, to appear heroic and Christ-like.

It seems that these saints were keen to cultivate these ideas about themselves – or at least that their hagiographers were keen to impress that perception on readers. And these references to asceticism and isolation, along with piety and prayerfulness, were endlessly reprinted and repeated, and still adorn biographies of these men on the pages of innumerable websites today: 'Illtud led a severe ascetic life . . .'; 'David, or Dewi, was a monk and a bishop in the sixth century. He was reputed to be an exemplar of the ascetic, spiritual life . . .'; 'St Cadoc (perhaps together with St Gildas, a close friend) led a solitary existence on an island off the coast of Brittany, not far from Vannes'.

Let's take a look at asceticism first. Remember that we're talking about people from the highest echelons in society – from noble and royal families; people who were often gifted large estates on which to build their monasteries; people who would have had the means to enjoy the finer things in life. It seems an incredible sleight of hand that they were represented as so self-effacing and abstemious.

What's also completely fascinating is that the connection between asceticism and 'saintliness' has continued to the present. In a fascinating paper on 'Reflections on Iconic Celebrity', the semiotician Fernando Andacht explored symbols used by celebrities to signal their status. He focused on three famous Argentinians: Eva Perón, Che Guevara and Diego Maradona, looking at the way they'd each developed into icons in the public imagination – Christ-like icons. Connecting them all is a dedication to ostentatious piety.

A novel about Perón by Tomás Eloy Martínez even bears the title *Santa Evita*; she's depicted on the cover wearing a monk's robe, with a golden halo blazing around her head. In real life, she achieved a saintly reputation through personally overseeing massive gift-giving to the poor and by emphasising her own personal sacrifice, in the service of others. In 1951, she wrote to the *Compañeras*, the women's movement that she founded, that her 'debt to the people is infinite, and I will only be able to pay it by burning my life for the sake of its happiness, and I understand that life is to be burnt up only for such a great ideal as that of Perón and of my people'. When, pressured by the military, she'd stepped down from the vice-presidential race earlier that year, she turned that into another opportunity to exhibit self-sacrifice: 'I do not forsake the struggle or the work; I forsake the honours.' But unlike so many medieval saints who were often said to have dressed plainly, Eva Perón appeared in public decked out in gold and gems. When Spain's dictator Franco criticised her, she apparently replied, 'The poor people enjoy seeing me beautiful. They do not want a badly dressed old lady to protect them. They dream with me and I cannot disappoint them.' And to some people, she really was holy. A woman suffering with polio is reported to have said, 'To be in the thought of the Lady, is like touching God with one's hands. What else can one need?'

Perhaps even more popular and globalised than Evita Perón's saintliness is the iconic image of Che Guevara. Rather fitting for someone who reportedly resisted being cast as a hero, the lasting image of Che Guevara was captured by a photographer at a protest rally. Eva Perón had risen, Cinderella-like, from a humble background to the highest status in her society, and dressed the part. Guevara, on the other hand, came from a middle-class background, and he dressed himself in a battered army uniform, denying himself earthly comforts; displaying his asceticism, wearing it on his sleeve. And he also turned down honours and accolades. As Andacht writes about Che Guevara, 'It is not hard to imagine how this passionate disavowal of any honor when it came from such a colourful and attractive figure *could not but arouse even more admiration.*' (my emphasis).

When it comes to Maradona, we're back to a rags-to-riches story. Rather like Evita, dressing up in her finery for the sake of the poor people, Maradona vaunted his opulence and his two Ferraris. In his autobiography, he explained that, whether he won or lost, what really mattered was that he did it 'with my own style, without betraying myself'. Through the medium of television, he invited his audience to admire his self-indulgence. And, in the way that saints become even more saintly by association with other saints, he had a tattoo of Che Guevara on his right arm. On the surface of it, Maradona's celebrity has less of an ascetic quality about it, but he was very open about his struggles with cocaine addiction; his own life of suffering. (And in fact, while each of these stories weaves in asceticism, it is also clear that prosperity is considered a blessing; asceticism as a virtue only works against that background, and not against one of poverty.)

Asceticism is never far away in celebrity culture. It seems to have come back with a vengeance in recent years, with journalist Kate Demolder picking up on the trend with a thoughtful article, 'How self-denial became the must-have trend of 2024'. It may be something that disenfranchised sections of society hanker after, but for those who have it all, having-not can be peculiarly alluring – a secular symbol of piety. Demolder writes that 'The middle-class ideal of the past decade, borne of the alliance between apps like Instagram and the celebrities who use it, has become that of complete self-deprivation.' She explores the potential underlying reasons for this ascetic instinct: potentially a reaction to a period of overconsumption (for some), possibly a response to 'powerlessness – buoyed by war, moral panic and climate change uncertainty'. There could perhaps be an analogy to be drawn with the political and economic insecurity of the third to fifth centuries. But ultimately, Demolder concludes that it is 'simply another style . . . just with an added layer of superiority baked in'. This style, this powerful symbol of status, has a long history.

And in fact, Andacht drew a direct comparison between the more recent 'Christomimetic' Argentinian celebrities he scrutinised and 'the holy men of the early Christian age . . . who outdid themselves in their hard, almost inhumanly ascetic and mortified existence to acquire a fame that was to be the very opposite of the pomp and extravagance characteristic of the Roman emperor'.

The idea of suffering and asceticism was one thing, but are we really to believe that all those sainted bishops were really that abstemious? While Christian hagiographers pushed that line, some pagan commentators' reflections escaped the censorship of the Church to survive to the present. The fourth-century Roman soldier and historian Ammianus recorded how, in the year 366, two rivals 'Damasus and Ursinus, burning with a superhuman desire of seizing the bishopric, engaged in bitter strife because of their opposing interests; and the supporters of both parties went even so far as conflicts ending in bloodshed and death'. Thugs on the side of Damasus pursued members of the rival faction into a basilica – and slaughtered them. Ammianus wrote that 137 corpses were discovered inside the basilica. Eventually, Damasus won the battle to become bishop of Rome (the post that would later transmute into pope). And Ammianus was clear about what rewards the bishop would reap: he'd be completely free from financial worries, receiving generous donations from wealthy women; he'd ride around in carriages, wear elegant clothes and serve up banquets 'so lavish that their entertainments outdo the tables of kings'. Ammianus did go on to suggest that provincial bishops tended to live more frugally, but all bishops were relatively wealthy, as befitted their high status in a highly stratified society. Perhaps some bishops did try to eschew worldly pleasures and luxuries, or at least, rein it in a little. But what really mattered was that they projected an *image* which included that ideal of asceticism, whether or not it was something they actually practised. It's still important to their image today. One Franciscan website claims, of Saint Damasus (as he would become, of course), 'As pope, his lifestyle was simple in contrast to other ecclesiastics of Rome.'

Isolation might be considered to be an extension of asceticism; humans are social animals, after all; self-denial of social contact also signals something superhuman, ethereal, separate from the mundane. Separation from society, turning away from the public gaze, shunning adulation, is another symbol that, seemingly paradoxically, increases the iconic status of the celebrity. It all adds to the aura of mystery. Lesser mortals are only offered brief glimpses of those elevated individuals. Early Christianity is replete with stories of people who lived as hermits, withdrawing from society – and were famous for it. If their intention really was to disappear from public consciousness, these famous hermits failed quite spectacularly in their ambition. Simon Stylites was famous for living on a pillar in fifth-century Syria; he's said to have climbed the pillar in order to get away from people, but he clearly wanted his asceticism to be *seen*.

The key to it seems to be to achieve *just enough* separation to create that romantic idea of isolation. But, of course, you can't separate yourself *too* much – you want people to notice, after all. You want to be isolated just enough to gain the desired effect, but certainly not to disappear from public consciousness. Once again, there are clues in the hagiographies that the *idea of isolation* is much more important as a symbol than an objective reality.

Archaeologist John Hines highlighted this paradox on an episode of that wonderfully erudite and diverse BBC radio programme *In Our Time,* hosted by Melvyn Bragg. The subject was St Cuthbert, a seventh-century Northumbrian saint.

John Hines described Cuthbert's early life, growing up in the Scottish Borders. He pointed out that Cuthbert would have been a member of the social elite; when he arrived at the monastery of Melrose, where he would train, he was riding a horse and carrying a spear – both symbols of his status. Cuthbert's life was described by Bede in the eighth century, but the much earlier *Anonymous Life of Cuthbert* contains more details, including briefly mentioning that he spent time on a military campaign, 'exactly what you'd expect of a young man of this rank', as Hines put it. After his training at Melrose, Cuthbert seems to have been sent to Lindisfarne, 'to enforce a more Roman style of discipline on this originally Irish monastery', Hines wrote. And Cuthbert did this in a clever way, respecting the Irish heritage at Lindisfarne – while replacing it.

Lindisfarne had been the episcopal seat of the seventh-century Irish bishop Aidan, who is credited with converting the population of Northumbria to Christianity (although there had been an earlier mission sent from Canterbury). Aidan came from a religious community on another holy island: the abbey on Iona, founded by the Irish evangelist Columba, and used as a base for spreading Christianity into Scotland. Just as at Lindisfarne, the relative isolation of the monks on Iona is often stressed, but it's important to recognise that it was just that – *relative*. In fact, both of those sites, Iona and Lindisfarne, were actually very well positioned to take advantage of trade – and generate wealth. So the leaders of those communities may have been escaping the public gaze (to some extent) but they certainly weren't aiming to cut themselves off from society, far from it. And, as we've come to expect, they were members of the social elite.

Columba, so the seventh-century *Vita Columbae* tells us, was a descendant of Irish royalty on both sides of his family. He studied under Bishop Finian, at Clonard Abbey – right next to the hill of Tara, where the kings of Ireland were traditionally crowned. For Columba, choosing to become a monk didn't mean turning his back on his social status and political influence – it meant advancing both. But after founding a few monasteries in Ireland (where monasteries formed some of the largest settlements, engaging in trade and industry as well as agriculture – up to the Viking period), Columba fell foul of other bishops and was exiled. (In his *Vita*, this was said to have come about because he illicitly copied a psalter, but the Annals of Ulster put it down to internecine feuding between clans.) Columba went off travelling, landing up in western Scotland, where, luckily enough, he had relatives among the rulers of the western kingdom of Dál Riata. He ordained another Aidan as king of Dál Riata, and this Aidan gave Columba the island of Iona – where the monk built his monastery. It seems Columba attended high-level meetings between Irish and Scottish rulers and may even have brokered a peace agreement between them. When he died, he predictably became a saint. And Iona remained a prominent centre of Christianity; a new seat of religious and political power.

In modern discussions of Columba and his monastery on Iona, the remoteness of the island always seems to be emphasised. But within a kingdom spanning the peninsulas, sea lochs and isles of western Scotland, with a strong seafaring culture, Iona occupied an easily accessible, central position – and as a bonus, wasn't too far from the north-east tip of Ireland. Columba's connections with nobility and royalty come as no surprise. Abbots were, as we have seen, useful to kings (and often related to them) – helping to legitimise their rule, operating certain monasteries as centres of learning and soft power, and training the sons of the elites for high office. The benefits were mutual – kings were useful to abbots too, as patrons, granting them land and other funds. Christianity was being used to confer divine authority on kingship, just as it had legitimised the Christian Roman emperors. Out in the wider community, affiliation with Christianity also indicated allegiance to the king. Strip away the religious aspect and what we see is the same wealthy, powerful families helping each other, competing with each other, periodically fighting each other, conspiring to hold onto their status and influence: bishops, abbots, kings – round and round it goes.

John Hines picked up on the importance of this political nexus on *In Our Time*: 'Without doubt there was a very close relationship indeed between kingship and the Church, not just in Northumbria but throughout Anglo-Saxon England and indeed throughout all of the different communities and populations of early medieval Britain.'

And then the discussion turned to Cuthbert's reputation for being a hermit on the Farne Islands. Oxford historian and cleric Sarah Foot described Cuthbert's search for solitude, going as far as to build himself a rock-cut cell on the smaller island of Inner Farne, where he could be even more isolated. 'This is a well-established means of getting oneself closer to God,' she explained. 'You cut yourself off from all the pleasures of the flesh and particularly from the company and distraction of other human beings' – in order to focus on prayer. John Hines added that Cuthbert wasn't just praying; he was growing crops on Inner Farne too. (To which Foot responded, 'He was praying through the work of his hands.') Hines also pointed out that, while Inner Farne may have been a few miles away from Lindisfarne (though still very visible from that island), it was actually closer to the mainland – just a mile away from the important royal seat of Bamburgh. 'So it's not remote and inconspicuous by any means,' Hines pointed out, 'and as for this romantic legend of Ecgfrith going out there to beg him to accept the bishopric – it's a story that represents very nicely the relationship between the rather ostentatious ascetic spirituality of being on his own – and the fact that it's being performed in direct view of the royal centre.'

We're reminded here of Samson – apparently seeking out splendid isolation on Caldey Island – conveniently close to the coast of Dyfed, and potentially the royal seat or *llys* there, on St Catherine's Island at Tenby. Our modern sensibilities also make these bishops and saints on their islands seem even more remote – we're so used to travelling overland, on well-maintained roads; in the Middle Ages, going by sea would have been much easier.

This conversation beautifully captures the way that myths of asceticism and isolation were constructed – and repeated – and how it's possible to deconstruct them. For the most part, what we receive today is the narrative perpetuated by cleric-scholars throughout history. Perhaps abbots and bishops like Illtud, Cuthbert and Columba would have seemed, when they were alive, a little less than ascetic to their close friends. But these ideals of self-denial and splendid isolation were clearly important to their image, and there was already a long tradition of (apparent and often ostentatious) asceticism in Christianity.

The desert monks of Egypt, described in the fifth-century *Historia Monachorum in Aegypto,* were famous for being cut off from society – but they couldn't be *too* isolated. Indeed, they seem to have been fully aware of and involved in civic political life. John the Clairvoyant, in the *Historia Monachorum,* is a good example. A bit of a local celebrity, he'd apparently renounced the world in its entirety but still managed to provide marriage counselling advice for local aristocrats. Some of these desert monks may have been very devout, and perhaps even annoyed by the steady stream of Roman bigwigs wanting relationship or legal advice. Others may have welcomed it. There were saints and charlatans, we can be sure, and perhaps, in some cases, not too much difference between them.

In the fourth century, Jerome of Stridon wrote about another famous eremite, Hilarion, who fled from a desert to find a more solitary life near Syracuse in Sicily, then Dalmatia, then Cyprus. Jerome explicitly says that Hilarion was trying to avoid people, even while it actually seems that he was creeping closer and closer to major population centres. Martin of Tours (who was actually bishop of Tours – not a very isolated position at all) also had a reputation for being ascetic and solitary. Apparently, he was tricked into accepting the episcopal role against his better instincts – we might imagine him acquiescing, 'Oh well, if I *must*.' He lived in a massive monastery that was apparently 'so sheltered and remote that it did not lack the solitude of the desert' – as Sulpicius Severus wrote in his hagiography for Martin. But the monastery was only half an hour's walk from the centre of Tours.

All these hagiographies, histories and myths contain facts and realities, submerged under wonderfully distracting currents and eddies. We peer through them to get glimpses of real people, the celebrities of their age. And their stories, their myths – those of St Cuthbert, of John the Clairvoyant and Martin of Tours are just like those of Maradona, Eva Perón and Che Guevara, indeed – aren't just about individual lives. They're intimately linked to wider myths of nationhood and identity.

Origin Myths

The saints, the material culture, the language – the connections between these regions of north-west Europe – Scotland, Ireland, Wales, Cornwall, Brittany – are striking. They transcend modern national borders and seem to speak of more ancient links. Coasts are permeable edges, not barriers, in this 'Atlantic Archipelago', as some historians have described it. The connections seem to be summed up in one word, *Celtic*. We talk about Celtic culture: Celtic languages, Celtic music, Celtic art, the Celtic Church. The word is hugely problematic, though – it's a very recent invention. It's sobering to reflect that no one in antiquity referred to any inhabitant of Britain or Ireland as a 'Celt'. We only think of these areas and their culture as Celtic because, in the early eighteenth century, a curator at the Ashmolean Museum in Oxford recognised the connections between languages spoken in these regions, and plumped for the word 'Celtic' to describe that linguistic family. (It was a word that the Romans had used for inhabitants of parts of Gaul, and had come to mean something quite generic, like 'ancient'.)

In the nineteenth century into the twentieth, in what was partly a reaction to overbearing English imperialism, people in parts of Britain and Ireland sought to recover and revitalise their identities and cultures, remembering, recovering and recreating a sense of what it meant to be 'Celtic'. This doesn't mean that modern Celtic identities are an entirely recent invention, a confection, just a romantic idea. Not at all. Culture is always being reinvented – it is a process, an endless tapestry. And the historical, cultural, linguistic connections between the rugged lands of the Atlantic Archipelago are real – it's just that, in the past, no one would have used the word 'Celtic' to describe them. So, yes, it's an anachronistic term, but it's useful, so I'll continue to use it here.

It's interesting that those Celtic connections seem clearer in the Iron Age, and then again in the late Roman and post-Roman periods. They seem to have been somewhat obscured during the centuries when (some of) these regions were under Roman control – and maybe we've made it worse because Roman history and archaeology tends to grab our attention, with its detailed accounts – of some things: its cities, its sophisticated baths and lovely villas with mosaic pavements and underfloor heating. (Who doesn't love a hypocaust?) Perhaps, even, the connections that seem to be revitalised in the middle of the first millennium represent the evolution of local, regional identities that once again are somehow set against, or apart from, the Roman Empire – just as, many centuries later, they would represent a reaction against English hegemony.

Historians have struggled to make sense of the cultural connections in the Atlantic Archipelago – and the way in which these regions seem to provide us with a different narrative to the usual story about the end of the western Roman Empire. That 'usual story' typically involves fragmentation of territories and invasions of people who are culturally and linguistically Germanic (a term that is equally problematic as Celtic, especially as language and material culture do not map neatly onto one another). Eventually, successor kingdoms assumed the names of those incoming Germanic groups: Franks and Angles eventually giving their names to France and England.

In the Atlantic Archipelago, migration has also been invoked to explain the origin of Brittany. In the sixth century, the historian Procopius wrote about a new kingdom being formed when the Franks entered into a treaty with the Armoricans; he also mentioned that several ethnic groups, who he identified as *Angilloi* (Angles), *Frissones* (Frisians) and *Brittones* (Britons), had migrated from Britain to the continent. Procopius was writing from several hundred miles away, in Constantinople, but another sixth-century writer much closer to home, the Welsh Gildas (who reputedly studied at Illtud's monastery and had a monastery named after him in Brittany), told a similar story. He mentioned refugees fleeing Britain in the face of Saxon onslaught – though he, like Procopius, doesn't say where they ended up. But it's clear that later writers believed that Britons, retaining their ancient name, *Brittones*, had carried that name over the English Channel to what had previously been known as Armorica or Aremorica ('the land facing the sea'), leading to it being renamed Brittania – Brittany.

There's another clue among the names of smaller kingdoms within Brittany. From the sixth to eighth centuries, Brittany appears to have been divided into three polities: Domnonée/*Domnonia* and Cornouaille/*Cornubia* in the west, and the Vannetais/*Gwened* (centred on the city of Vannes) in the east. Domnonia and Cornouaille are essentially the same (with slight variations in spelling) as the old names for Devon and Cornwall, in south-west Britain. (Those names were known since the Roman period, with the implication that these regions were originally Iron Age kingdoms.) Some historians have argued that the names of the Breton regions –and the British connection they implied – might have been invented by ninth-century writers at Landévennec Abbey. Others have suggested that the names mean something much more definite and real, representing 'united kingdoms' straddling the English Channel.

What we can say with some certainty is that the Breton names come *after* the British ones. The Breton *Domnonia* is first attested in the seventh century, in the *Life of St Samson,* and *Cornubia* in the late ninth. Armorica itself was being referred to as Brittania as early as the sixth century. It seems obscure not to recognise that an important connection between western Britain and Brittany was being forged (or consolidated) in those late-Roman and post-Roman centuries. As Caroline Brett and colleagues point out, 'regional names are not bestowed, and do not persist, without good reason: they must imply that regional identities in Brittany were formed under a strong and lasting influence from the corresponding British regions'.

It's generally very hard to work out what was going on with identities in those crucial centuries, through the demise to the end of the western Roman Empire. Romans famously thought of themselves as civilised, with anyone outside the Empire to be a bit, well, barbaric. But after nearly four centuries of Roman rule in Britain, the difference between 'Romans' and 'Britons' was less perceptible. (Though, as archaeologists Miles Russel and Stuart Laycock have argued, a large proportion of the country, especially away from the cities, remained quite 'un-Roman' throughout.) When the Roman army left Britain and the last imperial magistrates were kicked out, how did people think of themselves? As 'barbarians' once again, or still-civilised but un-Roman Britons? And how exactly did 'British' identity spread among the Gallo-Roman population of Armorica – with the arrival of elites persuading locals that they could step in and run things better than the Romans had done, perhaps?

It seems reasonable to infer that some people were moving from one (ex-Roman) province to another (ex-Roman) province – and in the process, forging new polities, new identities. But there's plenty of debate over the details, including just how much migration was actually happening – were there large numbers of settlers? Or just military elites moving in? Or old elites forging new alliances? The reality may have been less of a wholesale turnover in population (as the word 'migration' can unhelpfully imply) and more of an evolution – with shifts in political power, certainly, as elite families tried to maintain or expand their spheres of influence.

The movement of people around the Atlantic Archipelago wasn't restricted to this flow from Britain to Brittany. In some ways, it seems that once the Roman army withdrew from Britain, the contact with those nearest Atlantic shores took off – perhaps some ancient routes were revitalised after centuries of attenuation, especially between territories that had been inside the Empire – like southern Britain, and those that had remained outside – like Ireland. There's an impression that, once Roman frontiers no longer meant anything, movement – in all directions – was freed up. Although it's true that the relative isolation of Ireland, while Britain and Gaul were part of the Roman Empire, has been vastly overplayed. Writing in the first century CE, Tacitus said, 'The interior parts are little known, but through commercial interaction and merchants there is better knowledge of the harbours and approaches.' It's clear that people were travelling between Britain and Ireland, bringing with them plenty of objects, practices and ideas, during the last centuries of Roman rule in Britain. We can detect an echo of Latin in Ogham inscriptions: while Ogham was a local alphabet, used to write Irish, it was influenced by Latin grammar, and some of these inscriptions are thought to date to as early as the late fourth century. Other examples of cultural arrivals in

Ireland include extended inhumations, penannular brooches, Roman-style short swords – and Christianity (yes, St Patrick was a relative latecomer). These elements of Gallo-Roman and Romano-British culture can be tracked entering Ireland on its east coast and spreading south and west. As Richard Warner put it, 'The introduction of Christian missions into the same areas, from Gaul and from Britain, was simply part of that process.' The traffic was two-way, of course, with evidence of Irish clerics travelling widely; the Irish monk Columbanus travelled to Frankish Gaul and founded schools and monasteries there – and in Italy. (And although the 'Celtic', insular Church seemed to have an identity of its own, that didn't mean it was hermetically sealed from the rest of western Europe, particularly Frankish Gaul – where there were plenty of other bishops who seem to have had British names.)

Up in the north of Britain, in what is now Scotland, different kingdoms were emerging and vying with each other for power. In eastern Britain, old elites may have stayed in power by re-inforcing links across the North Sea; there was some migration too (if not the full-scale invasion and population replacement implied by later writers). In the west, in Wales and Cornwall, connections across the Irish Sea and the Channel seem to have assumed more importance – or at least, we see those links more clearly in those post-Roman centuries. And while we use that term 'post-Roman', we can see that elements of Roman culture were deeply embedded – and indeed, continuing to spread, especially through the medium of Christianity, as we have seen in the persistence and evolution of the old Roman education system, now being taught in monasteries.

In Brittany, whether through a major southbound migration from the south-west of Britain, or from reinforced connections and political alliances, the link across the Channel was clearly evident to medieval writers. And it was in vogue to connect ideas of belonging, of group identity, to one or more founding individuals. In Brittany, several origin myths emerged. One, recounted by Geoffrey of Monmouth in his *History of the Kings of Britain,* written in the twelfth century, described how a Roman senator, Maximianus, together with a Briton named Conanus, invaded Gaul and established Brittany. There's perhaps a hint of actual historicity here – the Roman's name is similar to that of Magnus Maximus, who was briefly a Roman emperor in the west (ruling Britain, Gaul and Spain) after seizing power in a military coup in 383.

There's a somewhat similar tale to be found among the writings of a sixth-century Roman historian based in Constantinople, Jordanes. His history is obviously fictionalised at times, with Gothic armies sacking Troy and fighting Egyptians. But he makes an intriguing mention of a British king bringing troops to Brittany in the 470s – to assist the Roman troops of Emperor Leo I, fighting against the Goths. Riothamus (which means 'great king') apparently brought a large army, which for some time was stationed north of the Loire – in Brittany. And perhaps once they'd reached Brittany, some of those British fighters decided to stay and settle; perhaps the emperor even made that deal with them.

Another origin myth of Brittany is intimately tied up with Christianity, with the recognition of not one, not two, but *seven* founding saints – who seem to have become more important to Breton identity over time. They are: Corentin of Quimper, Tugdual of Treguier, Paternus of Vannes, Paul Aurelian (who gives his name to St Pol-de-Leon), Machutus of Alet (Malo), Brieuc, and of course – Samson of Dol. They seem to have emerged, in an evolutionary fashion, from the great mass of Breton saints who are commemorated in the place names and saints' lists, gradually being whittled down to that list of seven. It's hard to extract robust details of their travels from their (usually much later) hagiographies, especially when some journeys were clearly invented to explain why a saint's cult had become associated with a certain place, and when miraculous voyages abound in the texts – as symbolic story motifs.

Corentin, whose attributes include being the patron saint of seafood, may not have done much sea-voyaging, as he's said to have been born in the Cornouaille region of Brittany. Tugdual or Tudwal was apparently a prince of Cornouaille, and travelled to Ireland and North Wales before returning to Brittany. The *Vita S. Paterni*, which may have been composed in the eleventh or twelfth centuries, claims that Padarn was a Breton who went to be a monk in Wales before returning to become bishop of Vannes. But, just to give a flavour of how unreliable these hagiographies can be, it's thought that this *Vita* conflated a Welsh saint of the same name with a recorded fifth-century bishop of Vannes; there were political reasons for stressing that British (Welsh) connection at the time.

Paul Aurelian, or Paulus Aurelianus, is said to have been Welsh, the son of a chieftain in South Wales. His hagiography was composed in 884 by a monk called Wrmonoc, at Landévennec Abbey, who once again may have woven in Welsh identities – including a king called Poul of Penychen and a St Paulinus who was the tutor of St David – with that of a Breton saint. Wrmonoc also claims that Illtud was the teacher of both Gildas and David. (He calls David *Aquaticus,* a nickname flowing from his particular brand of ostentatious asceticism: a determination to survive on just bread and water, abstaining from alcohol. In *Vita Pauli,* Gildas and David are portrayed as friends, but other sources suggest they actually led rival monastic movements.) Wrmonoc suggests that Paul Aurelian travelled from Wales to Cornwall and Brittany, but the confusion over identities throws those voyages into question. Machutus is another bishop-saint whose hagiography may have been stitched together from cannibalised traditions and cults. It's been suggested that there was a concerted effort to produce those 'authorised biographies' in the ninth century, stimulated by a reorganisation of dioceses in Francia. Machutus was said to have been educated at the monastery of Llancarfan in Morgannwg (Glamorgan), where he was taught by the famous Irish voyaging saint, Brendan, before he set off on his own voyages. (Nowhere else is Brendan connected with Llancarfan, but the hagiographers may have seen that his cult was becoming very popular – he could add some 'star value' to Machutus's story; it was useful to create those connections with both Wales and Ireland.) Samson's hagiography, probably written in the late seventh century, seems among the most dependable. As we've seen, it describes him travelling fairly widely, from Wales to Ireland, Cornwall and Brittany, where he's said to have founded the monastery at Dol.

The more militaristic explanations for the origin of Brittany and the saintly ones aren't necessarily exclusive. Drawing these threads together, we could speculate that migrations started with armies on the move, forming a bridgehead. Then more people – including, importantly, clergymen (some of whom would become saints) – could have flowed in, contributing to a sustained wave of migration. But we shouldn't take these histories too literally.

Modern historians take all these origin myths with a pinch

of salt – while recognising there's something meaningful in the spirit, if not the letter, of these tales. Rather than one or even seven key founding individuals and events, it's more likely that the stories reflect an ongoing *process* of contact, migration and cultural diffusion, a process that reaches right back, indeed, into prehistory. Simple, neat explanations linking the transformation of Armorica into Brittany with a general migration of Britons, including linking the arrival of the Breton language to a Cornish migration into Brittany in the fifth to seventh centuries (very much in vogue in the mid-twentieth century) are also treated with caution today; just as they are with the 'arrival' of 'Anglo-Saxons' into England.

More recent interpretations of the history emphasise the importance of *ongoing connections* between Britain and Brittany, as each area began to establish its identity in a post-Roman world. And it could be that leaders in western Britain were actively looking to expand their spheres of influence across the Channel, filling the power vacuums left by the departing Roman empirical administration. But importantly, all the while, the legacy of empire would play into those identities; leaders in these regions may have been rejecting government from Rome (or Constantinople) but the *idea* of *Romanitas* (or 'Roman-ness') was still strong – you didn't stop being 'civilised' just because you were now living in a new kingdom.

Even under Roman rule, various regions in the provinces had effectively been ruled by client kings; the *idea* of kingship had survived from the Iron Age, and now it resurfaced as the western Empire fragmented – except this time, it was legitimised and supported by Christianity, *Christianitas* being strongly associated with *Romanitas*. In the sixth century, these regional rulers were called *iudex* ('judge'), *praesul* ('protector') or *comes* ('count' or 'earl'). But by the seventh century, they were acquiring the title *rex*, 'king', which had biblical connotations too – harking back to the ancient Israelite kings, given this title in the Latin translation of the Hebrew Scriptures. In Brittany, Judicael was given the title *rex* in sources written not long after his death; in Gwynedd, Cadfan was the first British king to be recognised in this way, in a contemporary inscription.

We've already begun to see how closely connected kings and bishops were; sometimes they were literally, genealogically related. Caroline Brett and colleagues drew attention to the fact that both religious and secular leaders 'were drawn from elite families which had monopolised office-holding in western Britain for generations'. In some cases, there was very little divide between secular rule and ecclesiastical roles – in fact, there was a revolving door between them. Both Gregory of Tours and Gildas, writing in the sixth century, mention various rulers in Britain, with small kingdoms, similar in size to a Roman *civitas*; these rulers are warriors and often engaged in fighting each other, and with raiding – building up their power and wealth. They have British names – but they are Christian. Maglocunus or Maelgwn (whose name means 'Princely Hound' or 'Princely Warrior'), king of Gwynedd, was a monk for a while; Macliavus or Macliau was bishop of Vannes before he seized power in Brittany, becoming a count (effectively a king).

The hagiographies tell us that all these ruling and ecclesiastical families were connected, across the sea, across those 'Celtic' lands – and beyond. In an era where we have very little near-contemporary written documentation other than those saints' hagiographies, especially in Brittany, we're just glimpsing a religious tip of the iceberg. The saints are those whose names and stories have come down to us, but they're just the clerical members of high-status families who were well networked across the whole region: Ireland, Wales, Scotland, western Britain and Brittany. The voyaging saints, hailing from these elite families, were ideal emissaries to carry a family's name and fortune across the seas, forging useful alliances and consolidating dynasties – but now in the name of Christianity. The cults of saints helped to fix those names in popular imagination, to reinforce the status of their families and the places they had founded and preached in. Annual festivals on saints' days, rituals at shrines, pilgrimage – and all those 'voyages of the saints' – helped. (The strength of cult practices like this – focused on ritual rather than scripture – may even be one of the reasons that Carolingian clergy in Francia would later consider Brittany to be 'un-Christian', despite – or because of – all of its local saints.) In Britain, the strength of the early Church in the west also seemed to have been considered to be a threat to the hegemony of Rome, especially as they were professing a slightly different version of Christianity, following the teachings of a theologian called Pelagius. The Celtic west was always a bit of a law unto itself; even when it was infused with *Romanitas-Christianitas* – it had its own style, its own way of doing things.

The fact that Welsh, Cornish and Breton were mutually intelligible languages right up until the eleventh century speaks of a deep and broad social connectivity across these regions; a 'long-lasting undertow to the visible, high-level contacts'. It's likely that many people were also, at least, bilingual in the Roman period and beyond – speaking Latin as well as a regional Celtic, Brittonic language, with plenty of Latin words entering Welsh, Cornish and Breton.

The origin myths and hagiographies contain hints of history, with high-profile travellers – general-kings and bishop-saints – standing in for the much wider population movement and contact that must have been happening. These stories are also written much later than the events they claim to describe, looking back with a certain view of the past that was relevant to the identities and politics of their day (and that's fascinating too). We'll get closer to understanding the reality of migration in this period when we have more ancient DNA results from well-dated samples, which will illuminate those movements in more detail, with 'archaeogenomics' becoming a powerful tool to interrogate those demographic changes over time. For the moment, we can assume some migration was happening, while perhaps doubting that wholesale population replacements were underway.

We'll set aside the hagiographies for now, and we must wait patiently for archaeogenomics to work its magic and reveal the scale of migration around the Atlantic Archipelago at the end of the Roman period and beyond. But the histories certainly give us the impression that this was a period of social and political upheaval – and somehow, the spread of Christianity was part of that, or at least, was happening against that background. There's another strand of evidence we can turn to now, which can reveal more clearly how culture and society were changing in Brittany – at the time it was changing – and that's archaeology.

On the Ruin of Brittany

We've seen that the birth of Brittany was intimately linked with the story of the end of the western Roman Empire – this was precisely the time when Armorica became known as Brittany. But the historical sources for this period, and indeed for the earlier period – Armorica under the Romans – are very scanty. The peninsula simply isn't mentioned in written sources after the Roman conquest of Gaul in 58–50 BCE, right up until the late fourth century. And as we've seen, myths expanded to fill the gaps in the history. But even when people don't leave much behind in the way of written records, there are important clues to be gleaned from the remains of their material culture – the evidence that archaeology brings to light.

Archaeological investigations have revealed plenty of evidence of Roman culture in Brittany in the first to fourth centuries. As everywhere, it's most evident in larger settlements, and in Brittany there were five important regional hubs. These had been prominent in the Iron Age and went on to become Roman *civitates* and, eventually, modern cities: Rennes, Nantes, Vannes, Corseul and Carhaix. (The relative abundance of archaeological evidence in Brittany, contrasting with an absence of written documentation, is very similar to the situation in south-west Britain, where recent archaeological discoveries – including roads and fortlets – have taken scholars by surprise, showing that Roman influence and infrastructure extended much further west in Devon and Cornwall than had been previously assumed.)

The archaeology paints a general picture – where Brittany seems to have been relatively prosperous and well connected in the early Roman period. But then, in the third century, things appear to have taken a turn for the worse. The impression is of many towns and villas falling into decline, though not being completely abandoned; people continued scratching a living, amid the rubbish and rubble. This apparent economic downturn was happening at a time when we know that, more broadly, the western end of the Roman Empire was wracked with political instability; again and again, we see various military commanders trying it on and sometimes succeeding in seizing power in the western Empire. Historians have also suggested that Brittany's third-century demise could have come about due to a shift in the flow of commerce. A build-up of Roman troops on the Rhine frontier, ready to protect the Empire from 'barbarian' incursions, would have seen a heightened focus on trade routes connecting to south-east Britain – drawing focus away from the north-west corner of Gaul. It's possible that the political turmoil of the time was effectively a social response to an environmental challenge, with climate change ushering in a cool, dry period – causing widespread crop failure. (Britain was affected too, but less severely than Brittany; perhaps the presence of large Roman army bases in that province was enough to bolster the economy there.)

Whatever the precise reasons – and it's likely that several factors were at play – Brittany seems to have become something of a backwater, although archaeological discoveries reveal a few exceptions. Some relatively sumptuous villas and townhouses seem to have escaped ruination; somehow, their owners must have bucked the trend, weathering that economic downturn, riding the storm – well into the fourth century.

The fourth century appears to have seen a limited economic recovery, with coins and a limited volume of imported pottery trickling into Brittany. But the overall picture for the late Roman period – and, in fact, this is true for all of northern Gaul, not just Brittany – is one of decline. It must have been a tough period to live through, with all that political volatility, barbarian raids, coin debasement, high taxes and rural poverty.

Alongside the wider signs of economic downturn, there are signs of investment in defensive infrastructure. Town walls were strengthened; coastal forts were established. Some historians have suggested that this military investment in late Roman Gaul represented a sort of physical propaganda and sleight of hand: the new defences were allegedly designed to counter the 'barbarian threat' – whereas it was actually *internal* threats and social unrest that the Roman administration was mostly worried about. And not without reason – there are plenty of reports of revolts in Armorica in the early fifth century. We might look to more modern political scenarios for comparison here; it is not unknown, in much more recent times, for politicians to invoke a shadowy external threat. Fear can be a useful means of control.

What's particularly interesting is that this apparent militarisation of society isn't just seen in those larger built features in the landscape; we also see it at a more personal level. Around this time, we start to see more grave goods being included in graves. These include brooches and beads, but also military-style belts and weapons. It looks like there was a need to very visibly demonstrate the status of the deceased. As always with burials, we must remember that the dead do not bury themselves. The way in which they were buried may have followed their wishes, but in the end, it's their living relatives who are performing the ritual. They were demonstrating and cementing their own social status while honouring the dead. For men, often buried with weapons, status seems to be have been tied up with a warrior identity. You could perhaps argue that this was more symbolic than literal; more virtual than real. But even if largely symbolic, that idea, that impression of warriorness, was clearly important.

Similarly furnished graves appear around this time across northern Gaul, sometimes interpreted as representing the burial of *foederati* – barbarian mercenaries welcomed in by the Roman Empire. In south-east England too, similar graves may once have been uncritically interpreted as representing 'Germanic' incomers – the Angles, Saxons, Jutes and others described by the likes of Bede. While these graves undoubtedly indicate the influence of immigrants, and new cultural ideas, they may also be an indication of a wide response to social and political disruption (as I've written about more extensively in my book *Buried*).

In northern Gaul, the lined-up furnished burials known as 'row-graves', and sometimes interpreted as 'Germanic', contain Roman-style objects such as pottery and glass vessels, and sometimes a coin in the mouth, as per the Roman tradition. The most common objects found in male graves are belt fittings such as buckles, made in a Roman style; belts were a symbol of authority in western Roman society. Earlier interpretations missed the presence of weapons in Roman graves – making the 'early Germanic' less special in containing weapons. Axes are present in some, sparking a suspicion of Germanic connections, but might have been used in a Roman context by this time in northern Gaul. And although Roman citizens were legally prohibited from carrying weapons, many may have chosen to ignore that, especially in politically unstable times. Female burials often contain brooches of an undeniably Germanic style (trumpet-brooches, saucer-brooches, crossbow-brooches). It's clear that fashions and styles were being picked up from northern Europe – but it's impossible to tell whether a woman in northern Gaul wearing a Germanic-style brooch was Germanic *herself*. It's also important to note that while the overall style of the brooches might look very 'Germanic', the finishing decoration on them can be distinctly Roman; this is similar to the belt buckles that are often embellished using a Roman chip-carving technique.

Back in 1992, archaeologist Guy Halsall warned that the 'early Germanic' burials in northern Gaul had been simply assumed to represent a population of incomers. But careful dating seemed to dispel this idea – because the row-graves emerge *first* in northern Gaul. So they don't appear to be an imported idea from 'Free Germany' or Saxony to the north-east, where, anyway, the most common contemporary burial rite was cremation.

Instead of being the graves of 'Germanic' immigrants, it seems that these row-graves represent 'the traditional late Roman funeral custom but with the addition of more lavish grave-goods'. Why the change? Perhaps we can understand that by asking: why did people *need* to be buried with this extra stuff? And of course, as I so often find myself writing, people don't bury themselves – so the real question is: why did those burying the dead *need* them to have that extra stuff with them? The answer to that question must lie in what that *stuff* – the belts, weapons and cruciform brooches – symbolised and represented, and that was: status and authority, continuing into the afterlife.

Funerals represented an important social opportunity – for elite families to make sure their authority, wealth and status was on show, through largesse, feasting and lavish costume – on the living and the dead. Bodies would be soon buried and hidden from view, but for a while, they would be on show – with brooches, belt buckles and weapons gleaming. The death of an important member of society could spark a struggle for leadership in a community, but the funeral could help to ease those transitions, demonstrating the status of the wider family, pushing an heir to the fore. To Halsall, the appearance of these graves signalled not the arrival of a new 'ethnic' group, but instead, a period of elevated social stress and competition – with the need for families to display their power, to demonstrate and shore up their social standing. As imperial authority was waning, prominent families and community leaders would need to step up.

And, indeed, there are hints in the histories that certain families were competing for ascendancy in the early fifth century – with reports of *bacaudae* causing trouble. This word is tricky. During an earlier period when imperial hegemony was under threat, certain community leaders emerged, supported by disaffected peasants – and these rebels were termed *bacaudae*. By the fifth century, the word had developed to mean something more like 'bandit', with connotations of violent criminality.

But it may be that some of these *bacaudae* actually represented local ruling elites – taking matters into their own hands, seizing power and becoming tyrants (in the original sense). Landlords becoming warlords. There's a further clue from coins: in the areas where 'early Germanic' graves appear, there's also evidence of imitation imperial silver coinage. And another piece of (negative) evidence that feeds into this picture is the absence of such richly furnished graves south of the Loire, where Roman hegemony clung on longer.

In the north, those people would have had all sorts of reasons for behaving as they did, dressing as they did, burying their dead as they did. They would have been influenced by Roman ideas about aristocracy, 'barbarian' ideas of aristocracy, Christianity and other religious beliefs and practices. They were forging new identities, it seems; some of that would have been very definitely in opposition to Roman ideas – but some of it was very much drawing on Roman ideas about how to run society.

It's a compelling argument – that these richly furnished graves in the north represent heightened social competition for local, regional power, when imperial authority faltered. It doesn't mean that there was *no* immigration from north-west Europe – into Gaul, into Britain – in this period, but perhaps that this isn't the main reason for more lavish graves. In the end, it's probably a bit of both – local elites jostling for power *and* migration. Ancient DNA studies have suggested that there *was* significant inward migration in the first half of the first millennium, though it's presently unclear how much of this was taking place in the late Roman period, and how much in post-Roman centuries. It's complicated; people were most certainly moving around, and the social and political milieu was changing at the same time. One day we'll have more answers, a better understanding of the complex patterns, as archaeo-genomics starts to reveal the nature of migration as well as patterns of kinship.

By the early sixth century, though, things had definitely changed in Gaul. The Roman province was no more. In its stead was a Frankish kingdom ruled by Clovis, founder of the Merovingian dynasty. As for Armorica, its eastern reaches were gathered up into that kingdom, including the cities of Nantes, Rennes and Vannes. But by this time, as Gregory of Tours tells us, the western end of the peninsula had been settled by those British incomers, becoming Brittany.

It's very hard to test this archaeologically; British-made goods had been turning up in Armorica for centuries, even millennia, after all. But some specific links and claims have been made. It's been argued, for instance, that the existence of

Dorset Black Burnished pottery in Le Yaudet fort in Finistère is evidence for British soldiers (under Roman leadership) being stationed there in the fourth century. This doesn't seem to be an unreasonable suggestion; the use of *foederati* or mercenaries elsewhere in the Empire is well known. In Britain, it's thought that Germanic *foederati* were brought in – with some even suggesting that these soldiers could have formed the basis or vanguard of the 'Anglo-Saxon' migration into Britain (even if this was less profound a population movement than later histories might suggest).

But – as contemporary archaeologists are always keen to point out – *pots are not people*. Exchange of particular goods may indicate movement and contact – but not necessarily migration. People were clearly moving around – but they could have come and gone. And an artefact can pass through many hands on its way from its place of manufacture to the place where it ends up, waiting for an archaeologist to dig it up.

Just as difficult as it is to *prove* a British military presence in Brittany, it's much harder to *disprove* it. We know from historical sources that Roman troops were garrisoned in the main cities of Brittany, for instance – but there's no observable archaeological trace of their existence. It seems extraordinary, but even the presence of a large military force can be archaeologically difficult to spot. Still, it would be dangerous to assume a British military presence in Brittany in the absence of any evidence. And some historians have argued that Britain was never well known as a source of such *foederati* troops.

Very generally, the archaeology of late Roman and post-Roman Brittany provides us with a picture of gradual decline – and a certain militarisation of society. This, then, is the wider context for the cultural change that was taking place.

Because, amid all that turmoil and turbulence, Christianity was taking hold. By the time we get to the written histories, it's Christian clerics who are doing all the writing, and they tell us about the saints who lived in the fifth and sixth centuries — saints like Illtud and Samson. Christianity is intimately tied up with the origin myths of the polities emerging out of the post-Roman Dark Ages; Brittany, with its suite of seven founder-saints, is no exception.

So – might it possible to see traces of very early Christianity in the archaeological record? We have this picture of decline and those military-style belts and weapons appearing in burials. But is there anything else? Graves do seem the obvious place to start looking.

Finding the Christian Dead

There are many different types of funerary practice. They're tied up with tradition, with religious beliefs, with personal preferences. In western Europe, across the time frame we're exploring, some people were cremated and others were buried. Some were interred with grave goods and others without. Some graves were lined up in an west–east orientation, others were not. Perhaps, if we can chart all these variations, we'll be able to see changes through time which might reveal the spread of the new religion in the west.

In the third and fourth century in Britain, there was a change underway, as once-popular cremation burial was giving way to inhumation burial as the standard — or at least, most common — practice. A similar pattern is seen across the Empire, and this has been interpreted as a growing influence of Roman culture — but certainly not Christianity, as at this time only a very tiny proportion of people in the Roman Empire were Christian. But this is a very broad-brush picture of what was happening. If we look more closely, we see that funerary rites were geographically quite diverse over the crucial centuries of late Roman into post-Roman Britain. In western Britain, for instance, bodies were often buried in stone-lined cists – in what seems to have been a revival of a pre-Roman, Iron Age tradition. But there's even variation within a cemetery; some bodies may have been buried in cists while others were interred in simpler graves.

There is a really striking change in the style of burials in south-eastern Britain in the fifth and sixth centuries. This is when we see those 'Anglo-Saxon' graves, full of artefacts as well as the bones of the dead. Bodies were interred, fully clothed (we can tell from metal fastenings like wrist clasps, buckles, belts and brooches), adorned with other jewellery, with delicate bronze toilet sets, small knives and weaponry. They tend to be highly gendered – and it's these graves that display the male 'warrior status' that we also see in similar graves in northern France. They're often assumed to be non-Christian graves because they contain grave goods.

But rather awkwardly, a little later, some of the most richly furnished graves include some very beautiful gold pectoral crosses. They are most definitely Christian. And while it's true that certain clerics may have implied that grave goods were showy and un-Christian, the Church itself never forbade them. It's also the case that bishops and members of royalty were often buried with grave goods, even in later periods when the vast majority of graves were unfurnished (one rule for them . . .). As archaeologists Alain Dierkens and Patrick Périn neatly put it, 'A burial without grave goods is no more logically Christian than a richly furnished grave is indicative of pagan beliefs.'

But what about *orientation* of graves? In the past, some archaeologists suggested that this could provide an important clue – graves arranged in a west–east orientation were believed to signal Christian sensibilities. The idea is that the dead were buried facing the east, ready to spot Jesus Christ emerging in triumph on Judgement Day (like a Christian sun god). But unfortunately for this theory, plenty of non-Christian graves are lined up west–east, while early Christian burials are quite variable in alignment. A careful study of grave orientation in non-Christian medieval Iceland is particularly informative – it revealed startling inconsistency: graves could face any direction. The only rule appeared to be that, within a cemetery, burials tended to be lined up the same way – presumably for practical reasons more than anything else.

A large survey of burials in early medieval Gaul and Germania also revealed plenty of variety. Just as there had been no specific religious laws about grave goods, there was no legislation related to grave orientation in the early medieval period. Instead, graves often seem to have been arranged to accommodate other features in the landscape – which could simply have been the slope of the ground, or an existing founder's grave in a cemetery. And the Church largely stayed out of it – burial rites were considered to be private, family matters.

Much later, when churchyards developed around parish churches, graves did tend to be oriented west–east, but that may have been more to do with slotting graves neatly around the church itself. (Some parish churches started out as private funerary chapels for local aristocrats, later assuming a role for the wider community, with graveyards accumulating around them; another manifestation of that age-old tradition of clustering graves around the burial of a high-status 'founder'.)

But the period we're interested in, when Christianity was spreading, is much earlier – way before churchyards, and west–east oriented graves as standard; way before the Church got heavily involved with funerary rituals. Essentially, we're looking for Christian graves in cemeteries which would have contained plenty of non-Christians. In the middle of the first millennium, when Christianity was spreading through the Empire, most Christians would have been buried in among everyone else. The disappointing reality we have to face is that their graves were (and are) indistinguishable from those of their non-Christian neighbours.

But there are a *few* notable exceptions, which *can* be linked with early Christianity. They tend to be high-status examples. From as early as the beginning of the fourth century, in Gaul and Germania, we start to see what appear to be small Christian shrines appearing in cemetery settings. Such a shrine might be a *martyrium*, for a martyr; a *confessio*, for the grave of an unmartyred saint; or a *memoria*, which housed not a whole body, but just a relic of the saint. Those shrines could then become a focus for further burials. (If you could be buried close to a saint, you might hope that might help you when the Day of Judgement arrived.) In a few places, archaeologists have brilliantly been able to trace the development of a small funerary shrine into a later, substantial church – with examples at La Madeleine in Geneva, Saint-Denis in northern Paris and Saint-Germain at Auxerre. A religious centre would gain kudos from being associated with a saint; even better if he was actually buried there.

There's a particularly interesting example in Paris: the basilica of the Saints-Apôtres. This church was constructed in the early sixth century, for King Clovis – copying the church of the Holy Apostles in Constantinople, built during the reign of the emperor Constantine, in the fourth century. Clovis's basilica was also built over the grave, the *confessio*, of a local (unmartyred) saint, St Geneviève. In this way, it seems Clovis had succeeded in connecting himself with both Constantine and St Geneviève, as well as creating a handy mausoleum for himself and his wife, Clothilde – and their successors. And once again, we see that association of royalty and saints: how the social elite used those connections to legitimise and advance their status; how, in this case, a saint could be drawn into a royal narrative.

In west Wales and Cornwall, in the late fifth and sixth centuries, there are a few funerary monuments which are definitely Christian – and once again, they're linked to high-status individuals. They're standing stones, inscribed with Latin or Irish Ogam or Ogham, telling us the name of the deceased – usually a man, sometimes with a Christian phrase or symbol. Archaeologist Nancy Edwards has studied these monuments extensively and one of her favourite examples is an intriguing stone pillar from St David's Church in Bridell, Pembrokeshire. Down one side, there's a series of incised lines which make up an Ogham inscription. It reads: *Nettasagri maqi mucoi Briaci* – 'of Nettasagri son of the kindred of Briaci' – and it's thought to have been a grave-marker. It's one of nine or so stones in southwest Wales bearing Ogham inscriptions – bearing testament to the arrival of people from Ireland. There's other evidence of Irish being spoken in some parts of Wales, alongside early Welsh and Latin, up until the seventh century. Once again, we're seeing those strong connections between the lands comprising the Atlantic Archipelago. The stone also bears a Christian motif – a cross in a circle – but it's thought that this was added later, claiming Nettasagri for Christianity retrospectively. Interpreting these archaeological traces of Christianity is very complicated – nothing is as straightforward as it seems at first. There are other, later, stones, where a contemporary Christian connection is assured – where the inscription itself contains Christian references, just like the wonderful carved stones at Llantwit Major. Early traces of Christianity are frustratingly, but perhaps predictably, elusive.

Getting back to Brittany, it seems even harder to find any early archaeological traces of Christianity there. Only a handful of early medieval cemeteries have been excavated, and graves can be very elusive in Brittany; skeletal remains tend not to survive in the acidic soils found across much of the region, and stone-lined cist graves weren't used as much as in Wales and Cornwall. People in early medieval Wales and Ireland loved to reuse prehistoric monuments, including Iron Age circular enclosures and promontory forts, as burial sites; chapels were later built on some cemeteries. With the paucity of burial sites in Brittany, it's hard to know if similar practices were being followed there. They may have been – we just don't have any evidence. There's also a strong possibility that plenty of medieval traces have been obscured by much later church-building in Brittany, particularly in the sixteenth and seventeenth centuries, which saw the creation of many elaborate *enclos paroissiaux* – 'parish enclosures'. Drive through Brittany today and you find yourself marvelling at these monumental churches in almost every small town – they're usually right in the centre, next to the market square, with magnificent arched entrance gates. (It's strikingly different to Cornwall and Wales, where parish churches are often tucked away, a little remote from the centre of village life.)

There are just a few inscribed early medieval stones from Brittany. One is a pillar featuring a cross and the personal name *Gallmau*, from the church at Lanrivoare. And then, at Lomarec, there's a chapel containing an early medieval granite sarcophagus – bearing a curious inscription. Antiquarians became interested in this sarcophagus in the nineteenth century, but found it hard to decipher the inscription. It reads:

IRHA EMA + INRI

The latest analysis of this inscription suggests that it could date to as early as the fifth or sixth century – based on the shape of the letters. Reading it is more problematic, because of the acronyms and abbreviations; it could mean 'The king is entombed [or moulders to earth] here', or 'Here lies Haema, [buried] on the Ides of November; he retreated in peace' or even 'Jesus the Nazarene king of the Jews (INRI) pours forth blood'.

When it comes to smaller archaeological finds, the picture is very similar – there's simply not much from Brittany, especially compared with Ireland, Wales and Cornwall. Across those other regions, there's quite a lot of early medieval metalwork associated with churches – from plates and chalices to reliquaries and croziers – and nearly a hundred handbells. In Brittany, there are just six handbells. That's it. And those probably came from Wales or Cornwall originally.

This all makes sense in the light of what we've learned about early medieval Brittany. Elsewhere, such as in Wales, there's clearly a link between Christianity and high-status sites – or at least, that's where the religion is most visible. The political landscape of Brittany seems to have been flatter – but there were monasteries, or at least, there was *one*. Only three potential early monasteries have been excavated in Brittany, and only one of these is definitely monastic: Landévennec, in the far west.

While many burials may have dissolved into Brittany's acidic soils, and many early traces of Christianity may have been obliterated by those much later, wonderfully ornate *enclos paroissiaux,* perhaps it's better to start with an institution that we know was Christian in the Middle Ages – and then work backwards, looking for its earliest inception.

The next stop on the itinerary is the monastery of Landévennec.

Landévennec

The town of Landévennec is full of artists and artisans. On the day I visited, the sun was shining, and people were opening their houses and gardens to put on miniature exhibitions of art and pottery, drawing in eager tourists. Blue-painted shutters were thrown open on the houses lining the street. Window boxes cascaded with bright, lush plants.

In the museum shop, I found it hard to walk away without some silver Celtic-knot earrings (and a tea towel with a crab on it, but that's less relevant).

Up and over the hill, through the gateway, I walked into the precinct of the old abbey of Landévennec, with its romantic ruins still dominating the estuary. These include a very ancient oratory – a fifth- to sixth-century chapel that housed the relics of the saint – that was, much later, transformed into a laundry room.

The abbey church is there, with the bases of its huge pillars now used as plant pots for palms. The lichen-encrusted stone is decorated with carvings: an anchor here, a fleur-de-lis there. A drain covered with large stone slabs runs across what might have been a courtyard; it's an old stream, constrained and canalised to run right through the fortified abbey. Beyond that, in a long building that's identified as a ninth-century chapter house, and just to the north of it, are the hefty foundations of thick defensive walls which speak of the threat that Landévennec Abbey experienced from the sea in the ninth century, when marauding Vikings realised that monasteries could be immensely rich places: repositories of treasures, full of gold and gems.

I peered down from the walkway suspended above the excavated layers beneath the chapter house, and some metres below me, I saw a narrow, stone-lined cist grave. The occupant's skeletal remains had been removed, but there was more information about them in the beautifully conceived and realised museum at the top of the site, beyond the herb garden.

As you enter this museum, you're greeted by five, almost-full-size, undeniably spooky statues of the saint who founded the abbey in the fifth century. The painted eyes on these wooden carvings are eerie and piercing. These figurines range in date from the fifteenth to the eighteenth century – their subject was long dead by the time they were carved. His name was Winwalloe. It's a name that becomes mangled and transmuted as it travels from one language into another (although I always suspect the variation in spellings masks a similarity in the phonetic, spoken word): *Gwenolé* in Breton, *Winwallus* or *Winwaloeus* or *Wingualoeus* in Latin, *Guenolo* and *Winnold* in English, *Guenolé*, *Vennec* or *Venec* in French (giving us *Lan de Vennec*).

In the *Life of Saint Winwaloe*, written by Wrdestin in the ninth century (four centuries after its subject had lived), we're told that the subject of this history was born in Brittany, the son of a prince of Dumnonia called Fragan, who gave his name to Ploufragan, and Alba Trimammis ('Alba the three-breasted' – who was revered for her fecundity due to this anatomical adaptation to feeding three children at once). Winwaloe was said to have been born in Plouguin, and grew up in Ploufragan. As befitting the son of a prince, he went off to be educated by a cleric, Budoc, who later went on to become bishop of Dol. (According to the hagiographics, Budoc had been born in Brittany, then escaped a conflict with his mother, travelling to Cornwall and then Ireland, where he studied in a monastery at Ardmore, before returning to Brittany; he was also venerated as a saint after his death.)

Winwaloe was said to have wanted to visit Ireland to visit the shrine of the recently deceased St Patrick, but Patrick obligingly visited him in a dream and told him to stay put. With a few other men who'd been taught by Budoc, Winwaloe set up a monastery on a small island near Brest. That one didn't work out, and by some kind of miracle, he was able to sail across the estuary to the other side, where he founded what became Landévennec Abbey (presumably being gifted the land by a powerful relative), and predictably became a saint upon his demise.

Like his mother, and in a way which might seem to us, today, much more pagan than Christian, Winwalloe was revered as a fertility figure – as a 'phallic saint'. And it's not just Landévennec Abbey that bears his name – several churches in Cornwall are dedicated to him, including one at Landewednack (in Cornish, *Lanndewynnek*) and Gunwalloe (in Cornish, *Pluw Wynnwalow*), Tremaine and Poundstock, and one at East Portlemouth in Devon. In Norfolk, Winnold House was originally a Benedictine priory dedicated to St Winwaloe.

When he died, Winwaloe was interred at Landévennec Abbey, but when Vikings attacked the town in later centuries, the monks moved his body, first to Château-du-Loir and then on to Montreuil-sur-Mer, meaning the abbey church there also gained a dedication to him.

I turned away from the five pairs of painted eyes and entered the gallery. Inside, I was momentarily distracted by a tiny sculpture of a reclining woman with a squirrel on a lead, pointed out to me by my cousin, who knows me too well. There were chunks of dressed stone sculptures – lions and coats-of-arms. One damaged stone torso was arresting. Its head was missing, and its legs from the knees down. Also missing was what seems once to have been a large erect penis, the man's right hand holding what's left of the base of the appendage. Did this connect with Winwalloe's reputation as a phallic saint, I wondered?

Nearby was a brightly painted relief of what appeared at first to be a Virgin Mary, holding one child on her lap – but flanked by two others. Each child held the end of the scroll bearing its name emblazoned in gilded letters: S. Guenolae (a variant spelling of Winwaloe), on his mother's lap; S. Guernecs (Wethenoc) to the left and S. Jacut (James) on the right. The mother appeared to have her hands over one breast, with two more exposed just beneath. Here was Alba Trimammis.

There were smaller sculptures, too, including a beautiful ivory tau-crosier. It seems wrong to call it a crosier or cross, when the tau, or T, describes it so much better. Just below the cross-piece, it's carved with floral designs. The cross piece of the T is wrapped in the centre by a frieze depicting a seated man with tendrils of foliage curling around him. The tau-crosier was found during excavations in the nineteenth century, and said to have been buried with an abbot, although those bones have not survived. From its style, it's thought to date to the eleventh century.

Around the atmospherically dark gallery, architectural models of the abbey lay in pools of light, charting its evolution through the ages – from a modest chapel with a few outbuildings to a more sophisticated complex in the high Middle Ages.

But my eye was drawn to a pavement of fragmented terracotta tiles. It was discovered in the abbey church, in front of the choir. The tiles are square, chunky; they weren't made for a floor. They were originally used to create pillars, or pilae, to support a floor above a heated space —they are remnants from a Roman hypocaust, or underfloor heating system. They are an important clue. It turns out that the abbey was built on the site of a Roman villa – recycling its materials, and presumably taking over the agricultural estate of the villa. We've seen strong indications that Christianity and Roman-ness were bound up together – going back to the curriculum on offer at Illtud's monastery. But here, on the west coast of Brittany, was an astonishingly tangible demonstration of *Romanitas* evolving into *Christianitas*. The chronology of the buildings is complicated; it's thought that the Gallo-Roman buildings survived as part of the abbey for centuries, and were finally destroyed in tenth-century Viking raids – after which, any attempt at rebuilding was abandoned and the remains of the villa were just used as a source of building material.

And indeed, across the sea, back in Llantwit Major, there's a hint that Roman-ness wasn't just to be found in the range of subjects on offer at the monastic school – it was embedded in the landscape. People had lived in the Vale of Glamorgan for thousands of years, long before the monastery was even conceived, long before Christianity arrived in these islands. Archaeologists have identified burial mounds, ditches and banked enclosures dating to the Neolithic and Bronze Age. In the latter half of the first millennium BCE, in the Iron Age, people were in the area that's now Llanmaes, just to the north of Llantwit, enjoying a massive feast. They cleared up by burying their rubbish, leaving pig bones, pottery and great bronze cauldrons behind for future archaeologists to discover. The cauldrons and bronze axes found with them were made in north-west France. Although Llantwit Major is set back from the coast, it seems the Afon Colhuw, running through the town, may have been navigable back them – linking Llantwit into a network of maritime connections. There's an Iron Age hill fort overlooking the river, and two more, on the coast, at Summerhouse Point and Nash Point.

When the Romans turned up in Britain with their invasion force in 43 CE, they encountered varying levels of resistance from Iron Age tribes in different regions. Some tribal leaders were already allied with Rome, and practically welcomed them with open arms; others were less enthusiastic about the occupation. The people of south-east Wales, called the Silures by Roman writers, were particularly defiant and put up a fierce fight for more than thirty years – a whole generation of resistance. Eventually, in 75 CE, the Roman army prevailed and a permanent legionary base was installed at Caerleon, just east of Newport today, to keep an eye on the Welsh troublemakers. There was a smaller military camp 5 miles north of Llantwit, on the Roman road running east–west, the route inherited by the modern A48.

Closer to Llantwit Major, at Caermead, just north-west of the modern town, an archaeological excavation starting in the late nineteenth century uncovered the remains of a large Roman villa and outbuildings, arranged around a central courtyard, originally home perhaps to a retired Roman soldier, or a wealthy local farmer, adopting the trappings of Roman civilisation. The coins and pottery from the villa showed that people were living there from the second to the fourth centuries. Several burials were discovered at the site in subsequent excavations, and these were dated much later, to between the seventh and the tenth centuries. This is not unusual at all; there are plenty of records of villas being used as cemeteries, after the Roman house itself fell out of use. Sites like this appear right across Britain – from Ilchester Mead at Somerset, to Norton Disney in Lincolnshire and Winterton in Humberside.

The original excavations at the site of Caermead Villa, carried out by John Storrie in 1888, uncovered the remains of thirty-eight individuals and the complete skeletons of three horses, 'all found within the walls of the room with the tessellated floor; one was found lying over the skeleton of a man'. Violent interpretations were in vogue at the time, and despite the absence of any skeletal injuries, Storrie thought these people and horses had likely been killed on the spot where they were buried. Modern archaeologists prefer less dramatic interpretations; burials in old villas like this are conceived as 'rituals of termination' – saying goodbye to a place that held some memories or an idea of ancestral power, perhaps – or at least, reuse of a known ancient feature in the landscape. (In this way, they may be conceptually similar to the way that Anglo-Saxon burials can be found inserted into much more ancient Bronze Age burial mounds.) But with these villas-turned-cemeteries, there could be something else going on. Two other monasteries in South Wales, at Llandough and Bassaleg, are also known to have been founded near Roman villas.

The pieces of the puzzle are falling into place. The picture is starting to emerge. In Ireland, Britain and Brittany, the clues are there in the genealogies of the saints, their hagiographies, in the ruins of the ancient monasteries and the inscribed stones.

There's something fascinating going on here, in the north-west corner of Europe, this 'Atlantic archipelago', in the fifth and sixth centuries. We're right on the edge of what had been the Roman Empire; in Ireland, we're just beyond it. And as that empire began to fragment, people seem to have been grouping themselves into different polities and forging new identities. Those emerging identities are very complex – and present us with a strange paradox. On the one hand, they seem to be about escaping from Roman control, but on the other, they're all about emulating Roman-ness.

We talk about these centuries as the early medieval or 'post-Roman' period, but Roman-ness appears to have been very deeply rooted, among the social elites – and in regional systems of government and administration that survived the fragmentation of the western Empire: *Romanitas* and *Christianitas* forming different sides of the same, imperial coin. Roman history and ecclesiastical history are starting to look like the *same thing*. But we've pieced this together from such disparate fragments, scattered among place names, clues in later hagiographies, archaeological finds. Are we reading too much into it? Wouldn't it be great to have some more contemporary reports from those crucial post-Roman centuries in the middle of the first millennium? Well, we don't have such a thing, at least, not in Brittany (or Britain).

But whereas the historical evidence for these Celtic lands in this crucial late-Roman and post-Roman period is scarce – much of it written many centuries after events had occurred, and after key figures had died – it turns out there's some incredible contemporary documentary evidence – from neighbouring Gaul, as it became Francia. The picture of *Romanitas* evolving into *Christianitas* is about to shimmer into startling focus, as we move from Brittany into Gaul itself, to the fifth century, and the end of Roman imperial rule.

2

THE END OF EMPIRE

'This was the true origin of the Early Medieval
period – an inexorable process of Romanisation
over several centuries, both within and without.'

RICHARD WARNER

On the Persistence of Villas

The written history from Britain in the fifth and sixth centuries is extremely sparse. In fact, there's really just one near-contemporary source: Gildas's polemical treatise, *De Excidio et Conquestu Britanniae*; or *The Ruin and Conquest of Britain*. The later histories, most of them hagiographies, are fairly laced with propaganda and myth. Looking at the spread of Christianity, we learn something about the *who,* but the *how* and *why* remain fairly obscure. We've seen very clear indications that men from the social elite, the very highest echelons of society in Britain and Brittany, were choosing careers in the Church. But the detail is lacking.

And so it's even more astonishing when we look to fifth-century Gaul, still part of the Roman Empire – at least for a while – and find a veritable treasure trove of literature. There's so much more material to mine for clues – and some of it's even in the form of first-hand accounts. In fact, an awful lot of it comes from the pen of just one man: a prolific writer called Sidonius Apollinaris. He may not, of course, have been *the* most prolific, but through a quirk of fate, a very large bundle of his letters and eulogies have survived to the present. Eric Goldberg, a historian specialising in the Early Middle Ages, has called Sidonius Apollinaris 'the single most important surviving author from 5th-century Gaul'.

Reams of Sidonius's letters have survived: nine books, containing 147 letters, and 24 panegyrics or poetic eulogies. Sidonius collected them together for publication, rather like a memoir. It's important to bear this in mind when we read his words, because while he may have been writing in the first instance to friends and colleagues, he then meant them for public consumption. They were collected, curated and edited accordingly. And like any politician's memoir, they're meant to cast the author in a good light, of course. He may have felt the need to justify some of his actions in office, and to explain and justify – as we shall discover – a certain degree of political flip-flopping on his part. Sidonius lived through the end of Roman rule in Gaul, and his letters are an amazing window into a tumultuous time – and how the social elite were able to ride it.

Sidonius had a good pedigree; the Apollinaris family was very prestigious indeed. Sidonius's father had been prefect of Gaul under the emperor Valentinian III, and his grandfather had occupied the post before that. The Latin, *praefectus*, means 'put in front' or 'put in charge', and it was the highest-ranking administrative role within the empire, under the emperors themselves. The prefecture of Gaul was much bigger than just Gaul itself; it included the whole of the western Roman Empire, beyond Italy – including at its largest, Brittania, Gaul and Iberia.

Born in Lyon, probably around the year 430, Sidonius emerged into the very upper echelons of Gallo-Roman society – with all the opportunities that offered, but also with the expectation that he would maintain that privileged status. He did well for himself, marrying Papianilla, the daughter of Eparchius Avitus, a distinguished general of Gaul who briefly became the Western Roman Emperor in 456.

Sidonius himself became prefect of Rome in 468, and was awarded the titles of patrician and senator. The following year, he returned to his homeland of Gaul, entering into a high-level administrative position in Clermont (ancient Arvernis), one of the oldest and most important cities in France – a city that had been the capital of the Arverni people (whose name is preserved in the Auvergne region), before Gaul was invaded by Julius Caesar and became Roman.

Sidonius owned a country pad 14 miles to the south-west of the city: a beautiful villa. We know this because he wrote about his home there, at length, in a letter: *Epistula II.2* is an invitation to a schoolmaster friend to spend the summer with him at Avitacum. It's a fantastic example of the literary trope ekphrasis (painting a picture in words), and the most detailed description of a fifth-century villa in north-western Europe.

He opens his letter:

Sidonius to his friend Domitius: greetings!
  You accuse me of being a peasant, while I could just as well complain that you are still in town! Spring has changed into summer, and the sun, heightened up to its highest course, extends its ray up to the far pole of Scythia . . .

He urges his friend to leave the '*panting anguish of town and . . . hide yourself in the most merciful retreat from the harshness of the dog-star*' – picking up a theme from classical Roman poets: the idea of escaping the town to a country retreat.

And then he kicks off the description of the villa, starting with the bathhouse:

[It] clings to the roots of a wooded cliff in the south-west . . . First the hot room rises, which is equal in size to the sweat room, except for an apse with a basin, where the force of the boiling water, constrained in its courses, bursts out through the pierced sides of pliant lead piping. Inside, the room is heated and full of daylight, and this abundance of light inside forces

any modest people to consider themselves to be something more than naked.

Then the cool baths extend, which one may not impudently compare with the swimming pools built in public baths. The first has a roof which is pointed into a cone, while the ridges are covered from the four corners with imbricated rain-tiles . . . The interior face of the wall is covered with only the splendour of smooth stone.

He congratulates himself that there are no paintings of indecent naked bodies or oiled-up wrestlers. Instead, as befitted an author and poet:

Nothing will be found on these surfaces that would not be saintlier to see. Only a few verses, with the least immoderate temperament . . .

On the eastern side, an annex with a swimming pool, or, if you prefer Greek, a baptisterium, which takes in about twenty thousand modii, is connected to this hall. Having been washed clean, one comes from the heat to this place through a triple passage in the middle of the wall, opened up by arched intervals. In between are not piers but columns, which skilled architects call the signs of grand buildings. Into this pool, then, six protruding pipes with the likenesses of lions' heads, which, to those who enter quickly, seem to have a real set of teeth, sheer rage in their eyes, and real manes in their neck, pour out a stream, drawn from the mountain ridge and swayed by channels, and curved around the edge of the pool.

Sidonius spends a lot of time painting the picture of his impressively large bathhouse; it's obviously important to him as a status symbol. He then describes how you leave the baths, passing by the women's dining room, a storeroom and weaving room, enter a corridor and then emerge into the winter dining room, and another dining room, with the family silver on display, looking out over a lake:

> In this room there is an arrangement of dining couches and a fine table . . . Reclining in this place, you will occupy yourself with the pleasures of looking out, if you are ever idle during the meal.

He goes on to mention a room where you can rest and drift off, listening to a nightingale and swallows in the morning, cicadas during the day and frogs at twilight. And he describes the gardens of the villa: the lime trees around the buildings; the lake where you can go boating; the green park where you can play ball games. He briefly mentions the wider estate: 'extensive with woodlands, coloured by meadows, rich in pastures'.

As with the rest of Sidonius's writings, we do have to be a little careful about taking what he writes at face value. We must remember that this letter to a friend of his, just like all the other epistles that made it into those nine volumes, was also for wider consumption; he's carefully curating his public image, as well as exercising his literary flair. He's inviting a friend, but also letting us know that he's used to entertaining guests at his country getaway, and to enjoying leisure time on his estate as well. He's on display here as someone who enjoys the finer things in life, like any cultured Late Roman – and as a well-read, accomplished writer. His letter is clearly modelled on two of Pliny's letters, describing that author's own Laurentine villa, in the first century. But there's enough specific geographical detail in Sidonius's letter to be sure that he was describing a real place, and not just concocting a literary device.

Reconstructing the plan of the villa from Sidonius's description, it seems to have been L-shaped or C-shaped, arranged around a courtyard. Such a plan is well known from archaeological investigations of late Roman villas across the north-west provinces – what Sidonius describes seems to be a typical elite rural residence. Sidonius didn't build it, he acquired it through his marriage to Papianilla; it would have been built in the early fifth century at the very latest. He mentions other villas in his letters; it seems clear that his other posh friends lived in similar residences, at the centre of large estates.

Sidonius's letter tells us that the concept of a villa hadn't changed all that much since the first century, when Pliny wrote about his own home. That Roman way of life, and Roman culture, was clearly still something to aspire to – and a way of displaying social status. Sidonius demonstrates that in his style of writing, but also in what he was writing about: his villa seems quintessentially Classical in its architecture. (And it lacks the fortifications seen at some other sites in this period; he doesn't seem to have particularly worried about it being attacked). Roman-style bathing and dining customs were part of the package too.

The reason that this letter is so important is that it's evidence for a large, well-appointed villa, something rather like a stately home, still being occupied in the later fifth century. And in Gaul, as in Britain, the assumption has been that many villas had simply been abandoned by this time; some, perhaps, with people continuing to live among the ruins – among the crumbling, pale shadows of their former glory.

It's not just the histories that have produced that idea of the abandonment of villas – archaeology has provided apparently hard evidence for their demise, adding to the impression that all of Roman Britain – and indeed Gaul (and Brittany) – fell quickly into rack and ruin, with these high-status sites largely abandoned; used only as convenient quarries for dressed stone, and perhaps as somewhere to bury the dead.

But it's possible that villas were not abandoned as swiftly as we once thought. Many of our more well-known villas in Britain were excavated in the nineteenth century, by antiquarians keen to get down quickly to the Roman layers, particularly to uncover glorious mosaics. Those villas were simply used to illustrate the story told by Gildas and then others, rather than as another source of evidence, which could even be used to challenge the histories. They were much less interested, it's fair to say, in what lay above – and they lacked accurate dating techniques. This means we've lost a lot of precious evidence of the – more mysterious – late and post-Roman period.

Exciting evidence emerged recently from the earth under a mosaic floor at Chedworth Roman Villa, in Gloucestershire, owned by the National Trust. Archaeologists re-excavated the mosaic floor of a room that represented an extension to the original villa, taking charcoal and bone samples for dating from the foundation trench of the wall. The radiocarbon date that came back from these samples was so shocking that the archaeologists doubled up with another scientific technique, taking samples for OSL (optically stimulated luminescence) dating. And only then were they sure enough to share the news: the wall and the mosaic could not date to any earlier than 424 CE. Some people in fifth-century Britain, at least, were clearly still enjoying a life of luxury. They still had the means to commission an ornate floor for their villa; it was not left to fall into ruins. Those villa-owners clearly hadn't been plunged directly into destitution and despair, scratching around for a living as the economy collapsed around them.

The National Trust reported the news from Chedworth on its website. 'Up until now,' the article ran, 'it has generally been believed that following the economic crash at the end of the 4th century, all towns and villas were largely abandoned and fell into decay within a few years . . . [but] sophisticated life had continued within this luxury mansion decades after Britain ceased to be part of the Roman Empire and the country had entered the "Dark Ages".'

Chedworth raises the possibility that other villas, which were eventually abandoned and disappeared under fields, may have been occupied much longer than we've assumed. We mustn't rush headlong in the other direction, either – assuming that, actually, all villas must have survived for centuries, with life going on inside them as usual; there are also well-dated examples of villas that *were* abandoned in the fifth century. Chedworth perhaps opens our eyes to a more diverse pattern.

But we must also recognise that the villas which have been excavated are not the whole story. There's a big problem here with sampling. The nature of those sites is that they're *amenable* to archaeological excavation; they're the ones *we can* excavate – precisely because they're not buried under existing buildings. The excavated villas are necessarily those which became abandoned, which did not persist – whereas others lived on, in some way, with the possibility that they were continuously occupied, in one form or another.

In Britain, fragments of bricks, tegulae from mosaics and sherds of Roman pottery also often turn up around the centre of historic villages – sometimes close to the parish church. I saw an example of this recently, on a visit to the picturesque village of Norton in Suffolk. Archaeologists from University College London were finding traces of outbuildings associated with a large villa estate, hidden under fields of oats. But they couldn't investigate the villa itself – because it lay underneath the rectory, as the present owner knew only too well, having found fragments of mosaics when he'd laid a patio. I wondered how much of the church next door was built from the remains of the villa. In 2022, a comprehensive excavation of the ruined parish church of St Mary's, Stoke Mandeville, ahead of development, revealed Anglo-Saxon burials and the foundations of an Anglo-Saxon tower under the later Norman church; and under *that* were found roof tiles, painted wall plaster and three incredible stone busts, from what appears to have been a Roman mausoleum.

Archaeologist Eleanor Scott has suggested that burials at villa sites are also telling us something important: that they form a 'missing link' between the Roman villa and its continuation in the post-Roman era, often as a parish centre or parish church – as a religious focus for the community and somewhere to bury the dead. The Roman villa at Shakenoak Farm, Oxfordshire, excavated in the 1960s, provides a compelling example of a villa-turned-cemetery; twenty-two individuals were buried among the remains. Back in the 1970s, archaeologists were pointing to Shakenoak as evidence that British villa life gradually faded away, rather than falling off a cliff. But then this seems to have been forgotten – until recently, when the burials were radiocarbon dated – to the middle of the fifth century. The skeletons were male, bore signs of trauma (both old and happening around the time of death) and isotope analysis of bones and teeth suggests that they may have been from the south-west of Britain. They've been interpreted as belonging to a military band, who died in violent circumstances – but were buried respectfully, in relatively orderly rows. But that episode of violence didn't leave the Shakenoak villa site completely abandoned. Well-dated remains from the ditch show that farming, weaving and smithing activity was happening there into the seventh and eighth centuries. There's some place name evidence, too, to suggest continuity at Shakenoak, with the survival of a pre-Roman, Brittonic name for the stream – Yccen or Itchen – into the Middle Ages. There's also a possibility that Wilcote parish, in which Shakenoak lies, is an echo of a post-Roman parcel of land. Like Chedworth, Shakenoak suggests that it's time to bury the idea that villa life abruptly ended at the end of the Roman period in Britain. The authors of the recent 2023 study on Shakenoak saw evidence for continuity in the fifth-century archaeology, suggesting that 'a sense of this society's Roman past remained part of its self-understanding, even to the extent of carrying it through into a world that was culturally, linguistically and politically Anglo-Saxon'.

In France, archaeologists have written about the 'triple coincidence' of villa, cemetery and church. It seems clearer there, in Gaul, where there's more often an obvious continuity between the domestic life of the villa and its extended existence as a church. The thick terracotta tiles recycled into a floor at Landévennec represent a very real and physical demonstration of the way in which high-status Roman sites were converted into Christian centres. Llandough in South Wales seems to be a rare example of a villa that evolved into a large, early medieval cemetery – and monastery (and lies less than 2 miles away from the early medieval site of Dinas Powys, which appears, from the richness of archaeological finds there, to have been a particularly important place in the fifth to seventh centuries). This physical evidence of continuity is a powerful metaphor, too, for the way in which elite Roman families simply continued into the post-Roman era. Everything had changed – and nothing had changed. The power – at a local and regional level, at least – was still in the hands of those families who'd held it for centuries.

There's potentially some place name evidence too, in France. There are dozens of sites there with evidence of Roman buildings, a church and a place name ending in *-acum*. That ending seems to be Celtic, meaning 'place of'. We're reminded of Sidonius's villa at Avitacum. (Of course, many place names in France end with *-ville*, which sounds even more promising, but although this does mean 'farm' or 'village', it seems to come into use much later than the Roman period, from the eighth century). So it's a complex picture, but we can clearly see a connection between some Roman villas and churches.

Sidonius doesn't once mention religion in relation to his own villa – it's a beautiful house, a place for entertaining oneself and one's guests. Other villas, though, do seem to have become foci for religious activity, becoming burial sites, as we saw at Caermead, in Llantwit Major. There, as at French sites such as Chassey-lès-Montbozon, the villa does seem to have been largely abandoned, before being repurposed as a burial ground. At Chassey, part of the villa, a large room with an apse, seems to have then been rebuilt a bit later, to form a chapel or church. (This follows a pattern happening in burial grounds right across the Empire: cemeteries outside town walls get their own chapels, sometimes developing into larger churches. I've written about this happening in West Wales, in another book, *Buried* – the cemeteries come first, the churches later.)

A further stage of development might see a village growing up around the villa-turned-church. In some places, big residential villas persisting as such through the fifth century may have been the exception rather than the norm. The transition from a villa to a burial ground, to a church, to a village nucleus may turn out to be more common than once thought.

And it wasn't just the wealthy owners of the villas whose fortunes and habits would influence the continuation or transformation of these sites. The family living in the villa would have had many people looking after them and the estate. Could it be that the individuals buried in villa-cemeteries were descendants of the families who once farmed the estates? In his letter to his schoolmaster friend, Sidonius mentions fishermen on his lake and shepherds in the fields; these estates didn't look after themselves.

The villa was the high-status house at the heart of an agricultural estate. Around the Mediterranean, those estates were more focused on viticulture and olive cultivation. North of the Alps, they were centres for dairy, wool or cereal production – often with evidence of corn-dryers and large granaries. And these estates would have been full of people – agricultural labourers as well as household servants. All these people would have been dependants of the man in charge – of Sidonius at Avitacum – while for Sidonius himself, the villa estate would have been a primary source of income as well as somewhere to entertain friends and enjoy leisure time.

Besides this most detailed description of a high-status villa in fifth-century north-western Europe from the pen of Sidonius, there are a couple of other accounts of such residences. Paulinus of Pella, also based in Gaul, wrote about his houses, and there's a brief mention of a villa in Britain, in the *Confessio* of Patrick.

These villa-owners had a lot in common. They all came from noble families, which is not at all surprising – these were elite residences. Patrick is of course famous as a voyaging Christian saint. His father and grandfather before him had held high positions in the Church, and he claimed in his *Confessio* to have been captured from his father's villa at the tender age of sixteen, and taken away to Ireland. Paulinus of Pella wrote a biography called *Eucharisticus* ('Thanksgiving'), a tale of riches to rags, in which he described falling on bad times, becoming a Christian and briefly considering leaving his wife for a career in the Church.

As for Gaius Sollius Modestus Apollinaris Sidonius, better known as Sidonius – what was that high-level job that saw him returning to Gaul after being prefect of Rome? He was to be installed as bishop of Clermont.

Each of these men, born into noble families, seem to have found that Christianity offered them something important during a time of major political upheaval. Something to cling onto – as Roman hegemony faltered; as a serious invasion started to look inevitable in north-western Europe. But Christianity was also – and had been for some time – a way of taming the barbarians.

Soft Power and Culture Wars

> 'Normally when we see these colonial expansions and adventures, the first people to turn up are the men with bibles.'
>
> ANITA ANAND, *Empire Podcast*

By an extraordinary sleight of hand, the history of the Christian Church in the fourth and fifth century often seems somehow mysteriously divorced from the political history of the Roman Empire. Reading their hagiographies, you'd think bishops become bishops because of their piety and prayerfulness, not primarily because of the wealthy, powerful Roman families they grew up in. And pretty much every bishop became a saint once dead – including Sidonius.

Diplomatic expeditions to try to secure allegiance to the Empire, in barbarian lands, were also framed in religious terms – as though the political angle was simply too mundane, too sordid, even, to mention. We hear less about ambassadors, emissaries and diplomats; more about evangelists, missionaries and apostles. But they were the same thing. Evangelising missions were intended to prepare barbarian nations for a closer relationship with Rome. The aim was to achieve top-down conversion, starting with barbarian kings. The mission could involve political force or enticements; there could be economic benefits, and military assistance too. Promises of military help from Rome came with strings attached: conversion to Christianity (and importantly, not just *any* version of Christianity, but whatever was the current, centrally approved, orthodox variant) – with the allegiance to Rome that this signified – was essential. The traditional Christian and even some psychological explanations of conversions focus on the inner workings of the convert's mind and the attraction of a message of salvation. That may have played a role for some, but ignoring the political and military context of most conversion in the late Roman period and beyond is to be stubbornly obtuse. Being more gentle, you might say it was an instrument of cultural hegemony; but, in many places, you can also construe conversion as a tool of political subjugation and colonialism.

The Romans had been having trouble with barbarians, the

Goths among them, for quite a while. Going back to the third century, the Empire had been thrown into turmoil in what's become known in an uncomplicated way as 'The Crisis of the Third Century'. The Roman Empire had an uneasy, shifting relationship with those it considered to be barbarians, finding itself repeatedly invaded by some groups, while enlisting the help of others – and becoming increasingly, worryingly dependent on those barbarian mercenaries or *foederati*. (Meanwhile, forces within the Roman army also started to elect their own commanders – another destabilising factor).

Central and north-west Europe were full of barbarians who the Romans referred to as Goths. In the year 252 CE, Goths led by King Cniva attacked the north-eastern provinces of the Empire, defeating Roman forces at the Battle of Abritus (in what is now Bulgaria), and killing the emperor Decius. Seafaring Goths attacked the coasts. Other Goths teamed up with the Romans against their neighbours.

These labels and definitions are really far too neat. They're there in the history books, and were referenced in contemporary sources, certainly, but they're very hard to pin down. The identities of these various groups were bound up with different languages, different political allegiances, and shifting areas of geographical settlement and control.

The term 'barbarian' itself is problematic – it's a generic, fairly derogatory term applied by the Romans to anyone living beyond the fringes of the Empire. 'Goth' also seems to have been a very broad label, referring to people living in a broad swathe of northern Europe, beyond the borders of the Roman Empire, speaking a family of similar languages. The label doesn't map neatly onto political groupings, which anyway were very fluid and dynamic, with shifting alliances and areas of control. Ethnicity is an even more tricky aspect of this, combining aspects of ideas about ancestry, language and beliefs, as well as political and geographical control. Most of the time, we don't know how people would have defined themselves ethnically; we default to using names for groups of people or 'tribes' that were first written down by the Romans. And these may relate more to ideas about political control and territory than an any sort of genealogically defined identity – being less to do with ancestry and more to do with the region you lived in and the political leader you followed, and could end up fighting for.

In the end, we apply labels to groups of people because we need to understand and describe their interactions, but we must remember that these labels are somewhat arbitrary and blurred around the edges – and may differ from the way in which those people would have defined *themselves*. They also suggest a continuity, over centuries, which may not have been recognised at the time. But having said all that, employing the terms that were used in antiquity, even if imposed by others, may not be ideal – but seems to be the least bad option.

The story of Ulfilas the Goth aptly demonstrates these problems with labels, as well as revealing how the Roman Empire sought to soften up its adversaries – by sending in the men with Bibles first.

Ulfilas the Goth is known as a fourth-century Christian missionary, whose name means 'Little Wolf'. He wasn't a Goth because of his parentage – he was said to have been the son of Greek parents who came originally from Cappadocia (modern Turkey), within the Roman Empire. This was a population where Christianity, still very much a minority religion in the Empire, had started to take root. In the late third century, they'd been unfortunate enough to have been captured as prisoners of war from their homeland; they ended up north of the Danube, in Transdanubia (in modern Romania), beyond the limits of the Roman Empire. This was the land of the Tervingian Goths, a client state just beyond the official limit of the Empire, and it was here that Ulfilas was born, around 311.

Ulfilas's early years are somewhat shrouded in mystery; indeed, there are really only two sources from which to glean details of his biography: a later quote from a late fourth-century letter penned by one of his students, and a ninth-century summary of a fourth-century *Ecclesiastical History* by a church historian called Philostorgius. But somehow, his parents must have retained the privileges of the higher echelons of society, as Ulfilas was well educated, in Latin and Greek – and Bible studies. And so Ulfilas grew up as an aristocrat and a Christian (in a well-established community that already had a bishop). He was sent as an ambassador from the Tervingian Goths to see the emperor Constantine, probably in 336. Constantine, unlike his immediate predecessors, who had persecuted Christians, had started to see Christianity as politically useful (we must come back to him on that). In fact, some of his closest advisers were Christian bishops. While in Constantinople, Ulfilas was ordained bishop by Eusebius of Nicomedia (one of Constantine's inner circle of advisers, and the cleric who would baptise the emperor Constantine on his deathbed). So this is interesting as Ulfilas had been brought up Christian – a religion that had now not only become respectable but had gained imperial favour; and now Ulfilas was being promoted to a senior rank in the Church by a bishop close to the emperor himself.

A few years later, Ulfilas returned to Transdanubia – this time, as a missionary, and apparently sponsored by the Empire at its highest level. In spreading or reinforcing Christianity in his homeland, he would also be effectively strengthening links with the Empire. Ulfilas stayed for seven years, but it seems he rubbed the leaders of the Tervingian Goths up the wrong way. They were trying to pull away from the gravity of the Empire, and took a dim view of Ulfilas's attempts to reinforce Christianity – and Roman influence. They launched an attack on the Christians among them, who fled south, with Ulfilas leading them to safety in the neighbouring Roman province of Moesia. Ulfilas seems to have hung out there, as bishop, for the rest of his life, travelling to attend the odd church council. Presumably he thought that translating the Bible into a Germanic language (that we now know as 'Gothic') would help Christianity to catch on with the Goths, as this is exactly what he attempted. But just how accessible the resulting text was is questionable, as he seems to have translated each Greek word into a Gothic equivalent, while maintaining the syntax of the original.

In the 370s, when Ulfilas was an old man, a civil war broke out among the Tervingian Goths, between two factions, led by Athanaric and Fritigern. Athanaric was staunchly non-Christian, while his rival sought assistance from the emperor Valens, converting to Christianity – thus demonstrating his allegiance to Rome – as part of the bargain. (Other sources credit Ulfilas with converting the Gothic leader). Valens allowed Fritigern and his followers to settle within the Empire, to the south of the Danube, in return for military service. Fritigern would later turn against the Empire, teaming up with other Goths to vanquish Valens at the Battle of Adrianopolis in 378, and the Empire was eventually forced into letting these Goths settle in the Balkan provinces. (The united forces of Goths that prevailed at Adrianopolis would become known as Visigoths, including those who would settle in Aquitaine.)

Athanaric's fate varies depending on which version of history you read. The Greek historian Zosimus and others recount him negotiating peace with the next Roman emperor, Theodosius, and settling within the Empire. But Ammianus Marcellinus and Themistius both claim that Athanaric was expelled by his own people, and sought asylum in Roman lands as a refugee. Either way, it seems that Athanaric had been right to have been suspicious of evangelising Christians, acting as agents of Rome.

And we must also be somewhat suspicious of the histories that have come down to us. In the introduction of his masterful book on *Christendom*, Peter Heather includes a cautionary note about the biased nature of the documentary sources, most of which were written by 'true believers' (or people who at least purported to be such). These sources, describing the motivations of devout Christians, prioritise spiritual, devout explanations. On the one hand, as Heather points out, sociology and anthropology tell us that 'true believers are only ever a minority of the total human population'. This means that purely cultural explanations for Christianity's success – suggesting that it spread because of some sort of inherent spiritual and psychological superiority over all other cults and religions – cannot be the answer, however forcefully this is still argued in some quarters. The story of Ulfilas, Athanaric and Fritigern is a great example. We see conversion to Christianity as part of a straightforward bargain: an expression of allegiance that was necessary in order to secure military assistance from Rome, in this case. For wider populations, too, conversion was very often top-down, something which was demanded by kings of their subjects, after they had entered into certain alliances. As Heather commented, 'many kinds of coercion also underlay the emergence of European Christendom' – compliance was rewarded; non-compliance was punished.

There is a twist in the tale at the end of Ulfilas's story, which brings to light another crucial aspect of fourth-century Christianity: it was very far from being monolithic. In 383, Ulfilas, now in his early seventies, is thought to have travelled to Constantinople, having been called to attend a high-level church meeting. Unfortunately, he fell ill in Constantinople, and died there, but not, apparently, before writing a creed in which he rejected the particular version of Christianity he'd followed throughout his life – a version known as Homoeanism.

Ulfilas had lived through much of an extraordinary century, for Christians in the Roman Empire. At the start of the fourth century, Roman emperors were to be found persecuting Christians, who were seen as threats. The persecutions were brought to an end by an edict promoting religious tolerance, issued jointly by the co-emperors Constantine and Licinius in 313. After that, Roman emperors themselves became more interested in Christianity (with the notable exception of Julian 'the Apostate', whose few years reigning in the 360s saw an attempt to revive traditional Roman religion) until, in 380, the emperor Theodosius issued the Edict of Thessalonica, making Christianity, and specifically a version known as Nicene Christianity, the official state religion of the Empire.

Ulfilas's late conversion – from Homoeanism to the now-orthodox Nicene Christianity – lifts the lid on the complexity of Christian faith in the fourth century: there was more than one way of being Christian. From the time of Constantine onwards (the early fourth century), there was central guidance or endorsement from the Empire about which version was correct – or orthodox (literally 'right opinion' in Greek; the term 'catholic' carried a similar connotation, meaning 'universal', i.e. 'that which is (or should be) believed everywhere'). Emperors had stepped in at various times to resolve debates about orthodoxy within the Church, but the official view on the orthodoxy or 'right way' changed over time. A central point of contention was the nature of God and Christ – were they essentially one and the same in their divine nature, or were they just *similar*? It seems like such a subtle question and yet it had the power to divide bishops and their followers into factions – to drive culture wars. The subtleties of theological debate had real, political ramifications; your position in this debate could signal whether you were an ally of Rome – or not.

A Church council in Nicaea in 325 had resolved the issue in favour of God and Jesus being of exactly the same essence. But the debate rumbled on, and this Nicene version of Christianity was overturned by a meeting in Constantinople in 360, where it was decided that God and Jesus were just 'like' each other. This formulation became known as Homoean (from the Greek *homoios* – 'like' or 'similar'), and was the official, imperially favoured version of Christianity for twenty years, before being overturned again, with a return to the Nicene position, in 381. The emperor Theodosius branded Homoean Christianity as heresy, and sacked several bishops adhering to what was now determined to be unorthodox doctrine; to be a good Roman Christian, you had to stay alert and make sure you were following the *right* version of Christianity. But with all this flip-flopping over the official party line, it's easy to see how converts and bishops could suddenly find themselves at odds with whatever the imperial orthodoxy had become.

But if Christianity was to be the glue that held the Empire together, it was extremely important that everyone agreed to follow the *same sort* of Christianity. The integrity of the Empire depended on a standardised – orthodox or catholic – religion being followed everywhere. It signalled allegiance to Rome. So this wasn't just a spiritual requirement; it was quite mundane – there were huge political and economic implications. If sects splintered away, with their own sets of beliefs, their own thought-leaders, they wouldn't necessarily stay loyal to the Empire.

The Goths had converted to Christianity after 360, when Homoeanism *had* been orthodoxy, but in the late fourth century, when this doctrine was declared heretical, they would dig their heels in and stick to it, as did the Vandals. And in fact, their resistance to the Nicene Christianity now favoured by Theodosius and his successors signalled a growing ideological distance from the heart of empire; a growing unhappiness at being under the imperial yoke. While the Gothic leaders could still claim a Christian stamp of divine authority, they could also politically differentiate themselves from the Empire. The very ideology that the Romans had promoted among the barbarians, as a form of soft power, was now being used against them. Homoeanism became the brand of Christianity that would bind the barbarians together – against Rome.

As the fifth century dawned, the Empire's problems with barbarians – including various groups of Goths – were far from over. We return to the west, where the Empire was beginning to crumble.

Enemies Within and Without: Goths, Franks and *Foederati*

The withdrawal of the Roman army from Britannia in 410 CE gives us the impression of a precise end-date for Roman Britain.

And yet it's highly unlikely that the entire administrative structure of the province changed overnight – in fact, we know it didn't. And – as we saw so vividly with the links between Llantwit Major and Brittany and Gaul – the connections with the rest of what had been the western Roman Empire continued. Regional leaders may have been vying for power, without the Roman Leviathan to bring them all to heel. The throwing up of huge earthwork dykes perhaps speaks to that reality – but the finer-grained social hierarchy is likely to have held strong, for a while at least.

In Gaul, the end point of the Roman Empire is even harder to discern, but we do know that the process was more protracted than in Britain, with Roman control faltering in the early fifth century, then gradually falling apart in the latter half of that century. The once-unified territory started to fracture into smaller polities, with various barbarian groups seizing control and battling with each other for supremacy: Visigoths, Burgundians and Franks.

The Visigoths, or 'west Goths', were a group of Germanic-speaking people whose leaders may have come originally from north-west Europe; sometimes they fought against the Romans, and at other times, with them – as allied forces or *foederati*. The Burgundians seem to have come from Scandinavia while Frankish groups were originally from the lower Rhine area. Again, both Burgundians and Franks sometimes fought against Roman troops, and at other times, joined forces with them. (In fact, it's even more complicated than this, as some of these barbarians would also sometimes side with one 'Roman' faction against another.)

Although the Goths were often written about as 'invaders', much like the Saxons in Britain (and Saxons also attacked

Gaul), it's clear that Roman authorities in the early fifth century were also deliberately settling some Germanic auxiliaries and mercenaries in certain territories; Visigoths were invited into Aquitaine, for instance, to help the Roman state fight against the Vandals and Alans who had made incursions into Iberia. (We're reminded of the suggestion that the formation of Brittany could have been influenced by British mercenaries being brought in to settle in Armorica.) These planted communities of Rome-friendly Goths could spring into action when necessary, ready to help suppress uprisings, while in the meantime running productive farms in fertile areas that may have become deserted.

But inviting barbarians to settle in Roman provinces was always a high-risk strategy, with the possibility that these farmer-fighters might turn coat, and take up arms to attack the Romans — which, predictably, they did, from time to time. In these uprisings, the 'barbarian' armies seem to have been at a disadvantage compared with the professional Roman army, but the Empire's military resources were thinly spread in the fifth century, and the barbarians could sometimes gain the upper hand. In the first half of the fifth century, the Visigoths rose up, surging out of Aquitaine in an effort to seize towns in southern Gaul — and the Romans successfully beat them back. But they didn't go any further — and there doesn't seem to have been any attempt to wipe the Visigoths out after this insurrection. Perhaps the Romans were biding their time, just waiting for elite Visigoth families to merge with their own elites: to be gradually assimilated rather than summarily vanquished. But such explanations also miss out an influential section of society: the landowning elite, who may have seen themselves as 'Roman', and would also have been alert to political changes as new military leaders rose to prominence in their regional arenas. Their loyalty to Rome – versus their own families' best interests – would soon be tested.

The Romans were busy fighting among themselves too, with a succession of military coups in the early fifth century; power-hungry generals would suddenly declare themselves to be emperors, with the support of a local section of the army. These coups often seem to have started in Britain. There seems to have been something about having been sent to the far reaches of the Empire that got generals thinking that they could seize power for themselves. It was such a common occurrence and had been going on for such a long time, it was almost a tradition, with St Jerome commenting in the early fifth century that Britain was 'fertile in tyrants'. Usurpers who had first risen to power in Britain included Postumus and Carausius in the third century, Constantine the Great and Magnus Maximus in the fourth. In the early fifth century, another Constantine (III) thought he'd have a go, and he was ousted by yet another usurper, Jovinus – who enlisted the help of barbarian Burgundians and Alans to help him seize the throne. A group of Visigoths turned up, too, apparently to support Jovinus, but then they turned against him.

Once Jovinus was out of the way, Gaul fell back under the control of the central Roman government in Italy, and the emperor Honorius, and the Visigoths and the Burgundians settled down. Even a revolt among the famously independent-minded troublemakers in Armorica had been put down. For the decade between 440 and 450, Gaul seems to have been largely at peace. But soon, Rome's hold over its western provinces began to crumble, and we get the sense of the military elites across Gaul once again spotting an opportunity to carve up the province and seize power.

In 451, there was another threat from outside the Empire as Gaul was attacked by Huns, emerging from central Asia to take on the might of Rome. The Roman army was reinforced by Frank, Visigoth and Burgundian soldiers, and these allied forces prevailed in defending Gaul against the Huns. But in the end, the biggest threat came from within, with a string of military coups and murders leading to a high turnover of Roman military commanders and emperors. In 457, the Roman *magister militum* or commander in chief, Marjorian, was declared emperor by the army; a short four years later, he'd been murdered. The leading Roman general in Gaul, Aegidius, refused to recognise Marjorian's official replacement, and instead, seized the province for himself. Aegidius, followed by his son, managed to hold onto a portion of northern Gaul, ruling it as an independent kingdom, for a couple of decades. By this time, though, southern Gaul had fallen under the control of the Visigoths, who'd now successfully expanded out of their power base in Aquitaine to rule a kingdom that extended down across most of Iberia, too. And then, in 486, the Frankish king Clovis – once a Roman military commander himself – invaded and seized northern Gaul. In the fullness of time, the Franks would gain the upper hand right across Gaul, giving their name to the country that would eventually emerge: Francia. France.

The crumbling of Roman imperial power in the western Empire is an interesting phenomenon that demands explanation. Some cite the military prowess of barbarians, but the Roman army always seemed to have the martial edge. Others point to the destabilising effect of all the machiavellian plots and infighting among Roman emperors, would-be emperors and military generals. But those recurring power grabs could have been more of a contributing cause, or even a symptom, of deeper problems, rather than the primary driving force. The presence of very real threats to the Empire across multiple fronts was undoubtedly important. Military resources were stretched very thinly, forcing Roman generals into the position of seeking assistance from mercenaries, seeking fragile alliances with duplicitous barbarians. And it wasn't just generals who were looking for new allies. The landowning elite of what had been the western Roman Empire were keen to hold onto their land, power and status. A certain disaffection with empire, undoubtedly compounded by higher taxes, may have made affiliations with new military elites quite attractive. At the very least, collaboration could have been the only choice they had, in order to maintain their social status. Even that sounds too abstract – we're talking about people making choices about how to protect themselves and their families in a time of political instability. And somehow, religion was part and parcel of all this – bound up with old as well as new, emerging ideas about group identity. Your religion indicated not only who you were but who you were for, and who you were against.

Digging deep into the causes of the decline of the Empire, many historians see it as largely an economic problem. Encouraging barbarians to settle in the provinces – offering them favourable tax incentives – the Empire stitched itself up. With its dwindling revenues, it was struggling to fund its thinly stretched army or to pay *foederati* to fight alongside them. Mercenaries tend to get unhappy if pay day never arrives. (Power-hungry generals, untrustworthy allies, an overstretched military, and even the Empire's empty coffers, may be symptoms of a deeper malaise – proximate rather than ultimate causes of imperial diminishment. We'll return to this question.) It's possible – probable even – that many factors played into the decline and fall of the western Empire.

Discussing the tumultuous changes happening during the fifth century as an 'interesting phenomenon' is only something we can dare to do from our safe temporal vantage point, 1,600 years on. We may be fascinated by trying to find out what caused that political instability; it is interesting for its own sake, but also perhaps because it makes us reflect on our political landscape today (where, once again, culture wars are being used to define one group in opposition to another). Even the staunchest allies can be duplicitous in the fullness of time. Even the most permanent-seeming institutions, federations and kingdoms are not immutable, over thousands of years.

But what was it like 'on the ground'? What was it like to live through those tumultuous decades, through military coup after military coup, as emperors rose and fell with the regularity of changing seasons, when barbarians came to fight, to stay, to rule?

Once again, we're able to turn to contemporary Gallic writers to find out.

The End of an Era

As territories changed hands and new leaders and warrior kings rose to prominence and dominance, what happened to the rest of society? In Britain, as we've noted, we're largely left guessing – with very few contemporary documentary sources to help us peer through the gloom. But in stark contrast, the fifth century in Gaul is relatively well documented. We've already met Sidonius, writing his reams of letters in the later fifth century. But there are plenty of other sources – that can help us understand what was going on in the earlier part of that century.

While we have a relative embarrassment of riches when it comes to the literary documentation of life in fifth-century Gaul compared with Britain, it's very biased – in the sense of being an incomplete sample. It's the product of a very narrow slice of elite Gallo-Roman society, and it necessarily reflects the political concerns and ambitions of those prominent families who sought to maintain their status even while kings rose and fell. The peasantry, the common people, are conspicuously missing from this history, as is so often the case – and women are virtually silent, too.

But we can only work with the material that's come down to us – while being aware of its narrow scope. And a few aristocratic men have left us with astonishing insights into the events of that tumultuous century. Some penned chronicles, even if these histories are not as accurate or objective as we might hope for, but there are also some more personal, biographic accounts from this period. Let's start with a close-up look at two lives – of aristocratic Gallic gentlemen, both of whom were born in the late fourth century and lived well into the fifth, but whose fortunes varied widely.

A startlingly personal account comes down to us from Paulinus of Pella, who described the ups and downs of his life, set against the political events of the day, in his autobiographical poem, *Eucharisticus* ('Thanksgiving').

Paulinus of Pella was born into an aristocratic family in Macedonia, in 376 CE, where his father was *vicarius* (a high office – the deputy of the praetorian prefect). When Paulinus was still a babe in arms, his father was promoted to proconsul of Africa, and the whole family moved to Carthage (on the coast of modern-day Tunisia, very close to the modern capital, Tunis). Later, they moved to Burdigalam (Bordeaux), where Paulinus's grandfather was consul, and where the young Paulinus studied under Greek and Latin tutors. In his youth, he loved riding his horse – fast – engaging in falconry and wearing the latest fashions. Then his parents encouraged him to settle down, and he did very well for himself by marrying a woman with a huge estate in Gaul. Paulinus threw himself into renovating the grand house and extensive vineyards of his new property.

But his life of carefree comfort and luxury was not to last. Paulinus was wracked with grief when his father died. And his personal sorrow was compounded by political strife, when a Roman usurper called Priscus Attalus seized power in the region – proclaiming himself emperor in the west, with the support of the Visigoths. Paulinus had expected that he would naturally follow his father and grandfather into imperial service, but that career option had now been rudely whisked away. So, instead, he went to work for the new overlords, becoming a treasurer for Attalus, in around 414. But then the Visigoths dumped Attalus – and raided Paulinus's estate.

Paulinus's financial circumstances are somewhat opaque at this point in his autobiography. He was forced to flee, and writes about losing his earthly riches – but he still seems to have been able to access an income from familial landholdings, far away in Greece, where he mentions owning 'extensive farms'. He contemplated moving there, in fact, but then decided it would be too difficult to transfer his whole household to a foreign land.

It was at this time that Paulinus decided to convert to Christianity – and even contemplated abandoning his family to live as a monk. He doesn't mention who introduced him to this religion, but perhaps it was an aristocratic friend of the family. It seems that Paulinus saw Christianity as a way of reconnecting with his aristocratic Roman roots and values, the 'ancient tradition', as he puts it, using it to anchor himself firmly in that Roman aristocratic nexus and identity now reinforced by the Church, with Christianity having been adopted as the official state religion in 380. Again, we see that intimate link between *Christianitas* and *Romanitas*. Although Paulinus is vague about the details, it seems that he could also expect support – social and perhaps financial – by joining this network.

One by one, all the members of Paulinus's family died, even his two sons, leaving him completely alone. On his own now, he moved south to Massilia (Marseille), 'a city where indeed were many saints dear to me', as he writes, but also (perhaps more importantly) 'part of my family estate'. It was only a small property, though, and he seems to have struggled to make ends meet. He wanted to rent out some land and keep his house 'well stocked with slaves', but the plan failed, and he returned to Burdigalam 'as a wanderer, poor, bereaved of my loved ones'. But it turned out, luckily, that he did actually still have a house in Burdigalam. And even more fortunately, he could now turn to the teachings of his new faith to argue that, as 'nothing is our own; so that we may as surely consider others' goods to be ours, as we are bound to share our own with others'.

For someone who grew up as the son of a leading imperial aristocrat in the lap of luxury, who married a richly endowed wife, who still hoped to keep his house well stocked with slaves even when he described himself as destitute – Paulinus now expected society to support *him*. And then, suddenly, there was a boost to his fortunes – 'unasked, O God, didst speedily

deign to comfort me' – as a Goth bought his small farm in
Burdigalam (even if Paulinus considered the price a little low).
He finishes by thanking God and hoping that his fear of death
might be assuaged by the promise of salvation. Presumably he
died not too long after writing his memoir, penned when he
was eighty-three, in 459 CE.

It's a remarkable poem, revealing much about the politically
unstable times Paulinus lived through, about his own shifting
fortunes, and about the solace and support he gained from
Christianity, particularly after losing the majority of his land
and wealth, and then all his family as well, as he grew to a ripe
old age.

Although Paulinus found consolation in Christianity, he
didn't go further and pursue a career in the Church, despite
briefly having considered joining a monastery. Christianity
seems to have offered him solace, and that was enough, representing a romantic attachment to what he'd lost and where
he'd come from – a sense of antique Roman-ness. 'Paulinus',
the historian Ray Van Dam wrote, 'seems always to have been
looking backwards.' But perhaps that's because the Church
didn't offer him – in his state of (relative) destitution – a way
forwards.

Things were very different for Paulinus's contemporary,
the bishop Germanus of Auxerre (the churchman errone-
ously, anachronistically credited with being Illtud's tutor in
the *Life of Samson*). Germanus of Auxerre didn't pen his own
autobiography; instead, we learn about him from a very early,
near-contemporary *Vita Germani*, penned in the late fifth century, by another cleric, Constantius of Lyon.

Germanus came from an extremely well-heeled Gallic
family. He was born around 378 CE, in Auxerre, and received

a traditional Roman education at Arles and Lyon. He started his career as a lawyer in Rome, then returned to Gaul to take up a military role as a *dux* – meaning 'leader', translating literally as 'duke'; as such, he would have been a general, commanding legions, and tasked with assisting one of those high-level representatives of the praetorian prefect, a *vicarius*. So far, so traditional Roman aristocrat.

But then, rather suddenly, in 418, he was appointed bishop in his home town of Auxerre. We shouldn't really be surprised by now; it's just another example of that revolving door between high-level administrative and military positions, and ecclesiastical roles. As a bishop, Germanus was in a much better position than Paulinus had been, as a treasurer. Germanus's role in the Church wasn't tied to the fortunes of one particular ruler, which was risky in those politically unstable times; it seems the Church had, by this time, managed to establish itself as a sort of semi-autonomous civil service – maintaining administrative control and keeping its members in a secure job while kings and emperors fought it out among themselves.

As a bishop, Germanus, so his hagiography records, adopted an ascetic lifestyle. Just *how* ascetic, we may question; Paulinus, after all, seemed to consider himself utterly destitute while still owning property and hoping to keep slaves, and as we have already explored with those famously ascetic British saints, asceticism was something of an affectation of the wealthy and famous. (Among fifth-century Gallic bishops, Eucherius of Lyon was particularly famous for his asceticism; he took 1,740 litres of wine and 66 kilograms of cheese with him to his Lent retreat at the monastery of Île-Barbe.) Despite his new religious status and claimed asceticism, Germanus didn't adopt a hair shirt but kept on wearing his general's cloak – a strikingly obvious emblem of the link between Roman military authority and the Church. But it wasn't just the trappings of the military that he carried with him into his episcopal role.

Germanus was much more mobile than Paulinus. Perhaps that was also part of the key to his success. He didn't seem to be tied down by family; he travelled within Gaul, to Ravenna – and, in around 429, to Britain. His visit to Britain, on which he was accompanied by Lupus, bishop of Troyes, was carried out at the behest of the powerful bishop of Rome – and the timing of this is interesting too if we consider that the Roman army had already pulled out of Britain by 410, when British leaders finally expelled remaining Roman officials. Two decades later, there was clearly still an ecclesiastical administrative system up and running in Britain. But the bishop must have been worried that this north-western bit of the Church might break away – British clergy were turning their backs on the orthodoxy of the time, and instead following another divergent branch of Christianity called Pelagianism.

Pelagius was a British preacher, who moved to Rome towards the end of the fourth century. He'd caused some consternation by teaching that humans were not born sinful, and his controversial ideas had started to gain ground among the Roman elite. The Church was very keen to stamp out such things – they didn't take kindly to splitters, diluting the brand like this. It was important to the Church to maintain brand loyalty, to keep the whole business politically, ideologically and financially aligned. And the specific brand that had been chosen as orthodoxy included the idea, espoused by Augustine, bishop of Hippo Regius in North Africa, of original sin – diametrically opposed to Pelagius's view on humans' innate innocence. But this point of doctrinal dissonance once again distracts from the real importance of this theological point of difference – it was yet another culture war, with each side fighting for political dominance.

Whenever you see culture wars bubbling up, what you're really seeing is different factions vying for power. Contemporary culture wars often seem to be framed around what may first appear to be a simple question – but which turns out to be extremely complex. The Homoean and Pelagian heresies are like that too, and in fact the complexity and subtlety is crucial because it allows factions of quite sensible people to coalesce around opposing views. The heresies become symbolic: ciphers, flags around which to rally. And so what they actually represent is not really the question you think they're about on the surface, but different groups of people vying for political power. And you know one side is losing when history starts to record one possible answer to each of these questions as 'heresy' while the other answer becomes 'orthodox'. In this political context, it's pertinent that the Pelagian heresy seems to reflect the political situation in the western Roman Empire as those provinces fragmented and sought self-determination – pulling away from Rome (or indeed, Constantinople). Pushing this argument further, perhaps the Pelagian heresy isn't just *reflecting* that fragmentation but actually *embodying* it – because religion is completely intertwined with political power at this time. The Gallic and British bishops were, practically to a man, noble and wealthy; the brothers of kings, kingmakers, and often also military leaders. We talk about the military-industrial complex now; what existed in the first millennium was a military-religious-political complex.

Once in Britain, Germanus was able to draw on his training in rhetoric to talk the British clerics round to his side in this culture war – the right side, the 'orthodoxy', because it was supported by Rome. And then he was also able to offer military support, in person, leading troops to help the Britons fight off Pictish and Saxon raiders; he was a warrior-bishop, after all.

The *Vita Germani* also records that Germanus visited the tomb of the 'blessed martyr Alban' after he stamped out the 'damnable heresy' of Pelagianism. This is the earliest reference to a saint called Alban, whose life would be recorded in more detail in much later medieval sources. Some historians doubt that Alban was ever a real historical figure and suspect that Germanus may even have invented him – retro-engineering an origin myth for Christianity in Britain: a Saint Alban for Albion.

Germanus is then said to have travelled to Ravenna, apparently to seek forgiveness on behalf of the Armoricans, who had been rebelling again. He died there, in the 440s, at around seventy years of age. His body was brought back to Auxerre where it was interred in an oratory, and then later moved to a church that was dedicated to him.

It's interesting to compare these two lives, these two stories – and the role that Christianity played for each of them. For Paulinus, the religion provided a comforting link back to old Roman traditions and gentry, and perhaps some social and financial support. For Germanus, Christianity provided the next step in a high-level career that included legal, military and then ecclesiastical roles as he progressed from lawyer to general to bishop. In this last position, he was able to visit Britain in a diplomatic capacity, on a mission not to tame barbarians this time, but in an attempt to ensure that the once-Roman Britons were staying closely aligned with the Roman Church – not branching off on their own. This ostensibly religious mission had military overtones of course; in the febrile atmosphere of the fifth century, a culture war could easily develop into a real war and theological schisms could develop into political splits with economic sequelae.

While these two lives provide us with a personal perspective on the fifth century, other writers were attempting to write broader histories: chronicling the military coups, barbarian invasions – and yet another heresy-laced culture war.

This literature can be quite tricky to interpret: careful comparative analysis of texts has revealed that chroniclers would rearrange events, switch things around and even invent occurrences to suit a narrative flow. Historians warn that the chronicles can't be used as straightforward records of historical events – but they can still reveal a lot about the focus and concerns of their authors.

Exploring the literature relating to the end of Roman Gaul, the historian Steven Muhlberger drew attention to two mid-fifth-century chronicles that provide quite a striking contrast to each other. One was written by Prosper of Aquitaine, who lived in Marseille and published his *Ecclesiastical History* in 433. Another anonymous writer, from the same area, wrote his chronicle in 452.

Prosper didn't waste much ink describing the wars and invasions that must have taken place in Gaul during his youth, during the civil war in the first and second decades of the fifth century. He focused on the internal conflict within the Empire rather than barbarian incursions – although he does briefly mention that Spain was conquered by Vandals, and that Burgundians settled along the Rhine. Barbarian activities are marginal (figuratively and literally – being written in the margins) to the main story, which is about the Empire pulling itself together after a period of civil war. Prosper was a big fan of Constantius III – western Roman emperor for just seven months in 421 – because he finally beat the rebels and managed to settle the once-dangerous Goths in Aquitaine. (We may raise our eyebrows at this, because we know how that story would end.)

Prosper's history paints a positive, optimistic picture of the western Empire – finding its feet again after decades of civil war. Perhaps, writing from heavily Romanised southern Gaul, that's really how it felt to Prosper. He didn't hang around to see how it turned out anyway; he left Marseille for Rome soon after setting down his history. Still, for Prosper, the settlement of Goths in Gaul doesn't seem to have been a critical, trans-formative or worrying event.

The 'Chronicler of 452', writing just two decades later, painted a very different picture: 'At this time the condition of the state appeared to be intensely miserable, since not even one province was without a barbarian inhabitant, and the unspeakable Arian [Homoean] heresy, which had allied itself to the barbarian nations and permeated the whole world, laid claim to the name of Catholic.'

It's true that things really had taken a turn for the worse since Prosper penned his chronicle: Attila the Hun took it upon himself to invade Gaul in the year 451. But the Chronicler of 452 also had a markedly different take on the Gothic invasions of the early fifth century as well; he described how 'the madness of hostile peoples tore Gaul to pieces', and how 'Roman power was completely humbled by a multitude of enemies'. And it wasn't just Gaul that was being ravaged. The Chronicler of 452 also referred to the loss of Britain to the Saxons, and of Spain to the Sueves (from the Swabian region of what is now Germany);

this, very much, was a picture of the western Empire in crisis, fragmenting and assaulted by barbarians of all stripes.

This chronicler may well have been exaggerating the situation. As Muhlberger put it, 'His account of the dismemberment of the Roman empire is rhetorical rather than well informed or careful.' In this way, it's reminiscent of Gildas, who wrote about the scourge of the Saxons terrorising Britain in his searing sixth-century *De Excidio et Conquestu Britanniae* ('On the Ruin and Conquest of Britannia'). War and suffering were appropriate punishments for sin and immorality. The point of such texts is not so much to document history, but to convince an audience that society has fallen into such terrible depravity that it needs rescuing. And these chroniclers could advise on just how society could be saved by embracing (orthodox) Christianity, of course: *Christianitas*, as *Romanitas* had now become. (This is a very familiar strategy still employed by some politicians today to win support – they deliberately instil fear in the populace: fear of being invaded by others, fear of amorality, fear of societal breakdown, fear of change – and then, of course, they claim to have an easy solution.)

Both Prosper and the Chronicler of 452 are quite parochial, describing events from their perspective, down around the Mediterranean coast of Gaul – fairly oblivious of the north. For all of the second chronicler's bias and polemic, things may well have felt less secure on the riviera by the 450s. And the response to this unrest seems to have been to stoke up yet another culture war around a heretical version of Christianity – not Pelagianism this time, but Homoeanism once again.

During the fifth century, the Gallic aristocracy – whether more Roman or Gothic in their ancestry – was becoming increasingly divorced from the Empire, with the traditional high-level administrative career paths that led out of Gaul and towards the imperial centre increasingly denied them. The Church offered a semi-alternative system of power and status, and still linked back to the central power bases in the Roman Empire (which meant Rome itself, in the western Empire). Bishops – like Germanus – enjoyed the power and status of aristocrats, and could expect their heirs to succeed them. They could also expect to ascend to even higher levels of authority within the Church. But at the same time, that Church was looking like it could be in danger of splitting apart. In the west, people were still tending to follow the version of Christianity that had reached them first – Homoeanism – just like the Goths in the east had done.

Homoeanism (which taught that the Son was merely *like* the Father, not of the same substance) was now considered unorthodox and heretical – it wasn't 'proper' Christianity: catholic, orthodox, the *correct* doctrine, as endorsed by the Empire. It was a physical and spiritual threat. Steven Muhlberger bears quoting in full here:

'But it was not just that the barbarians were creeping closer to Marseille. It was also that they brought heresy with them. The defeat and resurrection of the despised Arian [Homoean] sect is a major theme for the Chronicler of 452. The special glory of Theodosius I was that he had expelled the Arians [Homoeans] from the churches they had seized under earlier emperors, and drove them out of the Empire. But the heretics had returned with the barbarians, and it was their help that made it possible for heresy to "permeate the whole world" . . . Not only Roman order but Roman orthodoxy was threatened, and this shaped the chronicler's view as much as the mundane peril.'

By this time, churches had taken over much of the administrative system of the Roman Empire, helping to redistribute wealth – and funnelling some of it back to Rome. And they acted as an important channel for mass communication, providing the means for the political aims and ambitions of the Empire to be broadcast on a regular basis, and understood right across what had become Christendom. So heresy wasn't just a spiritual scourge, it was a real threat to the coherence of the Christianised Empire. And plenty of people – especially literate aristocrats and businessmen – had a vested interest in preserving the social and political *status quo*.

The Chronicler of 452 was clearly worried about the political instability caused by the fragmenting of the Empire. And he wasn't the only one. There were plenty of doom-laden apologists writing in such despairing tones. But there's a discrepancy between what appears to be a continuous literary output – and what those writers were saying. They implied that a significant break with the past was underway; they were full of doom, writing of disasters, moral corruption, civilisation on the brink – and barbarian invasions. And yet, at the same time, many of these aristocrats (if not Paulinus of Pella) seem to have been holding onto their social status rather well.

Later that century, when things settled down, the texts take on a calmer tone. And what's remarkable and unremarkable at the same time is that the people occupying positions of power throughout the fifth century (at least the ones we can track) don't seem to change much, or at least – the families don't change. They're so embedded in the systems of power, administration – and knowledge – that were formalised and crystallised under the Empire, that they were able to adapt to changes at the top and keep things going much as they always had done.

Men from wealthy landowning families were still educated in Latin and Greek; still destined for high-level careers. They were able to keep managing business and the flow of trade and taxes; to keep economies functioning; to maintain – and even advance – their own dynastic power. (We may be reminded of some modern, populist politicians who are themselves aristocratic, born into the highest echelons of society, enjoying an elite education – and then deploring the demise of society, the loss of 'values', and turning to attack educational institutions.)

In his *Decem Libri Historiarum*, written in the sixth century, Gregory of Tours revealed how high-standing Gallo-Roman senatorial families simply continued in their traditional roles as diplomats, generals – and bishops – as Germanic conquerors carved up Gaul among themselves. As Ian Wood puts it, 'the doom-laden apologists were not the representatives of a class or society that was destroyed by the barbarian invasions . . . In fact they were members of an aristocracy that, in southern and central Gaul at least, survived relatively unharmed into the period of the successor states.'

And there's no better example of that survival instinct, of someone who managed to ride the storm and find a place for himself in one of those successor states, the Visigothic kingdom, than – you guessed it – our familiar friend Sidonius Apollinaris.

Working with the Barbarians

Peering back from our elevated vantage point in the twenty-first century, we might see 'Gaul' now as a natural polity, rather similar to modern France, and set in stone. But nothing in geopolitics is 'natural'. What became Roman Gaul was a territory divided into several kingdoms before the Romans progressively took it over in the second and first centuries BCE. Then, after the Romans, it broke up again. As military historian Hugh Elton put it, 'Gallic unity was only a result of having a place within the Empire.'

The Gallo-Roman author Salvian wrote about how the Roman state was already falling apart in early fifth-century Gaul. He was originally from the north but moved to the more politically stable Provence, where he became a priest. He described how local governors and aristocrats were managing to turn the political instability to their own advantage, grabbing more land for themselves, and exploiting people who (like Paulinus, perhaps) had fallen on hard times. The medieval historian Van Dam has written that Salvian's fifth-century Gaul was in some ways a precursor to medieval France, but that it also represented a return to a pre-Roman state, in which 'regional fragmentation had reappeared, imperial authority and public services had lapsed, and private initiative had become dominant'.

Even when Gaul was firmly a province within the Empire, in the fourth century, the centre of power, which had migrated to the eastern Roman Empire, seemed very distant. Laws passed in Constantinople took years to be implemented in Gaul – and historians note that some of the Gallic aristocracy even considered the eastern Roman ruler to be a 'Greek emperor' and nothing much to do with them. These attitudes are important as they remind us that even when the Roman Empire was *meant* to be one grand, unified thing, it was nothing of the sort – its cultural and political unity was something of an illusion. (The idea of Gaul being transformed by Germanic invasions in the late- and post-Roman periods also seems less novel when we remember that Julius Caesar was told by a king of the *Germani*, Ariovistus, that Gaul was actually a province within *Germania*.)

In early fifth-century Gaul, aristocratic Roman generals had repeatedly used Gothic mercenaries to help them seize power and break away from the central imperial regime, as well as to suppress local rebellion. Having helped to settle these useful allies in southern France, the Gallo-Roman elite were then tied into engaging with the upper echelons in this society – as Visigoth kings began to think about consolidating their *own* power. The histories describe some educated Romans moving to the Visigothic court in the early fifth century; some for financial reasons, but there were also hostage exchanges.

And yet, up until the middle of the fifth century, the forces of the Roman Empire – its army combined with its *foederati* – 'remained the most powerful shark swimming in the West European waters', as historian Peter Heather so vividly put it. The pendulum was about to swing, though. After 450, the balance of power shifted, but it was very messy. The 460s saw the Roman general Aegidius baulking at the installation of a new emperor, and starting to govern northern Gaul himself as an independent kingdom, forming a mini-dynasty when his son, Syagrius, succeeded him. That kingdom would be seized by the Franks in the 480s. In the south, the Visigoths expanded their kingdom to control a large chunk of south-west Gaul, with Burgundians seizing territory in the south-east.

Even while the Goths were going about wresting power from Rome, they didn't eschew the idea of *Roman-ness*. As we've seen, these Romanised barbarians and military elites were precisely the people who were originally paid to help Rome maintain control as *foederati*, settling in the lands they were tasked with policing, then seizing power for themselves – or perhaps, viewed from a different angle, hanging onto it, as usurper-emperors stabbed each other in the back and the western Empire crumbled.

When Sidonius visited Visigothic Gaul in the 460s (it seems it was still perfectly possible for an upper-class Gallo-Roman to travel between Roman Gaul and Visigothic Gaul at this point), he noted the persistence of Roman schools of higher education there. The Roman system of administration, culture, education – and social structure – was so embedded and worked so well, it wouldn't be easily dismantled. And the traditional elites had a vested interest in keeping it that way; it was crucial if those families wanted to maintain their power in society – even while seismic political changes were rumbling on, fault lines of power cracking open.

If we were to approach this in an abstract way, we might come away with the interpretation that Christianity had somehow inveigled itself into Roman systems of education, politics and administration. But again, that's *too* abstract. It's *people* who are creating these systems, this culture. It seems likely that some aristocrats would have seen the potential for Christianity to be a useful way of joining everything up, keeping everything running smoothly – and their status and their roles secure. But perhaps for others, it wasn't as explicitly intentional. Either way, now, the sons of both Gallo-Roman noblemen and Gothic kings were sent away to be taught Roman law and literature – and Christian scripture. The elite system of education, training those young men for kingship or positions in the Church, was still working well.

Interestingly, archaeologists looking at the material culture of southern Gaul don't see much of a change when the Visigothic elites were moving in – and they interpret that as meaning that the incomers were quickly and almost seamlessly integrating into existing society, rather than displacing it. Members of elite Gallo-Roman families had much to gain, too – if they could swallow their pride and bring themselves to work with the new barbarian elites, they could hope to hold onto their wealth and status even as political power shifted.

The economy of southern Gaul has been studied in some detail and shows us how the area transitioned from being part of the Roman Empire to being a separate state ruled by 'barbarians' in the form of Visigoths, Ostrogoths and, eventually, Franks. That contrast between part of the Empire and an independent state makes it sound very black and white, oppositional, 'in' or 'out'. And yet as we have seen through the lens of recent political and economic changes in Europe – particularly with the untidy business of Britain extracting itself from the European Union – there's always nuance. There are different levels of engagement between individual states and the larger bloc, in political, economic and legal terms.

Southern Gaul already had an identity of its own, within the Empire, and a longstanding tendency for its economy to have been quite self-contained, compared with other areas that produced more luxury goods for long-distance trade within the Empire. Historian and archaeologist Bruce Hitchner noted the 'virtual absence of south Gallic exports on any scale after the first century'. In the already politically unstable atmosphere of the fifth century, hikes in Roman taxes threatened further instability – with the potential to drive wedges between local elites and the labour force. For local landowning aristocrats, the benefits of leaving, rather than remaining in, the Empire may have started to look attractive. But that didn't mean a complete break away from existing trade networks and the fiscal and administrative systems of the Empire – far from it. Those systems were firmly embedded in the provinces – and enmeshed with systems of hierarchy and social status – through the Church, as we have seen. While what had been provinces 'officially' seceded from the Empire, they never extricated themselves from that administrative network – which was intimately enmeshed with the fabric of society and the function of economies. Talking again about southern Gaul, Hitchner writes that this region 'suffered no crisis of identity . . . it still belonged soundly to the Mediterranean economic system created by Rome'.

Sidonius lived right through these changes, and he documented them in his letters. He would find eventually himself in an impossible situation – torn between loyalty to the Empire and to local rulers in the Visigothic and Burgundian realms of Gaul. It may be that Sidonius published his letters in order to justify various actions over the course of his life, to friends and colleagues in his social sphere; he changed his mind and shifted his political stance a couple of times. He published his work in two tranches – the first in 469, when he became bishop of Clermont, when the Visigoths in Gaul were still loyal federates of Rome. The second volume was published in 476, by which time the Visigoths had rejected imperial overlordship and were indulging their own expansionist ambitions.

Sidonius was initially positive about Roman emperors making treaties or *foedera* with the Goths, seeing this as a sensible way of protecting the Empire (failing to predict that the barbarians would in fact turn out to be more dangerous as *foederati* than as foes). In his first published letter, he wrote very favourably about the Visigothic king Theoderic II, whose forces were occupying Narbonne at the time. Sidonius approved of Theoderic as an acceptable, Romanised barbarian, going so far as to describe how the king put a Romanly effort into his personal appearance – even taking care to clip the bristles beneath his nostrils on a daily basis. The king was assiduous in his royal duties and put on great dinners; visiting his house was a delight, combining 'Greek elegance, Gallic plenty, Italian briskness; the dignity of state, the attentiveness of a private home, the ordered discipline of royalty'. Interestingly, it seemed important to Sidonius that Theoderic adhered to religious *tradition*, even if it didn't seem all that genuine. 'Before dawn he goes with a very small retinue to the service conducted by the priests of his faith,' writes Sidonius, 'and he worships with great earnestness, though (between ourselves) one can see that this devotion is a matter of routine rather than of conviction.' He skipped over the king's Homoean (and therefore unorthodox) take on Christianity, and goes as far as to call Theoderic 'the support and preserver of the Roman people'. As long as the Goths were loyal federates, it didn't seem to matter if their theology was a bit divergent.

But in 466, Theoderic was murdered and replaced by his younger brother, Euric – who was not at all content to be a client king under the Roman Empire. In one letter, written around 469, Sidonius expresses his disappointment with an act of treason perpetrated by his friend, Arvandus, who was the praetorian prefect, the leading governor, of Gaul. 'I am distressed by the fall of Arvandus and I do not conceal my distress,' wrote Sidonius. Arvandus had been found guilty of collaboration with the Visigoth king, Euric, as evidenced in a letter. It seems that Arvandus was anticipating the secession of Gaul from the Roman Empire, and had been hoping to curry favour and stay on as the ruler of Gaul, as a client king under the Visigoths.

At the time, Sidonius was the prefect of Rome, with responsibilities that included overseeing a senatorial court which prosecuted high-level cases. Presumably, Arvandus would have been tried by this very court – but somehow Sidonius managed to be absent from the proceedings. He'd also let Arvandus know that his treacherous letter to Euric had been discovered – and advised his friend to confess to nothing. The last we hear of the matter from Sidonius was that Arvandus was tried in Rome, and condemned to death; Sidonius wrote that he would continue to pray that 'imperial generosity may . . . show favour to this half-dead man'. And it seems, according to later historians at any rate, that Arvandus may have been spared after all – that his death sentence was commuted to exile.

In the 470s, Euric and his Visigoths were knocking on Sidonius's door, repeatedly laying siege to Clermont. Inside its walls, Sidonius helped his brother-in-law, Ecdicus, to defend the city. Writing to another bishop, Basilius, in 474, Sidonius lamented Euric's expansionist tendencies – and now he did seem suddenly troubled by Homoeanism, saying that he feared Euric's lack of orthodoxy more than his military might. Suddenly, Euric was not the *right sort* of Christian. In plenty of his letters from this time, Sidonius seems to be expressing a crisis of identity, or at least, a certain regret about his earlier stance (when he'd been very accepting of the Homoean Goth *foederati*) as an embarrassing mistake. Confronted by the military ambitions of the Goths, he had to find a way to distance himself from them, and religious differences provided just that. Sidonius was also worried that the Church as an institution was not being supported; he was concerned that, in many cities, when bishops died, they were not replaced, and that 'the peoples, left desolate by the death of their bishops, [are] sunk in a gloomy despair at the disruption of their faith'.

Sidonius noted how quickly the Church was losing

followers – losing its control of the population – with churches falling into ruin, and congregations dwindling. 'What comfort is left to the faithful,' Sidonius writes, 'when not only the teaching of the clergy but even the memory of them perishes? . . . Examine more deeply these losses of spiritual members [bishops], and you will certainly realise that with each removal of a bishop you will have the faith of a people put in jeopardy.'

He may have genuinely believed this – but it's impossible to separate that spiritual sentiment from the more secular dimension; the Church officials united in their orthodox, catholic faith represented not only a last bastion of Roman control, but also a source of job security for Sidonius and his ilk. Though he couches his concern in terms of the 'comfort of the faithful', is he perhaps more concerned that, within the territory now controlled by the Visigoths, that alternative system of Roman power provided by the Church was under threat? Without funding, those high offices – including his own bishopric – would disappear.

Certainly, Sidonius saw the reinstatement of those positions as crucial: 'Work, therefore, that this may be the chief article of the peace – that episcopal ordination being permitted we may hold according to the faith, though we cannot hold according to the treaty, those peoples of Gaul who are enclosed within the bounds of the Gothic domain.' In other words, he seems to have been suggesting: we could make peace with the Visigoths if they reinstate bishops (and therefore both our soft power and job security).

Eventually, in 475, Clermont surrendered to Euric, becoming absorbed into the now independent Visigothic kingdom. Sidonius was exiled to Spain. And now he performed an extraordinary about-turn, forgetting his antipathy towards the

Visigoths and starting to write flattering poems about them instead. He penned a panegyric to Euric, praising him in ebullient terms as a noble warrior – and suggesting that, if the Visigothic king could see his way to becoming an ally of Rome, he could even help defend to the Empire against the Scythians. (I think we see similar *volte-faces* today when would-be candidates for election may tear into each other up to the point that one is chosen to proceed – when suddenly all the others cannot speak more highly of them.) Sidonius's poem urges Euric to be magnanimous, to think of himself as Roman now – despite the fact that Euric had declared himself independent. Sidonius's petition to Euric was successful; before long, he was reinstated as bishop of Clermont, having pragmatically accepted the over-lordship of the Visigoths.

It's very easy to see Sidonius simply acting in a politically expedient manner, following the way the wind blew, throwing in his hat with whichever authority prevailed. But the late Roman historian Jill Harries urges us not to be so overly simplistic – that the 'truth is more subtle'. And however adroitly Sidonius manages to shape-shift, depending on who he's writing to, who he's writing about, and the political milieu of the moment, Harries detects a firm underlying belief that is more robust. 'One constant feature', she writes, 'is Sidonius's ideal of Rome, the city that symbolised his aristocratic values and, through its rule, gave him and his peers the right, and indeed the obligation, to hold high office.' He believed in Rome – as an administrative system and a literary culture. (This was a deep and longstanding belief among elite Romans: that the Empire embodied a superior way of life that was nothing less than civilisation itself – and which depended on a wealthy, literary elite to run it.) It clearly wasn't an exclusive ideal.

Perhaps forced by the realpolitik of the times, Sidonius could accept Gothic rule – as long as (he could persuade himself) those Gothic kings demonstrated a willingness to behave like a Roman – not a barbarian.

Living through these politically tempestuous times, but managing to hold onto his job, his power and influence, Sidonius's story reveals how Christianity provided a way for Roman aristocrats to 'bridge the gap' – intellectually and practically – as the western Empire broke up into barbarian kingdoms. In a world where Roman imperial control was starting to falter, the Church offered a strong link back to the old ideas and values of the Roman Empire – as important to Sidonius as being eloquent in 'old-fashioned' Latin. Around him, other Gallic aristocratics tried to shore up their status, not by harking back to the glory days of the Roman Empire, but by strengthening their ties with the barbarians: the Goths who were now the predominant political force. They indulged in extravagant lifestyles and conspicuous feasting in a way that recalled Iron Age traditions, and prefigured later medieval customs – while wearing clothes that looked very much like those of Roman emperors and generals. Meanwhile, Sidonius hoped that, one day, a new Julius Caesar might rise to reclaim Gaul. He looked to Christianity as a way of preserving traditional Roman aristocratic roles, and a steadfast emblem of Roman-ness – even while the Empire itself fell apart.

Keeping It in the Family: Kinship and Dynasties

The richness of the textual historical record for fifth-century Gaul provides us with amazingly detailed glimpses into events and experiences – albeit through that narrow lens provided by the literate elites. But it also allows us to trace families through time, and see how interconnected they all were. Careful analysis of texts has shown that the transformation of Gaul into a Visigothic (and then Frankish) kingdom actually involved a lot of continuity among the ruling elites, with the same families holding onto power down through the generations, and plenty of close family connections between leading clerics and other aristocrats – which can be traced through hereditary names.

In fact, as the eminent historian Ian Wood wrote, 'Almost every major writer from fifth-century Gaul can be placed within a single, well-defined nexus of family, social and religious relationships.' All these very high-status men (and they were all men) knew each other; many were related – and some had direct connections with the centre of imperial operations.

We can start with our friend Sidonius Apollinaris – as we've got to know him so well – and map some of his genealogical network.

Both Sidonius's grandfather and father had held the high office of prefect of Gaul. Sidonius himself was urban prefect of Rome (essentially its mayor), and from 469 to his death in the 480s, bishop of Clermont. He was married to Papianilla, daughter of Eparchius Avitus, who had also previously held the position of prefect of Gaul and briefly reigned as western emperor. Another Eparchius, an earlier bishop of Clermont, from 462 to 472, was probably related to this emperor, Sidonius's father-in-law, too (as names were hereditary). Avitus's father was a man called Isicius, who was bishop of Vienne. It's thought that the previous bishop of Vienne, Mamertus, may have tutored Avitus. The younger brother of Mamertus, confusingly called Claudianus Mamertus, was also a priest in Vienne. Sidonius had also had a cousin and schoolfriend who was called Avitus – who must have had some connection with his father-in-law, too.

All these families – all these high-level administrative and ecclesiastical positions – are densely interconnected. And they're connected with the Gothic elites as well, with historical records of elite Gallo-Romans not only attending the courts of Ostrogoth and Visigoth kings, but also marrying Gothic princesses and being given land.

This strong link between religious and secular power wasn't new; it had deep roots in Roman society, going back way before Christianity spread through the Empire. In the days of the republic, in the second century BCE, Roman noblemen were routinely co-opted into one of the traditional priesthoods of the Roman state, the main three being the *pontifices*, the *augures* and the *decemviri sacris faciundis*. Sometimes, such a high-ranking priestly role would be the cherry on the top of a prestigious political career. But even young men could become *pontifices* or *augures*, suggesting that these posts were not always based on achievement, or seen as the pinnacle of a career, but could also be a means to an end – that end being political advancement. Fellow priests would back a colleague in the senate, when he ran for office – virtually guaranteeing his success. For existing senators, ensuring that family members were given a leg up into office meant that they'd have allies to help protect their interests.

We see exactly this pattern replicated in the Christian priesthood, in fifth-century Gaul, with Sidonius's illustrious political career culminating in being made a bishop. And, just as with those senatorial roles, the dynasties carried down through the generations: Sidonius's son, Apollinaris, would be a military commander, and briefly reprise his father's role as bishop of Clermont; his grandson would serve at the court of the Frankish king Childebert. We're seeing political dynasties occupying the highest positions in government and the Church, and the separation between those two systems looks more blurred than ever. What's also startling is that, while the imperial administration was starting to lose control in so many ways, the Church was becoming more and more prominent.

Historians have tracked the development of administrative systems linked to the Church by looking at records of bishops attending ecclesiastical councils. The third to fifth centuries in southern Gaul saw a proliferation of bishops, each of whom would have his own episcopal see – the name for the administrative area looked after by a bishop. The word 'see' in this context comes from the Latin, *sedes*, meaning 'seat'. (The Holy See, which is now practically synonymous with the Vatican City, is administered by the Roman Curia or 'Roman Court' – it's almost as though the Roman Empire never ceased.)

In most cases, bishops were installed in cities that were already operating as regional capitals – or *civitas*-capitals. And, in fact, by the fifth century, all but one *civitas*-capital in southern Gaul had acquired a bishop and become an episcopal see. There were also a few places, including Nice and Toulon, which got a bishop before they were recognised as a *civitas*-capital. This may just reflect the rate at which different towns were becoming urbanised and emerging as important hubs. These cities were already economically important, so the installation of bishops there doesn't represent a break from existing administrative systems, but just an extension or evolution of them. New bureaucratic roles within the Church also became more attractive as the power of the *curiae* (city councils) waned, with city budgets increasingly squeezed by the central imperial administration, struggling to fund its campaigns against the Persians.

What was happening in Gaul, and across the Empire, was that the Church was inheriting or taking over the secular Roman administration, depending on how you want to look at it. This transition was well underway even before Christianity became the official religion of the Empire; the educated sons of wealthy families were already finding themselves positions as priests, abbots and bishops. The fragmentation of the western Roman Empire may give us the impression that a massive revolution happened – but on the ground the political elites, those powerful dynasties, maintained their hegemony, thanks to their involvement in the most powerful cult that the Empire had ever generated. (It's likely that the original process of Romanisation, as the empire expanded, involved a similar process – where provincial elites would have bought into the imperial cult as a way of maintaining their power, authority and status. We often think about the expansion of the Roman Empire involving conquest and subjugation, but it simply wouldn't have worked if at least *some* of the local elites hadn't accepted and adopted Roman culture, together with its literary underpinnings, and the imperial cult – and there were plenty of incentives to do so.)

Although the records for Britain are so much thinner than those for Gaul, we can clearly see dynasties operating there too. Virtually every medieval saint is recorded as having come from a wealthy, noble family – whether that's explicitly stated in the hagiographies or just hinted at. Remember Cuthbert, arriving at Melrose on his horse, with his spear. At Llanilltud, the *Life of Samson* relates that one of Illtud's nephews was expecting to inherit the monastery. (Though Samson had other ideas, and after accusing the nephew of plotting to poison him, ousted him from that position.) On the ground, the lives of ordinary people may have changed less than we might imagine. The strictly hierarchical nature of society was maintained – the bishop, from an established, local, wealthy family, was still the most important person in town. The rich stayed rich and the poor stayed poor. Christianity reinforced that social structure, that inequality – while promising the poor that they would reap their rewards in heaven.

If we ignore the religious aspect for a moment, we're simply seeing the maintenance of sub-imperial, and then post-imperial, hierarchical administration. Putting back the religious aspect, the whole thing is shored up by a new idea of divine authority – one that could exist independently of an emperor, outside of an empire. For those elite families, it meant both that their social status could be secured and that regional administration could be smoothly maintained – even when new 'barbarian' kings arrived on the scene. And, in fact, the local elites running the cities of the Empire had always enjoyed a considerable degree of autonomy – central government and control was relatively light-touch. As long as local town councils were doing their job in collecting taxes, the emperor could largely leave them to their own devices. Draped over this system of devolved power, the imperial cult provided a useful reminder, a unifying ideology, and justified the existence of the elites. But Christianity could either reinforce that cult or short-circuit it. After all, now, an emperor – and indeed the Empire itself – was no longer necessary for 'Roman' civilisation to persist. What was emerging was a resilient model that would stand the test of time. Augustine of Hippo effectively predicted this in his *City of God*, written in the early fifth century; picking up a theme from the book of the Revelation in the New Testament, he posited that the Church could be eternal – or at least, less time-limited than the Roman Empire, which was merely serving as a useful vehicle for God's will for the time being.

But once again, I find myself falling into abstractions, writing of states and ideologies and models. That's one way of understanding what was happening. But in the end, it's all brought about by *people*; people with all sorts of reasons for behaving in the ways that brought about these changes. And what's impossible to ignore is that, for administrators switching over to working in the religious arm of the new system, there were significant financial benefits to be reaped. Being a bishop was becoming a very attractive career prospect indeed.

Jobs for the Boys and Tax Breaks

In the fourth century, Roman imperial administration had been overhauled, creating twelve (growing into fourteen) large regions known as dioceses (originally an entirely secular term, just meaning 'administration'), each governed by a *vicarius,* the regional representative of the praetorian prefect. There were two dioceses in Gaul. Another layer of management was introduced in the form of *comites,* or counts, who outranked the *vicarii.* Cities were important in the structure of the administration; a city and its surrounding countryside formed the *civitas* – essentially a 'city state' – the basic unit of Roman local government. (There are 114 *civitates* in Roman Gaul listed in the late-fifth-century *Notitia Galliarum* and they are strikingly similar to modern French departments, just as many of the *civitates* of Roman Britannia map rather neatly onto the modern counties of England). In each city, there were magistrates. But alongside those secular positions, as we've seen, there were ecclesiastical roles – with increasing administrative powers.

In the late Roman into post-Roman era in the west, a well-trodden aristocratic career, or *cursus honorum*, persisted – we've been able to track a few of these. But there were some differences to the earlier elite career paths. Where local aristocrats were formerly elected into public office, those appointments were now made by the *comites* or counts who looked after the dioceses of the empire. Bishops were officially meant to be elected by ecclesiastical councils, but it's clear that the self-declared emperors who kept seizing power in late Roman Gaul, and later, Visigothic kings, were actively involved in elevating their cronies into these influential roles. In the early fifth century, Constantine III and Constantius III – each of whom briefly assumed the western emperorship – both chose allies to be bishops, notably of Arles, which was becoming dominant as the western capital. Equally, bishops who fell out of favour politically were unseated, exiled or subjected to smear campaigns.

Beyond the usefulness of having friends in high places, all these appointments – whether secular or religious – required some kind of civic consensus to prevent rival factions tearing a city apart. And prospective bishops certainly didn't shy away from mobilising their supporters in order to help them get those top jobs. The records from fifth-century Gaul are littered with accounts of bishops and would-be bishops vying with each other for supremacy, cosying up with whichever secular leader seemed to be in the ascendancy at the time, and stabbing each other in the back.

As the Empire lost its central control over the provinces and dioceses in the west, cities in Gaul and Iberia remained locally governed by counts and bishops. Most of the documentary sources emphasise the bishop as the main governor – but then, most of the sources come from the Church itself, with churchmen writing all those *Lives* of bishops-turned-saints. Other sources show that, moving into the sixth and seventh centuries, cities were also governed by magistrates, sitting on city councils. These two pathways were not necessarily competing, but complementary, with a revolving door between secular and religious offices. But there was a really significant difference in these roles – when it came to taxes.

In the later Roman Empire, anyone holding public office was legally required to pay fees, or liturgies (literally: public works), in order to hold office. These liturgies provided the majority of the funds needed to run cities – to keep the roads mended, the aqueducts in good working order and the public bathhouses clean. (Magistrates were also responsible for collecting some other funds into the public coffers – various charges, rents and fines – although detailed budgets are lost to history.) But – crucially – ecclesiastical posts were exempt from such liturgies.

Other taxes were based on land ownership and agricultural production. It's hard to gauge wealth in early medieval Europe, or to translate it into terms that are meaningful today – but what we can say is that personal wealth was directly related to the amount of land someone owned; this was a largely agricultural economy. In the third century, the emperor Caracalla had granted citizenship to everyone living in the Empire, something which sounds lovely and magnanimous but which actually meant that everyone was now liable for taxes. How those taxes were collected was rather complicated (as it always is).

In the late fourth century, Roman taxes on food production,

which had been paid in kind (usually that meant in grain), were transformed into payments in gold, collected from wealthy landowners. These were scooped up by the provincial governor, then passed on through the diocesan administrator, to the praetorian prefect in Rome (or in the eastern empire, Constantinople). Another important change in the late Roman period saw tenant farmers being increasingly rendered as little more than indentured servants or serfs, tied to the land they farmed – usually on villa estates. So now, the landowners would collect in-kind payments from their tenants, while paying their own taxes in gold. That is, unless they could secure an exemption. This might be granted if they were deemed to be providing an important service – if they were barbarian *foederati*, for instance – or if the estate was ecclesiastical. And so there were two ways in which the Church and its clergy could excuse themselves from paying taxes: by avoiding the liturgies associated with other public roles, and being excused from the usual taxes on landholdings.

As imperial lands broke up into smaller kingdoms, such as the Visigothic and Frankish kingdoms in Gaul, the kings continued to collect taxes in much the same way. Kings were landowners too, and would collect taxes from their own royal estates as well as from the estates of other landowners (which they occasionally seized for themselves). But the number of tax-exempt estates was growing – especially those owned by the Church.

Various tax exemptions for the Church and its clergy had existed since the time of Constantine in the early fourth century; they'd even persisted through the reign of Constantine's nephew, Julian 'the Apostate', who'd removed other religious privileges from Christians. The exemptions weren't automatic, though; individuals and churches often had to argue the case. One of Sidonius's letters, written in 459, saw him writing directly to the emperor Marjorian, asking for personal tax exemption – as a bishop. Some churches, it seems, were exempt from paying taxes up to a point, but would have to cough up if their income exceeded that tax-free allowance. A petition from a church in Ostrogothic Italy, to the emperor Theodoric, asked for exemption from those higher-rate taxes too. The emperor agreed – for the church's existing landholdings – while stipulating that the church should pay full tax on any income from estates it acquired in the future. But as churches acquired more and more land from donors, they argued that they shouldn't inherit the tax liabilities; that all the farms coming into their possession should have tax-free status. The negotiations were endless. Meanwhile, lower-level landholders and their tenant farmers continued to pay their taxes, as their bargaining power was not as great. The hagiographies written about this time are full of cautionary tales of avaricious kings attempting to secure their tax revenues: the greedy kings against the pious bishops. God, it seems (as far as the hagiographers were concerned), was on the side of the tax-evaders. By the seventh century, the Merovingian kings who ruled France would realise that they were fighting a losing battle. They managed to exact dues elsewhere – demanding military service from their subjects and gathering extortionate legal fees from the law courts. And this meant they could let the Christianity off the hook. They'd been persuaded that the political costs – to them – of taxing the Church were just too high. Churches were duly granted absolute tax-free status.

The tax-free income that the Church drew from its estates was used in a number of ways. Individual churches had an increasing number of employees to pay; clergy, monks and nuns weren't paid for directly by imperial or royal taxes (although monasteries received royal endowments) – institutions had to find the money themselves, largely from the income generated by their own estates, together with gifts from wealthy donors and occasionally, if they were lucky, from the emperor himself. Churches also needed to pay for a lot of *stuff* associated with all of its rituals – for church plate, wine, feasts on saints' days, parchment to write on and oil for lamps. And it also needed funds for church buildings.

From the fifth century, there was an officially recognised, proper division of church income. This four-way division was referred to in some detail by Pope Gelasius, at the end of the fifth century, who wrote that 'all money received should be divided into four portions: that is, one for the bishop and his household for the purposes of hospitality and entertainment, a second for the clergy, a third for the poor, and a fourth for the repair of churches'. (That was the official line, although there's plenty of documentary evidence of bishops manipulating what presumably should have been an equal four-way division of funds, in their own favour.) In Spain, it seems a three-way division was employed – for the bishop, the clergy and the fabric of the church; the poor weren't specifically mentioned but there was still an expectation that the bishop would offer them some sort of handout. The Church had made itself responsible for looking after the poor, a lucrative business in itself, as cities grew and the problem of poverty – dirty, smelly, gruesome poverty – grew with them. The Church gathered funds from the state and from rich, private donors (promising to relieve those donors of their wealth in exchange for redemption and a pass into heaven) and directed some of that income to the poor and infirm, including making endowments for hospitals – helping to make the problem less visible.

Rich donors were also encouraged to invest in the fabric of the Church. And ecclesiastical buildings were going up just as other civic buildings were falling into disrepair. While historical sources imply that taxation was overly burdensome in the western provinces of the late Roman Empire, it seems that the tax burden may not have been that unusually high. (Just like today, people like to complain about taxes and to pre-empt tax hikes by complaining about them, before they happen.) But on the other hand, there is some evidence that local councils were struggling to maintain public services; for instance, private landowners were being asked to take on the responsibility of keeping aqueducts on their land clean, and some public baths were becoming run-down. And the record provided by inscriptions shows that most private investments into the civic built environment, rather than funding infrastructure such as walls and bridges (mundane, but essential), were being used to build churches. This could be interpreted as funds being diverted to serve a changing need in a changing society; historian Javier Martínez Jiménez suggested that donors were keen 'to invest in the spiritual and religious needs of the people, which were as high on the list of early medieval community needs as municipal infrastructure'. But then again, a church might have seemed like a much more attractive, prestigious thing to invest in than a bridge.

Godliness before cleanliness, then. But who determined that this should be the case? That the 'spiritual and religious needs of the people' not only outranked a need for well-kept public baths and other municipal public buildings and spaces, but required investment in prestigious, impressive buildings for the purpose, along with palaces for the bishops who were so generously looking after those spiritual and religious needs? Surely we must suspect it just may have been – the bishops themselves.

By funding such impressive architecture in the centre of cities, the urban elites connected themselves with this power – which transcended that of mere kings and emperors (while shoring it up) – just as their forebears would have done by helping to fund temples. And the new, imposing, ecclesiastical buildings were not only built to impress, they helped to embed Christianity in the heart of the city. In antiquity, civic cults had always helped to bind communities together; living in a city brought with it an expectation that you would engage with cultic rituals, including certain festivals and processions, honouring the gods (and the emperor) who protected the city and kept it prosperous. Those rituals were now being replaced with Christian ones, serving similar functions – and just as pagan cults had done, these included generic elements alongside local connections, including local saints, reinforcing a sense of connectedness with place, with the city. And of course, all of it helped to reinforce the pre-eminence of the same old social elites as well.

But all this investment in churches went alongside a disinvestment in other public buildings and spaces. Whether they fell out of favour or simply became unaffordable, the theatres and amphitheatres, forums and the public buildings around them fell into disuse and ruin – or were repurposed. Paved and cobbled streets disappeared under earth and gravel. Somehow those symbols of Roman-ness fell out of fashion – while the Church (in so many ways the ultimate symbol of Roman-ness) managed not only to hang on, but to increasingly dominate the central urban space.

Christianity was set to make an indelible mark on the urban landscape.

Godliness and Cleanliness: On Basilicas and Baptisteries

The physical evidence for the growing influence of Christianity is most evident in the cities of Gaul (another big difference with Britain where, although bishops were attested, archaeological traces of their influence are like hen's teeth). One thing that didn't change much as Gallo-Roman cities evolved into Visigothic ones was the presence of churches, and – usually in the city centre if there was room – with an episcopal complex for a bishop. Some were bigger than others. The episcopal group at Geneva and Lyon each included two churches; in Geneva, the bishop's complex was huge, occupying a quarter of the area of the town inside the walls.

In some Gallic cities, entire episcopal complexes were housed within the encircling city walls; in others, space inside the city was at a premium, and cathedrals and baptisteries were extramural. But for some, that wasn't prestigious enough. There's a nasty little story about Amator, bishop of Auxerre in the late sixth century, who found his extramural church too small for his growing congregation. He approached a wealthy man called Ruptilius, who owned a spacious house inside the city walls, and asked him if he could convert his house into a church. Ruptilius refused. Amator prayed for a miracle and Ruptilius duly fell ill. He panicked and handed over part of his house to the bishop.

Some public buildings were also converted into churches, which is perhaps not too surprising, given that Christianity had become the official state religion in the late fourth century. At Aix-en-Provence, the cathedral seems to have replaced a large building alongside the forum – either a temple or the basilica – in the late fifth century. When we hear the word 'basilica' today, we often think immediately of a church; the two words seem practically synonymous. But before Christianity came along, the basilica was just a generic public building. It was a large, long building typically found running along one side of a Roman town square or forum. And in turn, these Roman buildings were direct descendants of the Greek *stoa*, or *basilikḗ stoá*, to give it its full name – the 'royal covered colonnade' that would form one side of the agora (the precursor and equivalent of the Roman forum) in Greek towns and cities. Their architecture – with a tall central aisle flanked by two lower aisles, separated by posts or pillars – is distinctive.

These basilicas were public buildings for business and legal activities – a sort of town hall. The Roman versions tended to have an apse at one end, where you might find a statue of an emperor, or assembled magistrates sitting on a raised dais. The building was entered through the colonnaded long sides; the central aisle rose high, with windows in a clerestory above the level of the flanking side aisles. Similar basilicas were to be found in palaces (where they lived up to their original 'royal' designation).

A large basilica was a ubiquitous feature of Roman city centres – and a powerful symbol of Roman-ness. Imposing, perfect for public meetings and separate from the old temples, basilicas were increasingly adopted as meeting places by various cults, including Christians, in the late Roman period. Many previously secular basilicas were completely taken over – they *became* churches. And when Christians moved on from building modest 'house churches', to more ambitious and well-funded architecture, they built themselves new churches in the style of the old basilicas. To the extent that now, when we hear the word 'basilica', we don't tend to think of Roman town halls – our thoughts turn to Christian churches. The assimilation is complete.

In a dramatic break from the Roman tradition, enforced by law, of burying the dead outside the city walls, Christians started to bury their dead in and around basilicas in towns. And there may be a connection here with those rural villa sites, which also came to be used as burial grounds. In Britain, alongside smaller but more prestigious and well-appointed villa houses, some villa complexes included large buildings which archaeologists tend to refer to as 'aisled barns' or even 'farmhouses'. These were essentially slightly scaled-down versions of the basilicas – the aisled buildings found in town centres. Some of the rural aisled buildings may indeed have been used as barns; they may have been lived in, too; and they could potentially be used as larger reception halls, alongside the villas. If they were being used as a gathering space for the community around the villa, in the late Roman or early post-Roman era, they start to sound a bit more like parish churches. Villa chapels are hard to spot archaeologically – though fourth-century Christian tombstones found at villa sites in western Gaul are suggestive – but are well attested in the literature, with fifth-century Gallic church councils mentioning *oratoria villara*, villa oratories. Later, in the medieval period, exactly the same pattern would pertain – with lords of the manor building their own private chapels, next to their manor houses; some would be private oratories for the landowning family, others, estate chapels – used by the wider community (the same distinction may have existed in the early medieval period). Estate chapels may have then become foci for burial, and gradually evolved into parish churches – many still existing adjacent to a manor house. But it's important to note here that Christianity in the fourth and fifth centuries was still largely an urban phenomenon. The physical traces of Christianity in the countryside are all linked to wealthy landowners – and again, mostly about private cultic acts, rather than any kind of wider, systematic attempt at rural conversion. (By the sixth century, Gallic church councils record clergy in cities, rural parishes – and villas – but also stipulate that the important Christian festivals should be celebrated in episcopal churches in the city, not in estate chapels.) It's in cities that we see purpose-built churches being erected – with a distinction there too, between larger public buildings, associated with bishops, and smaller private chapels of elite families.

There were other urban Roman buildings that were pressed into Christian service – including baths. No Roman city was complete without a public baths; they were an obvious demonstration of civilisation. And they'd always fulfilled many different functions. They were, certainly, somewhere you could go to get clean and to keep fit and healthy. But they were also places to meet, eat, do business, or to relax and play board games. (Visiting the recently excavated baths at Silchester, where I was lucky enough to be given a guided tour by the generous and erudite lead archaeologist, Mike Fulford, I was struck by the similarity of the bath complex to a modern leisure centre – it was about *much* more than just washing.)

Bathing, and the buildings that facilitated it, became more and more important over the course of the Roman Empire. The architecture and engineering of bathhouses was an impressive signal of civilised Roman taste and know-how. In Rome itself, the imperial hot baths or *thermae* included gardens, libraries and lecture halls. They represented a very obvious and showy demonstration of imperial benevolence and public spending. They were architectural showpieces in the city, and the upper classes visited them to see – and be seen. But some public baths were there for everyone, as facilities that might be visited on a weekly basis. Farmers coming to market in a city might have visited the baths before going to a temple; in this way a mundane act of weekly bathing becomes associated with a more cultic aspect. Ancient historian Garret G. Fagan described the 'general function of Roman public baths' as 'reproducers of the social order in Roman communities'. And as the German classical archaeologist Dirk Steuernagel has put it, 'Baths were locations of religious practice since they were locations where people frequently met; they were permeated by religion since the urban life during Roman Imperial and late antique times generally was. Thermae offered themselves for the exercise of certain religious rites inasmuch [as] they were prominent parts of the public urban sphere.'

As the Empire wore on, some public baths acquired another explicitly religious function: they became used as Christian baptisteries. Writing in the second into the third centuries, Tertullian uses a certain word, *lavacrum*, in both religious and more mundane, bath-related contexts. The word *lavacrum* seems to have been a standard Latin term for 'washing' or 'pool', but it came to be associated with religious cleansing, sometimes used along with adjectives like *sanctum* and *regenerationis* – making the holy implication explicit. Other words which originally applied to particular pools in bathhouses, *piscina* and *alveus*, are also used to describe Christian fonts for baptism. The word 'baptism' itself obviously refers to what happens in a *baptisterium*, but a *baptisterium* was just a pool in a bathhouse before the word and the pool became adopted for religious purposes. A passage in an ecclesiastical history written by Socrates Scholasticus (c.380–450), describing events leading up to the exile of the archbishop of Constantinople, John Chrysostom, contains a brilliant detail about a bathhouse being pressed into religious service. Chrysostom had complained about a statue of the Empress Eudoxia being erected rather too near to the Hagia Sophia cathedral, and had fallen foul of the other bishops (who were presumably keen to show their support from the imperial family) who excluded him from worshipping in the Hagia Sophia. Undeterred, Chrysostom and his followers gathered to celebrate the Easter service in the public baths of Constantinople instead.

But to see the evolution of a religious function out of an originally more mundane purpose for Roman baths, in a Christian context, is to overlook the sacred connections that had always existed. Greek and Roman bathhouses were human constructions, but they were still recognised to bear some kind of connection to the concept of healing waters, sacred springs and wells. Bathhouses, long before Christianity adopted them, were often dedicated to gods or goddesses – such as Sulis Minerva at the famous Roman baths in Aquae Sulis, the city we know simply as Bath today. Votive altars and statues were erected inside bathhouses. In the Baths of Caracalla in Rome and the *Terme del Mitra* in Ostia, shrines to the Roman-Persian god Mithras were created in corridors underground. Our perspective from the twenty-first century perhaps makes the adoption of a bathhouse for religious purposes much more surprising than it would have been in the first millennium. It would be very strange to see a religious shrine or statue in a modern civic swimming baths today – but there was much less separation between the secular and the sacred in Roman times.

Bathing was an official part of public life, funded by the empire, and as well as shrines or statues of deities, there were plenty of imperial symbols in the baths, including statues of emperors. Baths themselves were powerful symbols of Roman-ness: beautiful, luxurious, civilised – they were a focus for the imperial cult that was also part of everyday life. (There's a connection back to Ancient Greek gymnasia too, where stat-ues of rulers and deities were on display.) Athletes and athletic contests – which also possessed a sacred dimension – were also attested in both inscriptions and mosaics in baths. (Sidonius was careful to point out, in the description of the bathhouse at his lovely villa, that there were no indecent paintings of wrestlers on the walls.) Many votive inscriptions have been found in Roman baths as well, including lead curse tablets. (These were small sheets of lead, inscribed with messages to the gods, often pleading for divine revenge on an enemy or thief.)

Some bathhouses were specifically associated with temples. At Lambaesis (modern Tazoult in Algeria), there was a *piscina* dedicated to both Aesculapius (the god of healing) and Hygeia (goddess of health), within a larger sanctuary of Aesculapius (which would have been a healing centre). There's another ex-ample in Algeria, at Thamugadi (modern Timgad – it's hardly changed its name). Here, a natural spring ran into a basin around which stood three temples, dedicated to *Dea Africa,* Aesculapius and Serapis (a popular Greco-Egyptian god). Just down the hill, the water from the spring fed the South *thermae.* There were also statues of *Dea Africa* and Aesculapius, as well as the emperors Valerianus and Galerius, inside the baths. There are plenty of other examples of statues of gods and votive inscriptions from Roman baths in North Africa. The baths were clearly part of the practice of public cults, overseen by high-status public officials.

So, when Christians started using baths for religious purposes, they weren't inventing something entirely new – just bringing a new religion into the mix. To begin with, Christians may have felt the need to disassociate themselves from the pagan cults also being practised at the baths; Tertullian mentions, for instance, that he avoids bathing when the *Saturnalia* festival is happening. This wouldn't be a problem for long, though. When Christianity became the official religion of the Empire, Christians seem to have entirely taken over some bathhouses, turning them into churches. The largest rooms – the cool *frigidaria* – were perfect for the job. There are plenty of examples of this transformation, including at the *Petits Thermes* of Madouros (modern M'Daourouch in Algeria), the *Thermes de l'Ouest* at Mactaris (modern Maktar in Tunisia) and the *Terme del Mitra* at Ostia in Italy. At Cimiez, in southern Gaul, a compact and bijou group of buildings was built for the local bishop among the ruins of a third-century bathhouse. So this isn't a subversion of the function of Roman baths, but rather just a Christianised version of what had always happened – and once again, we can imagine the same social elites taking the lead.

Churches grew out of baths, but new baths were also set up within basilica compounds in cities, and could help to generate income for the Church too, as records show was the case for the original Roman church of San Lorenzo in Florence. Thermal baths, long associated with healing as well as more everyday bathing functions, continued to be used by Christians in Late Antiquity and beyond. I've seen for myself one striking example of this transformation: the famous early church in the centre of Sofia, known as the Rotunda, which seems to have been part of a Roman baths complex (perhaps even the baths that were part of Constantine's palace) before it became an ecclesiastical establishment. Just a few centuries ago, a traveller to Sofia remarked on how prominent this building was at the time, standing tall compared with its surroundings; today it's surrounded by imposing 1950s Soviet buildings in a severe neoclassical style. Built mainly in red brick, the Rotunda is the oldest building in Sofia – its earliest parts dating to the fourth century. Behind the Rotunda, excavated open ruins include the remains of a hypocaust, where a floor was once suspended on pillars of pilae, allowing hot air to circulate underneath. It's thought that the Rotunda may have been used as a baptistery before being converted into a church, dedicated to St George. Inside, on the upper parts of the walls and the dome, there are partially preserved medieval paintings, including the archangel Michael. It seems miraculous that any of these paintings survive; the Rotunda was converted into a mosque during the Ottoman period, and then into a museum during the Soviet era. Today it's a church again.

The appropriation of the archetypal Roman basilica for religious use, of bathhouses and potentially villas too, demonstrates, in microcosm, how *Christianitas* captured *Romanitas*, or how Roman-ness developed into Christianity. These connections between the Roman Empire and Christianity have been hiding in plain sight. They are well known to scholars of classical studies and indeed of early Christianity, but somewhat obscure outside those circles – as though a veil has been drawn over them. But when we look at the career paths in fifth-century Gaul, all those elite Gallo-Roman families littered with bishops, at the archaeology of villas and cities, the illusion is shattered. Christianity, instead, seems inseparable from the Roman Empire; indeed, it seems in many ways to *be* the Empire.

But how did this happen? When we think of Roman religion, our mind turns to Jupiter and Juno, Venus and Mars, Mercury, Pluto and Minerva – and all the lesser gods that were adopted from other lands as the Roman Empire expanded and swallowed them up: Serapis, Mithras, Isis, Cybele, Sulis. A glorious profusion of divinity. So how did it change? How did what started as a minor sect within Judaism become so popular, displacing all the other gods and goddesses, replacing them with just one (even if that one was mysteriously three at the same time)?

And again, it's so easy to slip into that trap of talking about this new cult, this new religion as an 'it' – asking how *it* became popular, how *it* spread, how *it* came to dominate. *It* is an idea – in the mind of humans. So surely what we really want to know is *who* was responsible – for cementing this idea in the heart of Empire, and for pushing it out across a vast territory. We're off on our travels again, travelling back in time and to the other end of the Empire – to land in the early fourth century, in north-western Anatolia, in a city called Nicaea.

3

THE HEART OF EMPIRE

Gold coin showing Constantine with Sol Invictus, 313 CE

'So dear was he to God, and so blessed; so pious
and so fortunate in all that he undertook, that
with the greatest facility he obtained the authority
over more nations than any who had preceded
him, and yet retained his power, undisturbed, to
the very close of his life.'

EUSEBIUS CAESARIENSIS, *Vita Constantini*

The Council of Nicaea

In the spring of the year 325, hundreds of bishops from across the eastern Roman Empire arrived at the imperial palace in Nicaea, on the shore of the serene Lake Ascania, in north-west Anatolia.

Nicaea, or Nikaia in Greek, was one of the two major cities in Bithynia, the ancient kingdom occupying a strip of northern Asia Minor, from the Sea of Marmara, along the southern coast of the Black Sea. Previously named Antigoneia, the city had been called Nikaia since the end of the fourth century BCE, when Lysimachus, one of the generals who carved up the territories captured by Alexander the Great, seized it from his rival, the eponymous Antigonus. He couldn't keep the old name, and is said to have renamed the city after his wife, but the epithet also means 'victory'. (At the other end of the Empire, another Nikaia was founded by Phocaean Greeks and named after their victory over an adjacent tribe; it's still called Nice today.) Nicaea was economically important, owing its prosperity to its location – occupying a node on ancient trade routes connecting Europe and Asia.

Although Nicomedia, to the west, on the coast of the Sea of Marmara, was the official capital of Bithynia, Nicaea vied with it for supremacy. The kingdom came under the control of the Roman Republic in the first century BCE, and in 29 BCE, the senator and historian Cassius Dio said he thought Nicaea outranked Nicomedia. He may have been slightly biased, as it was his home town. But Strabo concurred, referring to Nicaea as 'the metropolis' – the capital. The first emperor, Augustus, ordered a temple to Rome and another to Julius Caesar to be built there, making Nicaea the provincial centre for the imperial cult. The bitter rivalry between Nicomedia and Nicaea continued for the next couple of centuries, with the various emperors favouring one over the other. The denizens of each city claimed priority, squabbling over the right to walk *in front* in the processions that accompanied provincial festivals.

But at the end of the second century CE, when three would-be emperors were battling it out for supremacy, Nicaea found itself on the losing side. The city had thrown its support behind the eastern protagonist, Pescennius Niger, while Nicomedia had quickly realised that Septimius Severus was likely to prevail – and they were right. Just as castles were slighted after the English Civil War of the seventeenth century, and monasteries in the reformation of the sixteenth, Nicaea was humbled, stripped of its titles. And yet it soon found its feet again, and continued to be a city where imperial cultic festivals and games were held, taxes were gathered into the imperial treasury, and the emperor kept a palace. It was here, in a hall at the palace, that the bishops assembled in 325.

Some were elders of the Church, distinguished by their years and wisdom. Others were younger and dynamic. Some had only just started out as Christian ministers. But they were all there with one important aim: to resolve an argument that was threatening to tear apart the early Christian Church. An argument about the very nature of divinity.

After weeks of debate, it was time to draw a conclusion. Some would be branded as heretics and expelled. The rest would agree on a form of words, an expression of belief they could all sign up to, creating a unity of message and purpose.

The final resolution would be passed at a meeting with a VIP in attendance – not just any old VIP, but *the* most important and powerful person in the world. The Roman emperor, Constantine the Great. In fact, it was Constantine himself who had called the meeting.

The bishops sat in rows along each side of the largest hall in the palace, according to their rank. Once everyone had found a seat and settled down, the room hushed and fell silent, waiting for the emperor to join them. First some members of the imperial family entered, followed by Christian officials. Then, at a signal, everyone in the room rose to their feet as the emperor himself appeared at the door and walked through the hall. He was resplendent in a purple robe, glittering with gold and studded with precious gems. He was also stunningly handsome, strong and tall – taller than anyone else in the room. But he didn't appear haughty; instead, he was pious in his demeanour. When he reached a certain point in the room, he stood and waited for a golden chair to be brought to him, and then he sat down. Everyone else now took their seats.

A bishop stood to welcome the emperor and give thanks to God. And then Constantine himself addressed the assembled clerics. He, too, started by thanking God and expressing just how grateful he was to see the bishops assembled, as he had asked, in pursuit of a common cause. 'In my judgement,' he continued, 'internecine strife within the Church of God is far more evil and dangerous than any war or conflict.'

Constantine had only just become the single, supreme leader of the Roman Empire – an empire that had grown so large, it had up until very recently been governed by two main emperors – one in the east, one in the west. But, rising to power in the west, Constantine had seized control of the eastern half of the Empire from his rival, Licinius, the previous year.

He'd thought that this victory marked the end of his troubles, bringing the entire Empire under his control, but then the news reached him of the disagreement among the bishops (some of whom may indeed have been more loyal to Licinius). And so he was delighted to see the clerics had come together at Nicaea. 'My wishes will be completely fulfilled when I can see you arriving at a consensus, in peace and harmony,' he told them. 'If you can put this controversy behind you and embrace peace, you will please the supreme God – and make me, your fellow servant, very happy as well.' The bishops listening to Constantine's exhortation to drive towards a peaceful resolution had walked into the hall through an honour guard of armed soldiers.

Then he opened the discussion and the bishops began to testify, sharing their opinions, voicing accusations and defending themselves. The debate soon became heated, but Constantine was able to expertly defuse tensions and steer the assembled crowd towards conciliation. Eventually, the argument about the nature of God was settled: the Father and Son were not just somehow similar, but of the same substance, the Council agreed. The date of Easter, another bone of contention, was also agreed. The resolutions were written down and the bishops signed the document – a statement of belief that would form the basis of what would be known as the Nicene Creed. Constantine then invited the bishops to a feast to mark the twentieth year of his reign and to celebrate this successful resolution of the Council of Nicaea. And a report of the meeting was sent to each province in the Empire, just to make sure that everyone would be completely clear, and singing from the same hymn sheet.

This description of the meeting is based on the account by

Eusebius, the bishop of Caesarea in Palestine, and penned after Constantine's death. But Eusebius had attended the Council himself — it's an eyewitness account, although written down years later. (I hope he had kept some notes and wasn't just relying on his memory.)

Eusebius was a fourth-century Christian priest and historian who recorded the events of Constantine's life — including the Council of Nicaea, when he first met the emperor — in a hagiography that is self-consciously prodigious in its praise; fulsomely flattering, oozing with obsequiousness. Constantine was, Eusebius wrote, 'the conqueror of the whole race of tyrants, and the destroyer of those God-defying giants of the earth who madly raised their impious arms against him, the supreme King of all'. Constantine, Eusebius gushes, was better than the Persian king, Cyrus (who, although feted as an illustrious king, had died in *the* most ignominious way, beaten by an army led by a *woman* — according to Herodotus, at least). Constantine was also better than Alexander the Great, Eusebius contends — Alexander may have been a successful conqueror and empire-builder, but he died at just thirty-two, 'carried off by revelry and drunkenness'. The great Constantine lived twice as long and ruled for three times as long as Alexander, over a truly enormous territory, stretching west to Britain, north to Scythia (central Asia), south into Africa, and east — somewhat vaguely — 'to the ends of the whole world'. And unlike all other emperors, Eusebius says, Constantine had been made emperor, not through the will of men but by *God*.

In the early fourth century, Christianity was growing in importance, but it was still very much a minority religion in the Empire. In fact, several of Constantine's predecessors had sporadically oppressed and victimised Christians. But now a Roman emperor was taking a personal interest in the operations of the Church, chairing a meeting of bishops from across the eastern Empire to discuss tenets of faith. This was extraordinary. Presided over by the emperor, the man holding the most secular power in the world, and attended by hundreds of bishops, the Council of Nicaea is widely recognised as *the moment* when Christianity and the Roman state joined forces. Whatever Christianity had been up until this point, however people had chosen to express their faith and build this religion, it would be something different from now on. Christianity would become enmeshed with the political project that was the Roman Empire.

Constantine was far from being the first Roman emperor to recognise, utilise and associate himself with divine authority. Emperors, after all, could all expect to be literally deified on their deaths. But Christianity seems like such a different beast to the panoply of the traditional Roman pantheon, with all those gods and goddesses, demigods – and the cult of the emperor himself. But it's the connection with this *particular* religion – knowing, with the benefit of hindsight, just how influential it would become in ensuing centuries – that makes us see this moment, on the shores of Lake Ascania in 325, as absolutely pivotal.

We will return later to the Council of Nicaea, to Constantine, presiding over events in his purple, gem-studded robes, as the supreme ruler of the Roman Empire. But first, let's look into why Constantine chose to favour this particular religion. What had made it possible for a Roman emperor to turn away from centuries of paganism and polytheism, and towards an ostensibly monotheistic faith? How, and why, did he break with Roman tradition – and find God?

Constantius, the Tetrarchy and the Sun

It seems that Constantine's father, Constantius, may have cottoned on to the usefulness of Christianity long before his son did. Constantius was one of four tetrarchs ruling over the Roman Empire at the end of the third century – under a system that divided the Empire into western and eastern portions, each ruled by an emperor, an *augustus*, and his deputy, a *caesar*.

The tetrarchy had been created by the emperor Diocletian, a military commander who seized power after the death of the previous emperor, Carus, in the year 284. Soon after his accession, Diocletian appointed another military man, Maximian, to become his co-ruler, or *caesar* (a term that had morphed from being the family name of Julius Caesar back in the first century into an imperial title). A couple of years later, Maximian adopted the more elevated title of *augustus*, placing him on a level with Diocletian. And then in 296, Diocletian founded the tetrarchy by appointing two deputy emperors, or *caesares*. Both of these were seasoned military men, and were well known to the two *augusti*: Galerius was Diocletian's son-in-law, and Constantius was Maximian's son-in-law. So, while the tetrarchy was not officially dynastic, it represented closely linked ruling families. It seems that Diocletian hoped that this system would help to remove some of the strife around succession.

Diocletian also oversaw a big administrative shake-up in the Empire, which saw it carved up into around a hundred provinces (where previously there had been only forty-eight), each ruled by an imperially appointed governor. Those provinces were grouped into twelve dioceses (which we have come across already in Gaul) – the word *dioecesis* in Latin coming from the Greek *dioikēsis*, meaning 'administration', 'government' or, more literally, 'housekeeping'. Each diocese was governed by an *agens vices praefectorum praetorio* – an 'agent acting in place of the praetorian prefect', or more simply, a *vicarius* – or vicar. The contemporary author Lactantius despaired of this extensive reorganisation and reform, which seems to have gone hand-in-hand with a hike in taxes. But the new system represented an attempt to create a stable, hierarchical pattern of rule across the vast, sprawling Empire, dividing up the job of ruling among those four emperors. While the tetrarchy comprised two super-emperors and two sub-emperors, each of them had fairly autonomous control over a particular territory – a district comprising several dioceses.

Diocletian ruled the eastern district, comprising the dioceses of Oriens (a region including modern Syria down to the Arabian Peninsula and Egypt), Pontica and Asiana (western and eastern Anatolia). Maximian's sphere was in the south and south-west: Africa, Hispania and Italia. Galerius presided over Pannonia, Moesia and Thracia in south-eastern Europe. Constantius's beat was in the north-west: comprising the dioceses of Viennensis and Gallia (making up what is now France) – and Britannia.

The tetrarchs – just like every Greco-Roman ruler before them – claimed a divine right to rule. The Homeric kings of earlier centuries had claimed to be descended from gods; by the time of the tetrarchy, it was enough to have a particular god as your sponsor. With four emperors now installed, it made sense for each to have their own deity, and the Roman pantheon helpfully provided a smorgasbord of possibilities. Jupiter was chosen as the patron of the eastern emperor,

Diocletian; Hercules was patron of the western ruler, Maximian. The divine patronage of each *augustus* extended to their respective deputies, but the *caesares* also seem to have had their own patron deities in addition. An inscription from North Africa records Jupiter, Hercules and Mars as the patrons of Diocletian, Maximian and Galerius respectively. No such inscription exists for Constantius, but there are some potential clues about the identity of his own patron deity. A record exists of a speech given at the wedding and inauguration of Constantius's son, Constantine. It describes his deceased father looking down and seeing the happy occasion: 'Divine Constantius, fortunate in your rule, and even more fortunate after your rule, for surely you hear and see these things, you whom the sun himself took up on a chariot almost visible, to carry you to heaven.'

There's also a medallion that was made to celebrate Constantius's victory over a usurper in Brittania, which bears the words *redditor lucis aeternae* – 'restorer of eternal light'. From these meagre clues, it's been inferred that Constantius's patron deity might just have been Sol, the sun god. Romans had been worshipping Sol, among all their other gods, for centuries by this time; that illuminating object of worship had been promoted by various emperors, who also used solar imagery on their coins, sometimes even depicting themselves as a sun god. Sol wasn't the only sun god in the Greco-Roman world, and at times, he was conflated with others, such as Apollo or Helios. But it's also been suggested that sun worship may have involved the idea that a single god, in a well-populated pantheon, was pre-eminent. This is known as henotheism (which comes from the Greek for 'one god'), and we can perhaps think of it as 'practical monotheism'. So it's not surprising that some historians have extrapolated from Constantius's apparent fondness for Sol – taking it to mean that he at least had leanings towards monotheism and that this perhaps might explain why he was a little more reluctant than his tetrarchic colleagues, particularly Diocletian, to persecute Christians (although, to be fair, Lactantius notes that he did follow Diocletian's edicts and destroy a few churches).

Even from this brief foray into the divine connections of the tetrarchy, then, we can see how certain gods in the Roman pantheon might at times have appeared more prominent than others – particularly when an emperor favoured one above the others. Individuals could have 'favourite' gods, either through official association or personal choice. The hard dichotomy between polytheism and monotheism starts to look more blurred than might be suggested by simple taxonomies of religion. But the idea that henotheism provided a 'philosophical bridge' for believers in many gods to switch to focusing on just one – with the implication here that Constantius's sun worship might have paved the way for Christianity to be accepted and adopted – appears to be too neat and simplistic.

A more comprehensive survey of the evidence, from inscriptions, coins and texts, actually reveals a striking lack of consistency and destroys that simple association of each of the four tetrarchs with a specific deity. If we take a look at gods shown on coins during Constantius's reign, some of them show Sol, certainly, but a whole host of other deities make appearances, including Hercules, Jupiter and Moneta (an epithet of Juno, as protectress of funds), as well as divine personifications of providence, felicity, security and the generic divine 'genius'. A further complication, of course, is that an 'official' identification of a tetrarch's particular patron deity may reveal very little about the personal faith of any of these men, anyway; it's likely to have been more of a ceremonial connection or brand, rather than a personal choice.

And what about that orator at Constantine's wedding and inauguration – was he really telling us something about Constantius's sun worship – or was it just a nice bit of poetic imagery and flowery metaphor? In the same speech, Maximian was also praised for bringing a new dawn to the empire, with Apollo (who by this time was practically synonymous with the sun god) appointing him to drive the sun chariot. The 'restoration of eternal light' celebrated on the medallion is surely more of a metaphor for the reinvigoration of Roman rule, rather than referring to the worship of Sol in particular (although in semiotics, more than one thing can be true at the same time).

It looks like each of the four tetrarchs chose a god to identify with, to represent them in the public eye – to associate their right to rule with divinity. Sol *could* have been Constantius's favourite god, his patron, but he is one god among others, as we might expect, and the solar imagery may simply be metaphorical in some cases. It's also important to reflect that choosing the sun god (whether Sol, Apollo or Helios) as a divine sponsor wasn't a novel departure for a Roman emperor; plenty of earlier emperors had done just that. In the end, it's hard to argue that Constantius was particularly or peculiarly drawn to monotheism; his coins reflect someone who was well immersed in the traditional polytheism of the empire, and seemingly happy to use all those symbols and associations.

Constantius's son, on the other hand, *is* famous for being a monotheist – for being the first Roman emperor to convert to Christianity. And, unlike his father, he wasn't content to accept the power-sharing arrangement that Diocletian had instituted.

A Vision of Victory

On 1st May 305, the tetrarchy was changing guard. The two *augusti*, Diocletian and Maximian, officially retired from office – and Galerius and Constantius stepped up, becoming the new western and eastern *augusti* respectively. New *caesares* were appointed, both nominated by Galerius: his nephew Maximinus and an old army friend, Severus. The new imperial system, with its two *augusti* and their *caesar* deputies, and a clear line of succession, seemed to be working fairly smoothly.

But in the same year, Constantius was in Gaul and about to embark on a campaign against troublesome tribes in the north of Britain. Claiming that he was ill and needed assistance, Constantius sent for his son, Constantine, who had been staying in the court of Galerius in Nicomedia. Constantine was released to join his father in Gaul, and together they sailed across the Channel to Britain.

A panegyric to Constantius, written in 297, described the campaign, naming those northern Britons for the first time in literature: the *Picti* or Picts, the 'painted ones'. They may not have been a single tribe, rather a confederation coming together to oppose the Romans. As for the paint, many historians have suggested that this refers to tattoos. The Romans viewed such body art as barbaric; tattoos were done on prisoners of war and runaway slaves – they weren't something that a civilised citizen would voluntarily seek out.

The Roman army seems to have reached the north of Caledonia, where Constantius was said to have been impressed by the white nights of summer. Just how successful the campaign actually was is debatable, but Constantius seems to have viewed it as a victory, declaring himself *Britannicus Maximus*, the Great Victor in Britain. But his days were numbered. Returning to York in 306, he died in the July of that year. Under the tetrarchic regime, the line of succession was clear: the western *caesar*, Severus, should have been the one to step up to fill the now vacant *augustus* position. Instead, the legions in Britain now declared Constantine as their chosen *augustus*.

Diocletian's conception of the tetrarchy had been specifically designed to remove such dynastic succession from the executive command of the Empire. But Constantine clearly saw it as his birthright to be an emperor, and the army around him in Britain appeared to agree. Another military coup in Britain, then – and yet another usurper seizing power for himself. The remaining three members of the tetrarchy were less than delighted by this turn of events. Galerius reacted by officially recognising Severus as the western *augustus* – but he also condescended to accept Constantine as the western *caesar*. That was never going to be enough for Constantine. Over the next eighteen years, he would battle it out with all the other rulers and their heirs until he alone was left standing – not as one of four tetrarchs, but as the single, supreme leader of a vast empire.

In 306, the same year that Constantine seized power in Britain, Maxentius, the son of the earlier western *augustus* Maximian, installed himself as the new emperor in Rome – yet another usurper seeking to inherit what had been his father's role. Maxentius styled himself not as *caesar* or *augustus* (roles that were starting to mean less and less as the tetrarchic system fell apart), but as *princeps invictus* (the 'undefeated prince'). Severus, still in control of northern Italy, didn't take kindly to this turn of events, and marched on Rome the following year. But when Severus arrived, his army abandoned him, defecting to Maxentius, who was now being supported by his father,

Maximian, who'd come out of retirement. Severus retreated to Ravenna, with his tail between his legs.

Maximian then tried to depose his son – unsuccessfully. He fled north to Constantine's court in Trier, and married his daughter Fausta to Constantine – in an attempt to create an alliance. But the western empire remained highly volatile. In 308, Galerius intervened to install an old army friend, Licinius, as *augustus* in the west, once again demoting Constantine to *caesar* – but Constantine refused to be contained in this way. In 310, Maximian rose up to lead an unsuccessful rebellion against Constantine in Gaul. He was captured and the official line was that he committed suicide, spurred on by Constantine. Constantine, though still married to Maximian's daughter, now tried to write his father-in-law out of history. He sought another source of legitimacy for his own rule, claiming an ancestral connection to a third-century emperor, Claudius II, which many historians believe to be spurious. But he also claimed a god-given right to rule, though which god or gods he believed had conferred that authority on him is an interesting question.

A praise-speech delivered at his imperial court in Trier in 310 mentioned a particular episode in Gaul that illustrated this divine favour. Constantine had visited a temple of Apollo to make offerings. The panegyrist describes how Constantine experienced a vision of this god (often conflated with the sun god by this time), offering him laurel crowns, and accompanied by the goddess Victory. At that moment, so the panegyrist wrote, Constantine knew himself to be the divinely chosen ruler of the world.

Some commentators have taken this to mean that Constantine worshipped Apollo at this time, or that he even *saw himself* as Apollo – but this really seems more like a standard bit of flowery rhetoric. And it surely tells us less about Constantine's personal faith – other than that he wasn't averse to making offerings to the traditional gods – and more about the type of propaganda that he saw as useful. Did he really have a vision at the temple? Who knows. The story fitted nicely with a familiar idea that sufferers of disease could attend the temple and Apollo would then appear in a dream to tell them how to heal themselves. And Eusebius, later writing the emperor's biography, relates several other times when Constantine had visions, so it wasn't out of character for him.

In his 1948 book, *Constantine and the Conversion of Europe*, the classical historian A. H. M. Jones suggested that what Constantine saw on his way to the temple could have been a real meteorological phenomenon – a solar halo, which was then interpreted as a heavenly sign. It was a controversial suggestion, greeted with scepticism. Some historians saw it as being overly reductionist, but others would continue to champion the idea. And whether or not Constantine's vision was based on a real phenomenon is perhaps beside the point. Whatever was actually seen – if anything at all – what's important is what the story portrayed: a divine sign, revealing that this highly ambitious warrior-emperor had supernatural backing. It affirmed his god-given right to rule. And *that* is the point.

Eusebius, later writing the emperor's biography, relates several other times when Constantine had visions, one of which came along in 312, at a time when Constantine was aggressively expanding his power base. No longer content with hanging out in the western provinces, he was now intent on installing himself as emperor in the historic heart of the empire – Rome itself.

By 312, Constantine and his army were marching down
through northern Italy to confront his brother-in-law and
rival, Maxentius. Their armies finally collided north of Rome,
where the Via Flaminia crossed the Tiber, at Milvian Bridge.
It's still a site of violent clashes in the twenty-first century – a
favourite battleground for fanatical football hooligans. In fact,
the bridge itself had been partly demolished by Maxentius in
an effort to defend Rome, and his troops had replaced it with a
pontoon. But this strategy backfired disastrously. Maxentius's
army was defeated, and when they attempted to retreat over
the bridge of boats, it broke up. Maxentius, and many soldiers
with him, drowned in the Tiber – sinking 'as lead in the mighty
waters', as Eusebius put it. (If Maxentius did drown, someone
must have fished his body out of the river afterwards, as other
historians report that his severed head was carried at the front
of Constantine's triumphal procession into Rome – or perhaps,
it wasn't his head at all.)

While Eusebius emphasises the role of Constantine as a lib-
erator, with the divine on his side, the other emperors in the
tetrarchy are described in truly demonic fashion, as 'enemies
of religion'. Here's a flavour of what Eusebius wrote about
Maxentius: 'To crown all his wickedness, the tyrant resorted
to magic. And in his divinations, he cut open pregnant women,
and again inspected the bowels of newborn infants. He slaughtered lions, and performed various execrable acts to invoke
demons and avert war. For his only hope was that, by these
means, victory would be secured to him.' Just to make sure
there's no doubt left in our minds about who's on the side of
righteousness here.

Constantine, in contrast, was now blessed with the divine
favour not of Sol, or Apollo, or any of the familiar Roman gods,

but a new one; it was in the run-up to this Battle of Milvian Bridge that Eusebius would eventually claim Constantine had another vision. In an earlier work, his *Church History*, Eusebius didn't mention the vision specifically, but said that Constantine 'invoked in prayer the God of heaven, and his Word, and Jesus Christ himself, the Saviour of all, as his aid' before advancing to battle. And afterwards, Eusebius described the victorious troops singing God's praises, and Constantine erecting a statue of himself in Rome, with a cross in its hand, and the inscription: 'By this salutary sign, the true proof of bravery, I have saved and freed your city from the yoke of the tyrant and moreover, having set at liberty both the senate and the people of Rome, I have restored them to their ancient distinction and splendour.'

In his later *Life of Constantine,* written after the emperor had died, Eusebius added more detail – and this is where he included the story of Constantine's vision, as well as the creation of a particular symbol to carry into battle. He adds a note that this account might seem unbelievable, but he'd heard it from the emperor himself:

> '. . . the account of which it might have been hard to believe had it been related by any other person. But since the victorious emperor himself long afterwards declared it to the writer of this history, when he was honoured with his acquaintance and society, and confirmed his statement by an oath, who could hesitate to accredit the telling, especially since later testimony has established its truth?'

Some authors, including Gibbon in his *Decline and Fall,* have suggested that this shows that Eusebius was applying a forensic level of scrutiny to his facts and sources. But – to me – it sounds strikingly reminiscent of those urban myths where the source is carefully emphasised – '. . . I heard it from a friend'. I'm also slightly suspicious of the fact that Eusebius didn't mention the vision in his earlier *Ecclesiastical History*, and only put it in writing after the emperor was dead and out of the way.

In the *Life of Constantine*, Eusebius once again described how Constantine, on the way to Rome, prayed to God. He explained that Constantine had already decided that the 'one supreme God' honoured by his father seemed to sponsor more successful outcomes in battle than the various other gods worshipped by earlier emperors. So Eusebius seems to have been claiming that Constantine's father Constantius had *also* been Christian, rather than a follower of Sol or any other non-Christian gods. It's a possibility – though there are no other sources to suggest that this was the case. (Historian Peter Heather adds a further political note to this possibility; he points out that Lactantius claimed the tetrarchic policy of Christian persecution was particularly pushed by the eastern *caesar* – Galerius, who could have been trying to edge out or embarrass Constantius in this way, if he suspected the western *caesar* was in fact Christian.) But back to the story – because this is the moment when the crucial vision appeared:

'And while he was thus praying with fervent entreaty, a most marvellous sign appeared to him from heaven . . . about noon, when the day was already beginning to decline, he saw with his own eyes the trophy of a cross of light in the heavens, above the sun, and bearing the inscription, Conquer by this (τούτῳ νίκα). At this sight he himself was struck with amazement, and his whole army also, which followed him on this expedition, and witnessed the miracle.'

Constantine went to bed, Eusebius tells us, pondering the meaning of this apparition, then had a dream that explained the sign in the sky:

> 'In his sleep the Christ [anointed one] of God appeared to him with the same sign which he had seen in the heavens, and commanded him to make a likeness of that sign . . . and to use it as a safeguard in all engagements with his enemies.'

And the next morning, Constantine did just that – commissioning a standard decorated with gold and precious gems. Eusebius says that he saw this standard himself, and he described it in detail.

> 'Now it was made in the following manner. A long spear, overlaid with gold, formed the figure of the cross by means of a transverse bar laid over it. On the top of the whole was fixed a wreath of gold and precious stones . . .'

There's something quite extraordinary about this when you think about it. Because what Eusebius is describing is actually nothing more than a *standard* standard – a very familiar staff or spear with a horizontal crossbar from which a banner could be hung: a *vexillum*. Roman army units had carried such standards into battle for centuries, and they were often depicted on Roman coins. Eusebius described the banner in this case, hanging from the crossbar, encrusted with more gems and embroidered with a picture of the emperor and his children. So Constantine hadn't invented anything new here. The cross-shaped design of the *vexillum* wasn't novel, and that structure would have been obscured by the banner anyway, when viewed from the front. It's very hard to argue that such a standard would have been intended as a Christian symbol.

But then Eusebius adds a further detail – inside the wreath at the top (itself a familiar decoration on a *vexillum*) was a particular symbol involving two Greek letters: the Greek letter P (rho) intersected by X (chi). As Eusebius explains, these are the first two letters of Christ's name. And so it is this *chi-rho* – and not the basic cross-shape of the standard itself – that is the real indication of Christianity in this object. (This Christianised standard would become known as the *labarum*, though this word isn't explicitly religious; it's been suggested it could come from a word meaning fluttering or waving, or it's possibly derived from *laureum*, for a wreath of laurel.)

As well as commissioning this new standard, Eusebius tells us that Constantine sent for Christian priests to come and tell him more about their religion – which he duly adopted. (This seems a bit incongruous with Eusebius's claims about Constantius – if his father really had been a follower of the faith, then surely Constantine would have had some working knowledge of it; and where did those priests suddenly appear from, en route to Rome?)

Then we have the Battle of Milvian Bridge, the death of Maxentius and the victorious Constantine entering Rome – and publicly professing his new religion:

'Thus the pious emperor, glorying in the confession of the victorious cross, proclaimed the Son of God to the Romans with great boldness of testimony. And the inhabitants of the city, one and all, senate and people, reviving, as it were, from the pressure of a bitter and tyrannical domination, seemed to enjoy purer rays of light, and to be born again into a fresh and new life.'

Eusebius describes Constantine's rise to power as a victory for Christians. Reading Eusebius, it's easy to come away with the impression that Christianity was not just widespread but already dominant at this point throughout the Empire. But in fact, it's estimated that in the early fourth century, only a tiny minority of the population was Christian. Across the Empire, there was an exuberance of different cults, gods and goddesses, the classical Roman deities being equated with Greek gods and goddesses, and with others followed in the provinces; individual cities had their own gods, too. Roman religion was pluralistic, but overarching all of it lay the imperial cult – a religious duty binding all good Romans together.

Eusebius's version of this story, in his *Life of Constantine*, was written some twenty-five years after these events. And Eusebius had not been an eyewitness – he's thought to have first met Constantine in 325. We're left wondering if Constantine really did tell Eusebius the tale as it's written, and if so, whether he might have been keen to project Christianity back into his past and spin this narrative of conversion. Or whether this was an elaboration and interpretation that Eusebius himself introduced to this eve-of-battle tale.

But there is another account of Constantine's vision and conversion to Christianity that was written down much earlier, by another author, Lactantius, only a few years after the battle of 312 – while Constantine was still very much alive. Lactantius was also a Christian, and very close to Constantine. He was an eminent rhetor, a teacher of Latin, and was tutor to Constantine's ill-fated eldest son, Crispus. (Constantine would later execute Crispus, on a charge of committing adultery with his second wife, Fausta; and she would be killed in a horrendous way – being boiled to death in a steam room. It was very dangerous to be part of the imperial family.)

Lactantius mentioned Constantine's vision in his historical narrative, *De Mortibus Persecutorum* ('On the Deaths of the Persecutors'). This work has its own curious history. It disappeared from view for around six centuries, and was considered lost until 1678, when the lost text was discovered – in a dusty old manuscript in the convent of Moissac in southern France. It described the persecution of Christians under various emperors, from Nero to Diocletian, ending with the rise of Constantine. The rediscovery of this text caused something of a furore as this text lays out a slightly different view of history to that described by Eusebius – both in terms of the broader context, and the details of Constantine's conversion story.

Whereas Eusebius tends to emphasise the persecutions that Christians had suffered before the ascent of Constantine, Lactantius refers to significant periods of time where Christianity was actually well tolerated in the Roman Empire – it wasn't all crucifixions, torture and being thrown to lions. In fact, the idea that Christians were *systematically* persecuted in the Roman Empire appears to be a myth – as is powerfully argued by historian Candida Moss. Although there were sporadic episodes of localised hostility, and Diocletian certainly was responsible for wider persecution of Christians in the late third century, the narrative of martyrdom in early Christianity seems to have been largely a – politically useful – fiction. There are also some crucial deviations from the story presented by Eusebius, when Lactantius describes the events leading up to the Battle of Milvian Bridge. He makes no mention of any sort of sign appearing in the sky, which everyone could see; instead, he describes Constantine seeing the sign of Christ in a dream:

> 'Constantine was directed in a dream to cause the heavenly sign to be delineated on the shields of his soldiers, and so to proceed to battle. He did as he had been commanded, and he marked on their shields the letter X, with a perpendicular line drawn through it and turned round thus at the top, being the cipher of Christ. Having this sign (XP), his troops stood to arms.'

At least, this is the translation that appears in most sources, including on plenty of church websites. But it's not quite what the Moissac manuscript says. It reads:

> *Facit ut iussus est et transversa X littera, summo capite circumflexo, Christum in scutis notat.*

Which translates as something more like:

> 'He did as he was commanded and marked Christ on the shields with a transverse letter X, with the top of the head bent round.'

A transverse or 'sideways' X is something a bit different from 'the letter X, with a perpendicular line through it'. It sounds much more like a simple cross shape: +. Then, with the 'top of the head bent round', it does suggest the upright stroke forming a rho, P. Lactantius seems to be referring, not to a *chi-rho*, then, but a *tau-rho*. This is another monogram that was used to represent Christianity, this time as an abbreviation for the Greek word σταυρόω, *stauroō* – meaning 'to crucify'. The *tau-rho* – essentially a P with a cross-bar – also acted as a visual metaphor, as the loop of the P suggesting a head on a crucified body. Another name for the Christian *tau-rho* is the staurogram – 'cross-image' in Greek.

So the details according to Lactantius – writing much closer in time to the battle in question (remember that Eusebius wrote his version decades later, after Constantine's death) – are different. There's no appearance of a celestial phenomenon, just a dream. And this time, Constantine is directed to mark not his battle standard, but the shields of his troops with a 'heavenly sign'. And that sign is different in the two accounts – in fact, it's three different things. In Eusebius's version, Constantine sees a cross in the sky, and decides to model his military standard on it (which, as we've noted, involved no modification of the usual design at all); then the *chi-rho* gets added to the top – as the first two letters of Christ, though the *chi-rho* was never said to have appeared in the sky. In Lactantius's version, there's no cross and no *chi-rho*, and instead a *tau-rho*, recommended to Constantine in a dream.

These tales of dreams and visions are the stuff of myth and propaganda. Their purpose is clearly to demonstrate that Constantine was divinely chosen, divinely protected and ruled by divine authority. In 310, it was Apollo and Victory who sponsored him; in 312 – according to Lactantius and Eusebius – it was Christ. Although this martial invocation of Christ (rather than the vengeful God of the Old Testament) might seem surprising, there are plenty of New Testament references to Christ as a divine warrior, especially in the Book of Revelation. Christianity was being used here in the same way that religion had always been employed to provide authority for Roman emperors – there was always a strong martial element, with the battlefield victories of the imperial candidate demonstrating their role within a Divine Plan, fulfilling their god-given destiny.

And it's very important to consider the motives of the writers, the people who deliver the story to us. In writing his *Vita Constantini*, Eusebius had a job to do extolling the virtues of the dead emperor – but also in claiming him for Christianity. Eusebius clearly had access to Hellenistic literature, and the biography he penned exhibits tropes familiar from earlier Hellenistic works such as the 'Alexander Romance' – where a general or king would experience a series of good omens as they rose to become a supreme ruler with divine favour and support. Most biographies of emperors contained some sort of prophetic fulfilment or omen explaining why their subjects obviously deserved their position; some emperors were even said to have performed miracles. The vision described by Eusebius – and later famously painted by Raphael's studio – also glimmers with a reflection of the apostle Paul's damascene moment and sudden conversion when a heavenly light flashed around him, leaving him blind for three days and leading to his sudden conversion, becoming a Jewish Christian, as related in Acts of the Apostles. (Though Constantine wasn't blinded by his luminous vision – fortunately; that could have been inconvenient on the eve of the big battle for Rome.)

But that shining apparition is also very similar to the vision described by the earlier panegyrist – the one where Constantine saw Apollo bringing him laurel wreaths. Could it be that these two visions were really one and the same event? In the 1930s, historian Henri Grégoire made the controversial suggestion that the vision on the way to Apollo's temple in 310 could have been later reimagined as a dream on the eve of the battle in 312. It was a fairly incendiary suggestion – and no wonder, as it suggested a very subjective interpretation of visions which had been described separately and specifically by both the panegyrist and Eusebius. Grégoire's alternative interpretation of the histories opened a can of worms. The foundation stones of the traditional story of Constantine's Christian conversion now started to seem a little wobbly. The implication was that Lactantius and Eusebius had both been rewriting a story that had originally been about a vision of Apollo/Sol.

Who knows if Constantine actually experienced those visions and dreams; we only have these second-hand accounts. We're being fed the story by two Christian authors, Eusebius and Lactantius, who both had their own agendas. Nineteenth-century theologians translating Eusebius's opus reminded us of this important fact in their introduction:

'He [Eusebius] was, above all things, an apologist; and the apologetic aim governed both the selection of his subjects and method of his treatment. He composed none of his works with a purely scientific aim. He thought always of the practical result to be attained, and his selection of material and his choice of method were governed by that.'

It's naive to take the history recorded by those Christian writers at face value; they had an important job to do in creating an origin story for Christianity itself. It may be that later in life, Constantine himself wanted to suggest that he'd been a follower of Christianity since the Battle of Milvian Bridge. That would have worked both for him and for the Church – it meant that the divine favour of the Christian god was with him from the start of his military campaigns, that his emperorship was endorsed by that god, and that the enemies of Constantine could also be painted as enemies of Christianity. But it's likely that this picture of Constantine's Christianity – particularly as it flows from the pen of Eusebius – is not something he would have necessarily recognised. If you take Eusebius at face value, Constantine was a sincere, committed Christian – from Milvian Bridge to his death. That image of the emperor – both chosen by God and choosing Christianity – was essential to the future of the Church. Historian Hartmut Ziche sums up Eusebius's construction of Constantine, as 'an emperor who was not merely tolerant of the Church but personally chosen by God; a sponsor of the Church not for political expediency but the salvation of the empire; the founder not just of a new eastern centre of government but of a new Rome, breaking with the errors of the old "pagan" capital'.

There's way too much vested interest to not even query the image of Constantine that Eusebius so fulsomely provides. We need to test this assumption that has become lore, ascending to the status of a historical 'fact'. So far, we've just been looking at what other people wrote about Constantine and his battle-winning conversion to Christianity. But what about the man himself? What did *he* have to say about it?

In His Own Words?

Historians have scrutinised Constantine's speeches, letters and laws, poring over them to see if there's an obvious flavour of Christianity after Milvian Bridge, and later in Constantine's imperial career. And this turns out to be one of those apparently simple questions that is devilishly difficult to answer.

According to Eusebius, when Constantine seized Rome from Maxentius in 312, he avoided making the customary sacrifice to Jupiter in the temple up on Capitoline Hill. Some historians have suggested that this demonstrates he was publicly turning away from the traditional gods at this point. Then again, it could be that he was just shunning this particular god – this Jupiter, who had, after all, been Diocletian's patron during the tetrarchy. Or it could just be that he was too busy. Or even that he *did* make the customary sacrifice, but it went undocumented. We can't read too much into this omission, if indeed it was that. (And we must remember of course that Eusebius had his own agenda.) We must turn, instead, to what Constantine himself said about religion.

Between 312 and 324, Constantine rarely mentioned religion in public statements. This does seem somewhat strange for someone who is meant to have undergone such a dramatic conversion on the way to the Battle of Milvian Bridge (at least, according to his later biographers). It suggests instead that he was keen to appeal to everyone – and not alienate anyone, whatever his own private beliefs might have been. In religious terms, he appears – publicly, at least – to have been something of a centrist.

But there's one particular decree, issued in 313, that's often put forward as evidence of Constantine being so nice to Christians, he must have been one. Known as the *Edict of Milan*, it laid out a policy encouraging a tolerant approach to religion. Only ten years before, the tetrarchs had issued a series of edicts demanding that Christians joined in with traditional Roman religion – particularly, demonstrating their loyalty to the emperor by performing sacrifices in the context of the imperial cult (essentially a slightly more bloody version of pledging allegiance to a flag). Resistance to these demands was met with reprisals: imprisonment, torture and execution.

The 313 *Edict of Milan* rowed back from that dictatorial and repressive approach, stating that anyone who wished to follow Christianity could do so freely. But in fact it wasn't just about Christianity; it stipulated that all restrictions were to be removed and the right to freedom of religious belief extended to everyone – and to all religions. But the *Edict* did single out Christians in another way – decreeing that properties which had been confiscated from them would be restored. (That special consideration may just have been making up for the fact that Christians had been particularly picked on, under the tetrarchs.)

However, this *Edict of Milan* turns out to be a bit problematic. Firstly, it wasn't actually an edict, it was a letter. Secondly, it wasn't just written by Constantine, it was co-authored by Licinius, who had succeeded Galerius as the eastern emperor at this point in time. Indeed, some scholars have even argued that the *Edict* was essentially Licinius's work, even though it was issued in Constantine's name as well. Thirdly, it may not actually have been written in Milan – though Licinius had certainly been there early in the year, getting married to Constantine's half-sister, Flavia Julia Constantia. This is very nitpicking, though, as the preamble to the letter describes it as being conceived (if not written) in that city:

'When both I Constantine Augustus and I Licinius Augustus auspiciously met together in Milan and held a discussion of all matters pertaining to the public advantage and safety, we decided that, among the other things which we saw would benefit the majority

of men . . . were those which ensured reverence for
the divinity (*divinitas*), so that we might grant both
to Christians and to all men the freedom to follow
whatever faith (*religio*) each one wished, in order that
whatever divinity there is in the seat of heaven may be
appeased and made propitious towards us and towards
all who have been under our power.'

The letter presents the idea that religious tolerance would be
in the best interests of the population generally – and the emperors themselves, who only refer to their own beliefs in that
most vague and general way: 'whatever divinity there is in the
seat of heaven'.

An important point about this letter is that it was about extending tolerance and restoring property to Christians in the
eastern provinces that Licinius presided over. He sent it to the
governors of each of these provinces, across Asia Minor, Syria
and Egypt. And this may have brought those eastern provinces
into line with the west, where it's possible this level of tolerance already legally existed – at least, according to Lactantius.
He claimed that one of the first things Constantine had done
when he was declared emperor by the army, in York in 306 CE,
was to issue new legislation. This in itself was extraordinary as
only *augusti* were meant to make law, while a *caesar* (the rank
Constantine had accepted from Galerius) could only instruct
governors and make decisions on existing points of law.

And yet Lactantius, writing in around 315, claimed:

*Suscepto imperio, Constantinus Augustus nihil egit prius, quam
christianos cultui ac Deo suo reddere. Haec fuit prima ejus sanctio
sanctae religionis restitutae.*

('Having assumed emperorship, Constantine Augustus did nothing before restoring to the Christians their worship and their God. This was his first sanction of the restoration of the holy religion.')

If this actually happened, this new legislation would have applied to Christians across the territory that Constantine had inherited from his father: Britain, Gaul and Spain. Many historians doubt Lactantius – as a Christian apologist – on this. But if we take Lactantius at his word, while bearing in mind that there are no other sources to back him up, perhaps passing a law like this would have been very useful, politically. Firstly, it would have marked Constantine out as rather different to the other three emperors, who were still persecuting Christians. Secondly, it would have loudly proclaimed his status as a law-giver (note that Lactantius actually calls him *Augustus* in this passage). And thirdly, it could of course be that Constantine genuinely believed in religious tolerance as a public good; a way to promote harmonious relations (especially in growing cities), suppress dissent and curb unrest.

Whether or not this earlier law was ever passed, the 313 *Edict of Milan* certainly gave Christians the right to reclaim property that had been taken from them during the persecutions under Diocletian. In fact, they had been lawfully entitled to own property since 260 CE, a right granted to them by the emperor Gallienus, effectively recognising Christianity as a lawful religion more than half a century earlier. The tetrarchs had then removed that right from Christians – so the *Edict of Milan* represented a return to that earlier, more tolerant state, with confiscated property restored to its owners. And that legal right to own property was extremely important to the

Church – it made it financially viable as an organisation; it could accumulate assets.

But aside from this note about property, the *Edict* was about much more general religious tolerance – while being very vague indeed about the religious inclinations of the two emperors themselves. The pronouncement ends with an urge for their commands to be carried out forthwith, for the sake of attracting unspecified 'divine favour', to ensure the continued success of themselves and the Roman state. Constantine and Licinius ruled over a huge territory, which despite the homogenising influence of Roman culture, involved a great diversity of beliefs and practices. There was no advantage for the emperors in publicly sharing what they really believed.

When it comes to more targeted communications, though, Constantine offers us a glimpse of where his loyalties lay. Writing to Caecilianus, bishop of Carthage, in 313, he signed off referring to 'the Divinity of the Great God'. The bishop would surely read that, not as referring to Sol or Jupiter, but to the solo God of Christianity. It's a very firm expression of monotheism – without specifying a particular god. (And, in fact, it follows a henotheistic trend which had become written in stone in the preceding third century, with more and more *pagan* inscriptions referring to *Theos Upsistos,* the 'highest God'.)

Other letters and statutes of Constantine's, preserved in Eusebius's *Life of Constantine,* refer to a 'supreme power' (using the Greek word *pantokrátor,* a term first coined in a Jewish context in the Greek translation of the Hebrew Bible, the Septuagint), as well as discouraging the erection of cult statues, the consultation of oracles and the performing of sacrifices. Meanwhile, under Constantine, bishops were given access to imperial funds to enlarge their churches to accommodate all the new converts when 'the madness of polytheism [has] been removed'. Once again, the problem is that many of these letters and pronouncements come to us via Eusebius, who clearly had his own agenda and may have been very selective about what he included in his biography of the emperor. He's also often describing letters and laws rather than quoting them verbatim. That phrase, 'the madness of polytheism', is Eusebius's. Some historians take him at face value; others are much more sceptical. There's a particularly lengthy document known as the *Oration to the Saints* (more fully as the *Oration of Constantine to the Assembly of the Saints*), a defence of Christianity that is often assumed to be a real speech given by Constantine, but some historians doubt its authenticity, suggesting it could have been by Eusebius or even a later author.

When Constantine celebrated his tenth anniversary in 315, Eusebius tells us that he offered 'prayers of thanksgiving to God, the King of all, as sacrifices without flame or smoke'. But there wasn't anything stopping other citizens from making traditional sacrifices.

In a letter to the prefect of Rome in 318, and in a public speech the following year, Constantine seemed to come out against those who used 'magic arts' and divination – but there were important conditions. Magic arts were alright as long as they were used for positive purposes and didn't harm anyone; legal divination in public shrines was also permissible. And previous emperors had also expressed concern about illicit divination; there was nothing new or particularly anti-pagan about that stance. Constantine continued to support the legal, above-board use of diviners or *haruspices*, including as part of the emergency response when state buildings in Rome were struck by lightning in 321.

In 323, Constantine wrote to Helpidius, the *vicarius* of Rome, to condemn reports that Christians had been forced to take part in the 'lustral sacrifices' and to stipulate that anyone involved in such coercion would be beaten (if poor) or fined (if rich). While the letter demonstrates support for the Christians – who presumably had petitioned him about this unfair treatment – it didn't in any way outlaw the traditional cults.

But events of the year 324 saw religion developing into a 'wedge issue'. Constantine's power-sharing arrangement with his eastern counterpart, Licinius, was breaking down. And religion was a way of demonstrating political allegiance – in a way that it often still is, today. Licinius favoured the traditional gods, so any followers of those cults in Rome could look dangerously like supporters of Licinius. And this was more than just a culture war. In fact, Constantine had already seized a chunk of Licinius's territory – much of the Balkan Peninsula – back in 316. There had been an uneasy peace since then, but Constantine would never be satisfied with being a co-emperor; he was after world domination. He used the excuse of routing a Visigoth incursion to send his army into Thrace, meeting Licinius's troops near Adrianople (modern Edirne). After a massive battle, Licinius withdrew his defeated army to Byzantium. While Constantine's forces laid siege to the city, his son Crispus led a naval offensive against Licinius's fleet in the Hellespont (the modern Dardanelles). From Constantine's perspective, both operations were successful, and Licinius gave up Byzantium, retreating east with his army across the Bosphorus. But Constantine and his troops followed, defeating Licinius's army once again, at the Battle of Chrysopolis. (The site of the battle is now the district of Üsküdar within the sprawling city of Istanbul, which spans the Bosphorus today – a huge city, home to 15 million inhabitants.)

After that Battle of Chrysopolis, Licinius retreated to lick his wounds at Nicomedia. Meanwhile, his wife, Constantia (Constantine's half-sister), pled for mercy on his behalf. Constantine spared Licinius at first, but just a few months later, in 325, thought better of it and had his former co-emperor arrested and hanged. One explanation or excuse was that Licinius had reneged on the *Edict of Milan* and had started to persecute Christians again; meanwhile, the Church was loyal to Constantine. According to Eusebius at least, Constantine became more overtly Christian at this stage in his career, retrospectively claiming that he'd fought the civil wars against the remnants of the tetrarchy for religious reasons, as he battled his way to absolute power.

Eusebius also recorded that, following his victory over Licinius, Constantine installed new governors in the eastern provinces and sent out letters, including a new law which decreed that 'no one should erect images or practise divination and other false and foolish arts or offer sacrifice in any way'. While some historians claim that this law meant that Constantine was effectively making Christianity the official religion of the Empire, others once again urge a much more careful scrutiny of Eusebius's account; he describes the content of this law rather than quoting it directly, for instance. And there's a stark discrepancy between what Eusebius tells us and what the non-Christian teacher and author Libanius wrote later, in the 380s, stating that Constantine had 'made absolutely no alteration in the traditional forms of worship'. Constantine's follow-up letters to the new eastern governors emphasise toleration again, and crucially, do not outlaw these other cults. Although Constantine may have had an aversion to gory sacrifices, he doesn't seem to have attacked the old beliefs more generally.

With Licinius out of the way, Constantine was now the one, supreme emperor. He renamed Byzantium *Nova Roma* – New Rome – as the new capital of the Roman Empire. It was a great choice for a capital city: a virtually impregnable fortress on a peninsula jutting out where the Bosphorus meets the Sea of Marmara, on a crossroads of trade routes – from Asia in the east to Europe in the west, from the Black Sea in the north to the Mediterranean in the south.

Constantine announced plans to reconstruct Byzantium in 324, with a series of ambitious new building projects in his capital, including a new palace and a hippodrome. Some historians point to the start of construction of impressive new churches (Hagia Sophia, Hagia Eirene and Hagia Dynamis) as an indication that Constantine was uniquely sponsoring Christianity. Although Eusebius claimed that the city was purged of 'idol worship', the historian Zosimus recorded the building of new temples to the goddess Rhea (mother of the Olympian gods and protectress of the city), to Tyche (goddess of good fortune), and to Castor and Pollux (protectors of sailors and patrons of horsemen). Various pagan statues were brought from Greece and also set up in the new capital. It's also perhaps pertinent that the new showcase churches bore dedications familiar from pagan temples – wisdom (Sophia), peace (Eirene) and power (Dynamis). And the early fifth-century historian Philostorgius reported that Constantine marched around the perimeter of the city on foot, spear in hand – in the way of a traditional Greek purification ceremony or *lustratio*. Constantine led the procession, acting in the traditional role of *pontifex maximus*, or chief priest.

In 326, Constantine was back in Rome to celebrate his Vicennalia, his twentieth anniversary. Whether or not he'd refused to sacrifice on the Capitol after his victory in 312, this time he does seem to have publicly snubbed that tradition. But he did provide funds for the completion of a big basilica on the forum, the renovation of the Circus Maximus, and a couple of churches on the edge of Rome. Then he returned east to the city that would become known as Constantinople – his New Rome – and never went back to its namesake.

In 330, the official ceremony to refound and rename the city as Constantinople included, according to a sixth-century source, a chariot being driven around the hippodrome carrying a gilded wooden statue of the emperor with a figurine of Tyche, goddess of fortune and protector of the city, in its right hand. This performance would be related every year, for two centuries. (And the gilded horses that stood with the chariot throughout the year, between these events, may well be those that were taken by the Venetians in 1204 – still adorning St Mark's to this day.) In the centre of the new capital, a porphyry column was erected, as a very tall pedestal for a golden statue of Constantine, looking very much like Sol, complete with a spiky sunray crown. (The column, looking a little worse for wear, is still standing in Istanbul.) So none of this seems very *Christian*.

But then, in 331, Eusebius tells us, the emperor ordered (non-Christian) temples to be destroyed and their treasures brought to Constantinople. Yet again, there's no trace of any actual law that was passed to close or destroy temples, and this claim of Eusebius's seems at odds with Libanius's note that there had been no change in the traditional forms of worshipping under Constantine. Indeed, in the mid-330s, towards the end of his life and his reign, Constantine permitted the erection of a new temple at Hispellum, a hundred miles to the north of

Rome, dedicated to himself and his family; the town was even renamed *Flavia Constans* in his honour. Constantine permitted the priests there to preside over festivities connected with his cult – though he ruled out any other 'contagious superstition' there. It seems he was perfectly happy for the imperial cult to continue, then, as long as it didn't involve animal sacrifices. In his court, Christians rubbed shoulders with pagan officials; the prevailing mood appears to have been one of religious toler-ance – and less polarised than we might imagine. The historian Harold Drake has even suggested that, 'on a number of levels, Romans for most of the fourth century did not see religion as the critical issue it subsequently became'.

Eusebius's biography of Constantine, as well as the letters of the emperor that he presents, are full of references to a singular God, 'Lord and Father of all', 'Lord and Saviour', and the 'Divine Faith'. But even Eusebius seems to acknowledge a certain conflation, a syncretism, with Sol, when he describes Constantine's recommendation of Sunday as a day of rest:

> 'Accordingly he enjoined on all the subjects of the Roman empire to observe the Lord's day, as a day of rest . . . And since his desire was to teach his whole army zealously to honour the Saviour's day (which derives its name from light, and from the sun), he freely granted to those among them who were partakers of the divine faith, leisure for attend-ance on the services of the Church of God.'

This passage also tells us something about the wider social milieu – while it says that Constantine wished his 'whole army to honour the Saviour's Day' (bearing in mind this was Eusebius's interpretation), there's an acceptance that while there were 'those among them who were partakers of the divine faith'; this implies – and accepts and tolerates – that were some who were not.

Towards the end of his life, according to Eusebius of Caesarea, Constantine embarked on an expedition against the Persians – but he didn't get very far at all. At Nicomedia, just east of the Sea of Marmara, Constantine suddenly fell ill and never recovered. He was baptised on his deathbed, by the other Eusebius, bishop of Nicomedia. (Which seems rather late if we're to believe he had been Christian for decades by this time; baptism into the religion was an important ritual for adults.)

It's very hard to know what to make of all of this. Some historians read Constantine's letters and edicts and see him becoming more firmly Christian over time, especially after 312 and then again after he'd finally pushed Licinius out of the way in 324. But even when we seem to have Constantine's own words, they've come down to us, filtered and carefully selected by those influential Christians in his entourage – people like Eusebius and Lactantius. We're getting their – carefully curated and theologically finessed – view of this emperor. It's very hard to know whether Constantine personally bought into this cult, and, if he did, whether he was approaching it in a syncretic way, synonymising the Christian God with Apollo or Sol. As we've seen, the distinction between monotheism and polytheism is much more blurred than we often assume. Unsurprisingly, different historians, looking at the same textual material, have drawn disparate conclusions.

Before we make up our minds, there are other sources, other means of communication, which we can turn to. Not written on parchment or papyrus, copied by the faithful down the centuries, but inscribed and depicted on stone, bronze and silver.

Inscriptions and Symbols

The literate nature of our society still seems to prioritise the written word; images can be reduced to illustration, decoration, even meaningless abstraction. And yet inscriptions carved in stone, and symbols struck in bronze, can be firmly dated and may tell us things the literature does not. And having found that literature is much less certain than we might have expected it to be – particularly when it comes to Constantine's conversion and faith – we can look around for visual evidence, and ask whether he was consciously projecting an image of Christianity during his lifetime.

In 1954, archaeologists W. F. Grimes and Audrey Williams led an excavation in central London, along the eastern bank of the Walbrook. Their team dug through the rubble left by the Blitz of the Second World War, all the way down to water-logged Roman layers. The dig uncovered a large aisled building with an apse at one end. Within it, the archaeologists discovered a small statue of Mercury, a bearded head of the Egyptian god Serapis, and another head, possibly of Minerva. There was also a marble bust and head of the Persian god Mithras, together with a marble relief of this god slaying a bull – a central theme in his myth.

A slab of marble confirmed that the temple was a Mithraeum, a temple of Mithras:

[Pro salute d(ominorum) n(ostrorum) Au]g(ustorum)
[et nob(ilissimi) Caes(aris)]
[deo Mithrae et Soli] Invicto
[ab oriente] ad [occid]entem

Which translates as:

> 'For the welfare of our August Emperors
> and most noble Caesar
> to the god Mithras and the Unconquered Sun
> from the east to the west.'

The inscription has been dated to 307–308, when Galerius was *augustus* in the east, with Maximinus as *caesar*. In the west, Maxentius was now ruling Italy from Rome, but Constantine had already seized power in the most western provinces, controlling Britain, Gaul and Spain. It seems likely that an inscription from Britain would have recognised Constantine, rather than Maxentius, as an *augustus*. The inscription shows how Mithras and Sol were often conflated. So, here is a Mithraic temple in Londinium, dedicated to Mithras and Sol, and appearing to mention Constantine – who was in Britannia in 307 – and there's nothing Christian about it. This, of course, predates the Battle of Milvian Bridge and Constantine's claimed conversion. But what about the famous symbol that Constantine is meant to have carried into battle just five years later?

The symbols seem like a good place to start – the stories are so rich in them. And both Lactantius and Eusebius describe an archetypal Christian symbol – the *chi-rho* (or *tau-rho*) – being carried into battle by Constantine in 312. It's become an oft-quoted historical 'fact'. But right from the start, going back to those sources, there are discrepancies: in which symbols were being displayed, and where. Lactantius said the *tau-rho* was inscribed on the shields of Constantine's troops while Eusebius, writing decades after the event, recorded the *chi-rho* being mounted on a military standard. Was either symbol actually present at Milvian Bridge? Can we get any closer to the truth?

We don't have the standards or shields from the battle to look at, unfortunately. Indeed, it would be extraordinary to have well-dated archaeological evidence of this nature. Even when weapons survive in the archaeological record – escaping the fate of most objects, which is to be recycled or to rust away – it's hard to date them precisely. And even if such objects had miraculously survived, it would be especially difficult to link them to one particular year and one specific battle.

But take a stroll along the Via Triumphalis in Rome today and there's a monument, still standing, seventeen centuries after it was erected. It's a huge triumphal arch, commemorating Constantine's victory over Maxentius, and dedicated just three years after in the Battle of Milvian Bridge, in 315. It bears a perfectly legible inscription and it's liberally encrusted with sculptures. Given that it was intended to celebrate that particular victory, hot on the heels of Constantine's conversion, according to his biographers, we would surely expect to find some Christian reference or symbolism on it.

The Latin inscription on the arch reads:

IMP CAES FL CONSTANTINO MAXIMO
P F AUGUSTO SPQR
QUOD INSTINCTU DIVINITATIS MENTIS
MAGNITUDINE CUM EXERCITU SUO
TAM DE TYRANNO QUAM DE OMNI EIUS
FACTIONE UNO TEMPORE IUSTIS
REM PUBLICAM ULTUS EST ARMIS
ARCUM TRIUMPHIS INSIGNEM DICAVIT

Which translates as:

'To the Emperor Caesar Flavius Constantinus the Great,
pious and fortunate, the Senate and people of Rome,
because by divine inspiration and his own great mind
with his army
on both the tyrant and all his
faction in one instant in rightful
battle he avenged the state,
dedicated this arch as a mark of triumph'

So it does contain a reference to the divine – that *instinctu di-vinitatis* – Constantine's victory was 'instigated' or 'inspired' by the divine. It sounds rather vague. Some have suggested that this phrase does invoke the Christian God – but others argue that it's less definite. In fact, careful comparative analysis has shown that when the term *instinctus* arises in a Christian context, it usually refers to pagan or demonic influence. And it's a perfectly familiar phrase in non-Christian texts, where it was associated with a variety of gods, including Apollo. This inscription, then, appears to be quite firmly religiously neutral (and therefore, rather diplomatically, acceptable to both pagans and Christians).

What about the imagery on the arch? Can we find any traces of Christian iconography there? There's plenty of sculpture there to scrutinise. There's a frieze showing Constantine setting off to battle in his chariot. Above the frieze, on the east facade, there's a roundel that clearly shows Sol, the sun god, in his chariot, pulled by four horses. It seems we're being unsubtly invited to notice a similarity between the depiction of Constantine and the sun god. And in another scene,

Constantine is shown with his right hand raised – a gesture often seen in depictions of Sol. In one of the lateral passageways, a bust of Constantine faces a bust of Sol. And finally, the arch was also carefully positioned so that a visitor approaching it along the Via Triumphalis would see a colossal statue of Sol, just over a hundred metres away, perfectly framed in the archway. If Constantine *was* Christian at this point, he certainly wasn't displaying any such affiliation through this monument. There's not a single Christian symbol on it – and conversely, a lot of Sol, and the emperor himself represented as god-like (which was quite typical for Roman emperors).

We should be a little careful, though. In common parlance, we might say that 'Constantine erected this arch', but of course he didn't, really. He may not even have ordered it to be built. The arch was dedicated to Constantine by the 'Senate and people of Rome'. And whichever committee designed it – because that certainly wasn't Constantine himself – careful analysis of the sculptures suggests some had been repurposed, perhaps taken from an arch that was originally designed for Diocletian. This is an important caveat, but even so, we can still presume that Constantine was at least broadly happy with the messaging on what became his monument. And there's not a single mention of Christ, no depiction, not even the smallest *chi-rho* tucked in among all that ornate sculpture. The arch is not, in the slightest bit, Christian.

But let's not give up just yet – we've only just started. Archaeology provides us with another vast store of symbols to explore, and one that effectively records the whole imperial career of Constantine. This source is well dated and absolutely replete with meaningful images and, indeed, lettering – it's old coins.

Physical currency is still brimming with visual symbolism today, with portraits of monarchs, coats-of-arms, famous cultural icons and commemorative images of certain events. Across the Roman Empire, where perhaps only one in seven people were literate, coins represented an incredibly important means of mass communication. They could be used to advertise the death of an emperor, to announce the accession of a new one, or to celebrate an anniversary, a military victory or an imperial festival.

Numismatists have pored over coins minted during Constantine's reign – there are well over a thousand different designs known – and they bear a plethora of messages. Most coins from the early years of Constantine's reign depict the head of the emperor, crowned with a laurel wreath, on the front, while the reverse shows divine Genius, bearing an overflowing dish and a cornucopia or horn of plenty – a promise of prosperity. Constantine is effectively saying, 'You can trust me with the economy, life will be good in my Empire.' Similar designs continued to be minted after 312, the year that Constantine defeated Maxentius at Milvian Bridge, but other deities also made appearances. Jupiter, holding up Victory on a globe and sceptre, was a recurrent theme, but even more common was Sol Invictus. The sun god was often accompanied by the words *soli invicto comit* – 'to the unconquered sun, companion [of the emperor]'. Mars and Hercules also popped up occasionally. In terms of the deities appearing on his coinage, then, Constantine, like his father, was employing traditional and well-understood symbols, involving a diversity of divine beings – although it does seem that Sol was a firm, recurring favourite.

The appearance of non-Christian deities on Constantine's

coinage, continuing long after his battle at Milvian Bridge, is an incontrovertible, well-dated fact. It's certainly awkward for those commentators who are keen to hang onto the idea that Constantine was a committed Christian after 312. Sometimes they try to get around it by suggesting that he was simply playing along, trying to keep the majority, non-Christian population on side, for a while at least. This does seem a bit like special pleading. So does the protestation that Constantine wasn't personally overseeing the design of coins or the inscriptions on monuments. We're being asked to believe that Constantine was a dedicated Christian despite the evidence to the contrary.

After 320, though, there does seem to be a noticeable shift in the design of Constantine's coins. Depictions of Sol became less common, replaced by a penchant for more martial themes. Some coins show a military standard flanked by two bound captives. Many of these were minted to celebrate anniversaries of the emperor's reign, and include lettering on the banner hanging from the standard: VOT X, XX or XXX, depending on the date. VOT stands for *vota*, as the emperor would have renewed his imperial vows on these occasions. Another design, appearing from around 325 CE, on coins minted in the eastern Empire, features the emperor with his eyes raised to heaven. Some have suggested that this 'eyes to the heavens' pose could indicate Christianity. But while the upward gaze may have symbolised religious piety, it's not especially Christian – it's a common enough motif, copied from much earlier, pre-Christian Greek coins.

Another design that some scholars have suggested might have had Christian connotations shows a snake impaled by a military standard. Eusebius described a very similar image in the imperial palace: a painting of the emperor in the act of stabbing a serpent. But even Eusebius didn't imply that this was Christian symbolism in any way – or that Constantine was attempting to look Christ-like with it. In fact, it seems unlikely that it would have had any Christian connection because such an image could have been considered quite heretical at the time; in the fourth century, images of Christ – and especially of Christ fighting the Devil – were considered to be idolatrous. Instead, the image could have been a visual metaphor for over-coming an enemy. The representation of enemies as serpents or dragons goes way back, not just to the Old Testament but to even earlier Levantine myths. Interestingly, Constantine some-times described his rival in the east, Licinius, as a serpent or dragon. So it's somewhat more likely that the serpent-stabbing coin, and perhaps the palace painting too, commemorated Constantine's victory over his last remaining tetrarchic rival in 324, the year when he became the single ruler of the entire Roman Empire.

But what I've not mentioned until now is that there is some-thing else on the serpent-stabbing coin which does appear to be more explicitly Christian – it's a *chi-rho*. It appears at the top of the military standard that is piercing the snake – making this standard look very much like that detailed description of the original *labarum* penned by Eusebius.

So could this be the smoking gun – the pictorial, numismatic evidence to support Eusebius's story? It *could*, but it only ap-pears in the 330s – nearly two decades after Constantine was supposed to have gone into battle with that divinely inspired *chi-rho* standard. So why did it take so long for this apparently crucial cipher to appear on a coin? Any connection with the Battle of Milvian Bridge seems a bit tenuous, so many years

The dig at Llantwit Major, with earlier features – children's graves and a smithing hearth (the orange patch) – starting to emerge from layers beneath the Norman walls (2023).

© GeoArch/Tim Young

Aerial view of Llantwit Major – with St Illtud's church on the right, the dig in the centre and the Bristol Channel in the distance.

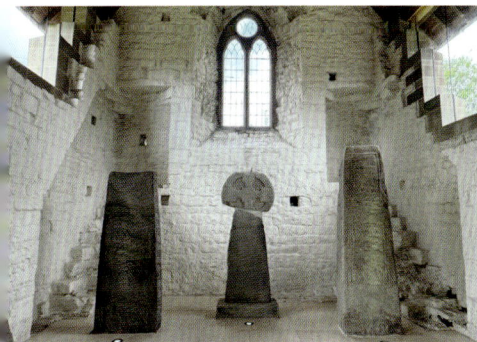

The medieval crosses in the Galilee chapel at the west end of St Illtud's church.

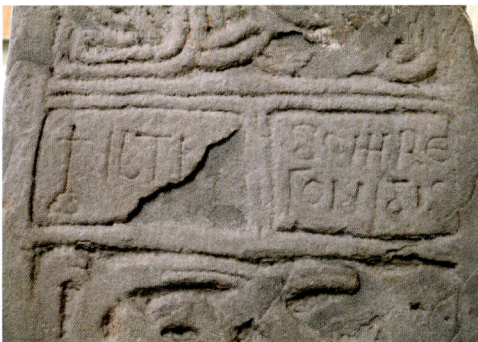

© G. A. Bell/Alamy Stock Photo

The letters ILT[U] carved on the back of the tenth century cross that once stood in the church of St Illtud.

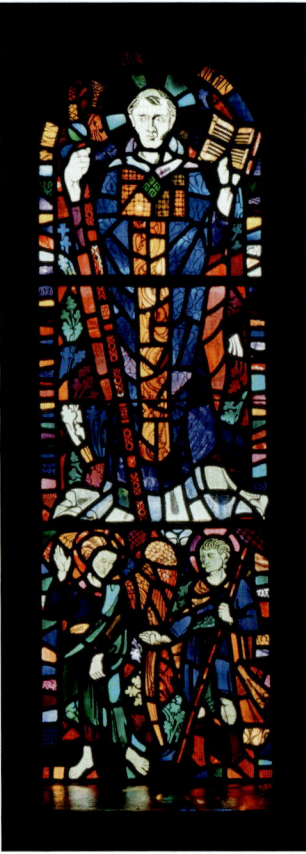

Lullingstone Roman Villa, as it might have looked in 360 CE (Artist: Ivan Lapper).

A 1920s stained glass window showing St Illtud as a mature man in the panel above, and below as a young knight accompanied by an angel. From St Illtud's priory church on Caldey Island.

Aerial view of Landévennec Abbey.

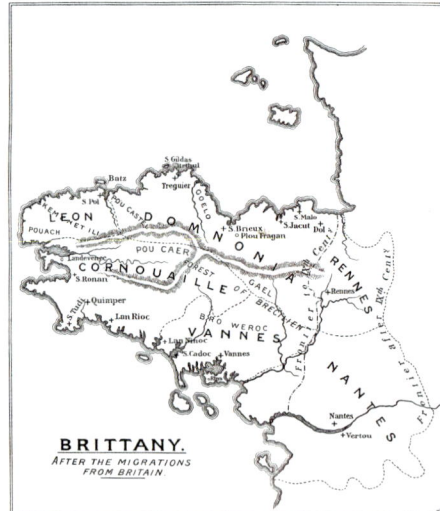

A map of Brittany as it was in the tenth century (from *Lives of the Saints* by Sabine Baring-Gould, first published in the late 1800s).

The Rotunda of the Agios Georgios church in Thessaloniki, built in the 4th century mausoleum for Emperor Galerius, then converted into a church and later into a mosque under Ottoman rule.

Bishop Ulfilas explaining the gospel to the Goths (note the ahistorical winged helmets!); woodcut from 1880.

The basic architecture of a Roman basilica.

Terme del Mitra, in the Archaeological Park of Ostia Antica, Rome, Italy. Part of these Roman baths, built in the second century, were later converted into a Christian cult space.

Byzantine mosaics clinging onto the dome of the Rotunda, featuring saints with their names and professions.

Modern Iznik (ancient Nicaea) on the shore of the azure blue Lake Iznik (ancient Lake Ascania).

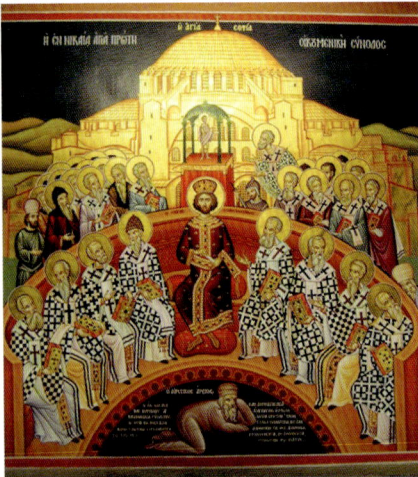

Constantine presiding over the Council of Nicaea, in his purple, gem-studded robes, while the condemned Arius crouches at the bottom. Icon from the Great Meteoron Monastery in Greece.

Fresco depicting the Battle of the Milvian Bridge (1517–1524), in the Hall of Constantine at the Vatican Palace, Rome.

Statue of a louche and imperious Constantine in York. (Artist: Phillip Jackson, 1998)

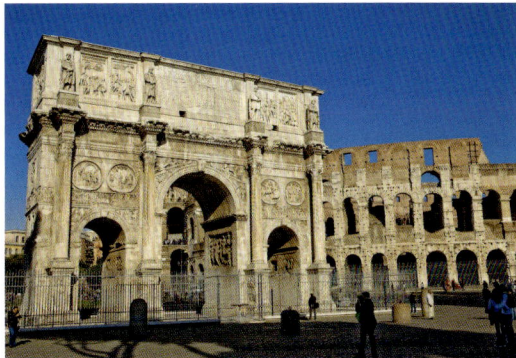
The Arch of Constantine, commemorating his victory at the Battle of Milvian Bridge – with not a shred of Christian imagery to be found on it.

The beautiful and ancient Hagia Sofia in Istanbul.

Inside the Hagia Sofia – now converted into a mosque again, but with Byzantine murals surviving on the walls.

Roundel (*tondus*) on the arch of Constantine – thought to be a genuine Constantinic component – showing Sol, the sun god, in his chariot being pulled by four horses. Below it, the frieze depicts a triumphal procession, followed up with an imperial cart bearing an emperor – although ostensibly Constantine, this may be Constantius II (his head is now missing), re-purposed from an earlier monument (Rose, 2021).

Coin of Constantine I, 318 CE, with the sun deity Sol on the reverse; minted in Londinium (modern-day London).

Coin of Constantine I with legend CONSTANTI-NVS MAX AVG on obverse (left); on the reverse, a standard – topped with a chi-rho – stabs down into a serpent, with the lettering SPES PVBLIC-A ('the hope of the people') and CONS below (indicating the mint of Constantinople) – 326 CE.

Constantine medallion with a tiny chi-rho on the front of the emperor's helmet, 315 CE.

Gold coin of Ptolemy III Euergetes (pharaoh of Egypt from 246–222 BCE), with an eagle grasping a thunderbolt and a (very much pre-Christian) chi-rho between its legs.

The mosaic from the Hinton St Mary Roman villa, with the bust of a man and a chi-rho behind his head, together with two pomegranates, in the central roundel, with busts of figures (seasons or winds perhaps) in the corners.

Bellerophon slays the Chimera on the mosaic in the adjoining room of the Roman villa. Archaeologist Richard Hobbs has suggested that this image of Bellerophon could have been an allegory for Constantine rushing his foes, while hunting scenes to each side are typical of mosaics commissioned by wealthy landowners – the landed gentry of the era.

View of the agora of ancient Corinth, from the *bema* where St Paul would have stood on trial.

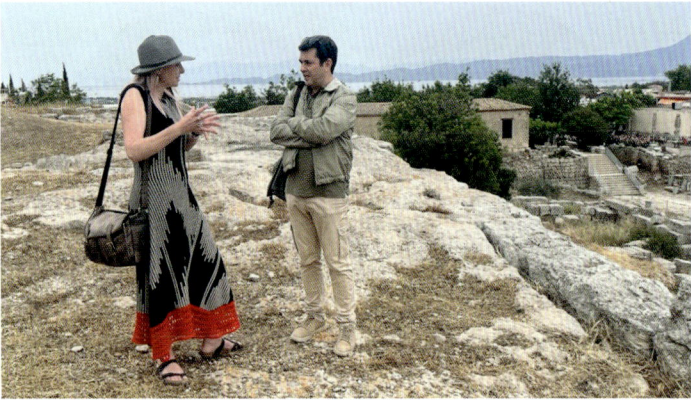

In conversation with Socrates Koursoumis, at the incredible archaeological site of ancient Corinth of which he was director for many years.

The dig at Carlisle cricket ground that revealed a huge Roman bathhouse (June 2023).

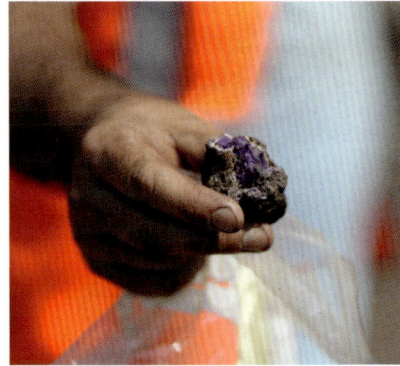

A muddy lump breaks open to reveal stunning imperial purple pigment – in the hand of Wardell Armstrong LLP Archaeological Director, Frank Giecco (Carlisle, June 2023).

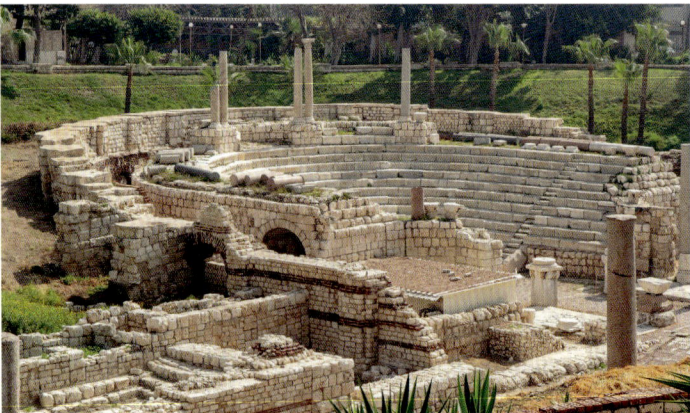

The ancient Roman Odeon at the Kom el Dikka archaeological site in the centre of modern Alexandria.

later. And of course, let's remember that Eusebius didn't mention the *labarum* in his earlier *History of the Church*, only in his much later *Life of Constantine*, written after the emperor's death. So who knows which actually came first. Perhaps I'm too suspicious — but maybe, just maybe, it was *this coin*, depicting a military standard with a *chi-rho* on top, that inspired Eusebius to come up with that detail for his great origin myth, his conversion story.

This may be overly sceptical, as there are a few other coins with a *chi-rho* associated with a banner. There's another late Constantine coin that shows two soldiers holding a standard with a *chi-rho*, this time on the banner rather than perched on the top. Then there are some earlier examples of designs involving a *chi-rho* — not on a standard or banner, but on a helmet instead. The earliest of these is actually not a coin, but a commemorative silver medallion produced in Ticinum (modern Pavia, in northern Italy). There's no mintmark on this medallion so it's hard to date, but it appears stylistically similar to coins minted at Ticinum in 315, to mark his decennalia (tenth anniversary). If that date is correct, this means the medallion was created just three years after the Battle of Milvian Bridge. But even then, it could be that this 315 coin was minted to celebrate another victory, in 314, where Constantine had fought against Licinius's troops at Cibalae (now Vinkovci in Croatia). On this medallion, Constantine is depicted in a frontal pose, looming over a horse, and wearing an elaborate helmet, with a tiny, almost imperceptible *chi-rho* in a roundel on the crest. And there's at least one other Constantine coin showing a small *chi-rho* on the side of the emperor's helmet.

Again, there's an echo here in Eusebius; when he described how Constantine ordered the *labarum* to be made, he also mentioned that 'the emperor was in the habit of wearing these letters on his helmet at a later period'. But could it be that Eusebius was inspired by coin designs to come up with this idea? Perhaps this is to be way too sceptical, too conspiratorial. And you might be thinking – what does it matter? Even if Eusebius was prompted by these coins to come up with the idea of the *chi-rho* on Constantine's standard at Milvian Bridge, or on his helmet later on – the cipher is there, all the same, struck in bronze, during Constantine's lifetime: a tiny Christian symbol.

At least, that's the conclusion we jump to. Because we tend to look at that *chi-rho* symbol and assume that it meant, as Eusebius was so careful to point out – 'Christ'. But – it's not that simple. And this is where the story gets *really* interesting. (Mostly because this is the bit that the history books usually leave out, whether through accident or intent.)

Firstly, the *chi-rho* symbol itself is not straightforward. It was an inveterate shape-shifter – it had a propensity for morphing into different forms, sometimes with a horizontal bar added, or with the P replaced with a straight line, making it look more like a straightforward cross. In some of these incarnations, it looks very similar to the eight-pointed stars or sun wheels that often appeared on ancient coins. One coin expert has even suggested that the symbol used by Constantine – especially if on his shields, as Lactantius suggested – might actually have been a sun wheel, its spokes arranged around the central shield boss. This could have had broad appeal for soldiers who were probably more familiar with Sol Invictus – as a god in his own right, or as an epithet for Mithras, also a very popular god with the military. Or it could have been that the thought behind using such a device (if it was used) could have been deliberately blending or 'syncretistic'; perhaps it was a powerful symbol that could have represented Mithras, Sol and possibly Christ at the same time. Indeed, some historians have suggested that Constantine was *consciously* conflating Sol and Christ – after all, merging deities had been a fairly common practice across the Roman world; Greek and Roman gods had an assumed equivalence, and local gods in the provinces were often conflated with deities from the Greco-Roman pantheon. There are other connections between the iconography of the two deities; the use of a solar halo to denote Sol, also used for Christ – and for saints – may also have helped to merge the idea of those two divine identities.

This is all very well, but the tiny symbols on the Constantine coins are very definitely *chi-rhos*, and most definitely not sun wheels. And it's also hard to argue that what Eusebius was describing in his *Life of Constantine* was actually a sun wheel, because he describes it in such detail – as an intersecting X and P, which he explicitly says are the first two letters of Christ.

But there could be other readings of the *chi-rho*. It's even been suggested that, if the letters on the coins were meant to be read as Latin rather than Greek, then the monogram could have been a contraction of the word for peace – PAX . . . PX. It's possible that it was designed to have been read in many ways – though this hypothesis feels a little far-fetched and far-reaching.

We end up back with the undeniable appearance of the symbol on Constantine coins (albeit just a few), alongside the description of the *chi-rho* in the later writing of Eusebius as an overtly Christian symbol. But *still* – all may not be what it seems. As a Christian writing about Constantine's life, Eusebius made an explicit link between the *chi-rho* he describes being placed on Constantine's standard and Christ. But what's interesting is that he seems to have been the first person in history to have made the connection between the *chi-rho* and Christ – or at least, the first person to have written about it, that we know of. It's not that the *chi-rho* cipher itself had never been used before this. There are plenty of other examples of this Greek monogram being used – just not in a Christian context.

The *chi-rho* had appeared on another Roman emperor's coin nearly a century before it popped up on a handful of Constantine's. A coin of Decius, who was briefly emperor from 249 to 251 CE, includes a *chi-rho*. The monogram appears in a legend on the reverse, relating to Aurelios Aphianos, who was chief magistrate of Maionia in Asia Minor, where the coin was minted. Here, the letters P and X combined as a *chi-rho* (or more correctly, in this case, a *rho-chi*, which looks exactly the same) appear as an abbreviation for *archōn*, ἄρχων – 'leader' or 'ruler', referring to Aphianos's role as chief magistrate. (*Archōn/ archē* had a wider meaning and was used in military contexts too; the Greek equivalent of a centurion, for example, was a *hekatontarch* – literally: leader of a hundred.) The design of this Decius coin also includes the Phrygian goddess Cibele, drawn by panthers. And indeed, Decius was famous for persecuting Christians in the mid-third century. No one suggests that there's any connection between the *chi-rho/rho-chi* and Christianity on *this* coin.

Going back much earlier – before the Common Era, before Christ – we find a gold coin of Ptolemy III, the ruler of Egypt from 246 to 222 BCE. This coin has a head of Zeus Ammon on one side, and an eagle with a thunderbolt (both linked with Zeus/Jupiter) on the other. The legend reads ΒΑΣΙΛΕΩΣ ΠΤΟΛΕΜΑΙΟΥ – *basileos ptolemaiou* – Ptolemy the King. And tucked in between the eagle's legs is – a *chi-rho*. A definite, unequivocal, unambiguous, pre-Christian *chi-rho*. It's been suggested that these letters could have been the initials of the master of the mint, or perhaps the minter himself. But perhaps it's more likely that, once again, they stand for *archōn/archē*. In that case, this *rho-chi* could relate to the primacy of the Alexandrian mint, or the seriation number of the coins – or for the sovereignty of Ptolemy, together with Zeus.

Symbols can acquire layers of meaning over time. Even if the *chi-rho/rho-chi* on those third-century BCE Ptolemaic coins started off as a mint mark, it could have developed an association with Jupiter just by virtue of appearing together with an eagle and a bolt of lightning. And as the classicist Álvaro Sánchez-Ostiz has argued, the inclusion of the *chi-rho/rho-chi* on Constantine's coins is much more likely to follow these earlier manifestations, to carry a familiar, time-honoured message about leadership, supremacy, and perhaps Jupiter as well. There could have been another politically, iconically useful connection as well – with Alexander the Great, someone else who was said to have seen a favourable omen on the eve of battle (in his case, an eagle and lightning) just before he went to war with the Persians. Alexander also positively associated himself with Zeus in his iconography.

The coins are incredibly important – because they reveal a tradition with a long history of using a *chi-rho/rho-chi* to mean *archōn*, leader. The existence of the *chi-rho* (or *rho-chi*) on Constantine's coins is an archaeological and numismatic fact, but it seems we can't simply assume it carries any Christian meaning at all. It only appears on a few coins, and always in a military context, on a helmet or a standard. And crucially, whenever it had appeared on coins before Constantine's time, it had just meant *archōn*. Similarly, if Constantine really did put a *chi-rho* on his standard in 312 (and we do only have Eusebius's word for that), it seems much more likely that it would have been used by Constantine to mean what it had always meant up until that point: not *chi-rho*, but *rho-chi*, standing for *archōn/ archē* – victory, leadership, supremacy (possibly with a nod to Jupiter and Alexander) – rather than 'Christos'.

So it seems there's very good reason to doubt Eusebius's claim. And even if he was factually accurate about the standard being made with a *chi-rho* on top, and if that really was meant to denote the first two letters of Christ, as he says – this would have been the *first time* the symbol had ever been explicitly used in this way. It's worth stressing this. There are *no* well-dated and unequivocal uses of a *chi-rho* meaning 'Christ' before Eusebius wrote his *Life of Constantine* in the late 330s.

This doesn't mean that archaeologists and historians haven't made claims for earlier Christian *chi-rhos*. They have – and these interpretations have become so widely reported and accepted that they have ascended to the status of facts. And yet they are just interpretations, and all seem to be based on a dangerously circular argument.

There are some engraved gemstones from rings featuring *chi-rhos*, stylistically dated to the late third century. Based on the numismatic evidence, it may seem somewhat more likely that the meaning of these is actually *rho-chi*, standing for *archōn*. We certainly can't assume they are Christian.

There's a mosaic pavement from Hinton St Mary in Dorset, England, thought to date from the fourth century, with a *chi-rho* that, once again, has been assumed to carry Christian meaning. (This interpretation even appeared in the British Museum's *History of the World in 100 Objects*.) But again – it's an entirely circular argument. The design of the mosaic includes a central roundel with the bust of a clean-shaven man with a *chi-rho* behind his head. It's claimed by some to be the oldest portrait in the world of Jesus Christ. To either side of his head floats a pomegranate. Around the edges of the mosaic, there are semicircular lunettes, one depicting a tree while in each of the other three, a dog chases a deer. There are more little busts in the corners; two flanked by flowers and two by pomegranates. They've been suggested to represent either the seasons or the winds, although some scholars have suggested – with actually nothing other than wishful thinking to support this assumption – that they could be evangelists. In the room next door, a smaller mosaic on the floor presents a familiar scene from Greco-Roman mythology: the hero Bellerophon slaying the dreaded chimera.

Is the image in the central roundel of the larger mosaic really a picture of Christ? The only reason to infer this at all is the inclusion of the *chi-rho* – and we've seen just how slippery that is. That inference rests on the huge assumption that this *chi-rho* could only have been intended as a Christian symbol. Some have suggested instead that the portrait is Constantine; after 312, the *chi-rho/rho-chi* became a symbol of him and of his leading city, Constantinople. The pomegranates and hunting dogs don't help us with identification, other than the fact that they're not particularly Christian. I think that Bellerophon, next door, is sending us quite a strong signal that the eyes staring out of the centre of the larger mosaic are not those of Jesus.

Other British mosaics, from villas at Frampton and Lullingstone, also contained *chi-rhos,* and once again, scholars have leaped to the conclusion that those symbols are Christian. The Frampton mosaic was discovered in 1794, and hasn't survived – we're just left with descriptions of it from the time of

213

excavation. Similarly to Hinton St Mary, there seem to have been various hunting scenes depicted, as well as Bacchus riding a leopard, a Cupid surrounded by a dolphin border, two lines of text referring to Neptune, and a panel which may have shown another Bellerophon slaying a chimera. At the entrance to an apse, a border of acanthus scrolls was broken in the centre by a circle – containing a *chi-rho*. Scholars pushing a Christian interpretation here suggest that Bacchus and Bellerophon could represent Christ, which seems a bit of a push. Everything seems resolutely pagan. It seems somewhat more likely, once again, that the *chi-rho/rho-chi* refers instead to something imperial, possibly Constantine himself, rather than Christ.

At Lullingstone villa, there was a painting on wall plaster of a *chi-rho/rho-chi*, inside a wreath, and flanked by the letters alpha and omega. The painting appears in a part of the villa that was thought (because of that wall painting) to have been converted into a chapel in the mid-fourth century. The wreath suggests a triumphal victory. There are more paintings around it: birds on either side of the wreath, and a series of figures, standing with their hands raised in a classical praying gesture. The mosaics in the villa are determinedly pagan: Bellerophon appears once again, slaying the chimera; busts representing the seasons appear in the corners; Zeus, as a white bull, carries off Europa, while a line of text refers to jealous Juno. Was this just an old floor that survived the conversion of part of the villa into a 'Christian chapel', or could the *chi-rho/rho-chi* in its victory wreath mean something different, something non-Christian? The addition of the alpha and omega seem to reinforce a Christian message: the phrase 'alpha and omega' – referring to God as the beginning and the end – appears four times in the New Testament, in the Book of Revelation. But if this mosaic *chi-rho* was actually intended as a *rho-chi,* standing for *archōn* as it had done in the past, then the extra Greek letters make a word: *archō,* 'I rule'. There are so many layers and possibilities here.

It's important to say that I'm not arguing that the painted *chi-rho/rho-chi* at Lullingstone was definitely not intended as a Christian cipher – but that it's certainly possible it wasn't, given the antiquity of this monogram. That means it's not enough – on its own – to stand as conclusive evidence. It's not impossible for there to have been Christians in late Roman Britain, in the fourth century – but were there enough, and was the religion deeply rooted enough to persist when Britain exited the Empire, with the withdrawal of Roman troops in 407 and the booting out of Roman magistrates in 410? It's hard to know, given the patchiness of the historical record, and given the fact that the religion seemed to be spreading at just the time that the Empire was crumbling. British archaeology, we must admit, is sadly equivocal – there are simply no buildings that can be definitely proved to have been churches, even private house-churches. And in some ways, this is quite surprising, given that we have a record of bishops from York, London and Lincoln attending the Council of Arles in 314, and British clerics also attending ecclesiastical councils at Serdica in 343 and at Ariminum in 359. We must be cautious – remembering that absence of evidence is not evidence of absence. But we must also guard against leaping to conclusions and engaging in wishful thinking. *And* we're getting distracted from the story of the *chi-rho.*

Back to the mosaics, and heading over to northern Italy, there's another early mosaic *chi-rho* that seems, on the face of it, to be more firmly Christian. Indeed, it comes from a Christian context: the basilica of Aquileia, in northern Italy – an important town that was even known as *Roma Secunda* in the time of the Empire. The basilica was rebuilt in the eleventh and fourteenth centuries, but its mosaic floor – only discovered in the early twentieth century – is thought to date back to its earliest inception, at the beginning of the fourth century. The basilica was built during the reign of Constantine, soon after the *Edict of Milan* was written, apparently using government funds, and under the auspices of Bishop Theodore. The north hall of the basilica is thought to have been built first, and the mosaic pavement here is purely decorative. But the mosaic in the south hall includes one large panel showing Jonah being pulled out of the mouth of a tenacious sea serpent. A dedicatory text, written in mosaic, mentions Theodore, and includes a *chi-rho*. If this mosaic was created in the early fourth century, does the *chi-rho* refer to Christ – or to Constantine? It could be either, or both, of course.

Perhaps relevant to the mosaic at Aquileia is a bronze coin minted in that city in 320–324. The design on the reverse includes bound captives flanking a standard – a familiar scene. A mintmark of Aquileia appears below, while what looks like a *chi-rho* floats over to the left. Rather awkwardly, though, this coin was struck in the name of Licinius – Constantine's eastern rival, who was decidedly pagan. So this appears to be good evidence that the symbol was still being used in a non-Christian way – by this other emperor – around ten years after the Battle of Milvian Bridge.

The *chi-rho* would certainly become a Christian symbol – that's not in doubt – but the big question is: *when*? And given that its use predates Christianity, it would be foolish to expect a sudden, neat transition – right across the Empire, at the same time. And how convenient, too, for this

symbol – a time-honoured emblem of leadership and victory –
to be claimed for Christianity.

So I'm left wondering if Eusebius really might have been responsible. Did he effectively *invent* the Christian *chi-rho*, niftily
changing the order of the letters? I can picture him, sitting
down to write the *Vita Constantini*, a handful of Constantine
coins on his desk, and his eye alighting on those tiny letters,
musing to himself – *archon . . . Christos*? That would have been
a stroke of genius. If *Romanitas* was to be synthesised with
Christianitas, what better way of reinforcing that association
than to layer a Christian interpretation onto an existing
symbol of Roman leadership and empire? And, in fact, there's
yet *another* layer to this detective story. Eusebius would have
been very familiar with the Greek translation of the Hebrew
Scriptures, and in those scriptures, the Greek word *archōn* is
used as a title for kings and officials, but also – you've guessed
it – as a divine title for Christ, as well. Eusebius would have
known that, when he claimed the *chi-rho* on Constantine's
shields stood for Christ; he must have known it could be read
in two ways – it was *chi-rho* and *rho-chi*, then: Christ *and* ruler.

However it happened, this Christianising of the *chi-rho* would
surely have taken a while to catch on. Only the literate would
have been immediately aware of the wordplay, after all. And the
chi-rho undoubtedly carried the original meaning of leadership
with it as it became increasingly used in a Christian context, by
subsequent emperors who were more demonstrably Christian
than Constantine. One such emperor was Magnentius –
yet another usurper, who served in the Gallic army under
Constantine's son, Constans, before killing him and taking
his place. Magnentius ruled from 350 to 353, and issued a coin
with a far larger *chi-rho* than on any of Constantine's coinage.

It takes up almost the whole of the reverse, with just enough room for a little alpha and omega on each side of it.

Was Magnentius Christian? He's said to have asked for help from the bishop Athanasius, but he also repealed laws that had made pagan worship illegal. Some historians have suggested that Magnentius's use of the *chi-rho* on his coins publicly announced his Christianity; others have suggested it was 'deChristianised'. But perhaps it simply hadn't become widely recognised as a Christian symbol even by this time, despite Eusebius's best efforts, and the letters still referred to imperial leadership.

We haven't even looked at the other symbol yet, the one Lactantius said was carried into battle on the shields of Constantine's troops – the one that seems more like a *tau-rho* than a *chi-rho*. Unlike the *chi-rho*, the *tau-rho* or staurogram does appear to have been used in a Christian context before Constantine. That's if we can trust some fragments of biblical text written on Egyptian papyri that are thought, based on palaeographic analysis – scrutinising style and vocabulary – to date to the second century. If the date's correct, it makes the staurogram the earliest, definitely attested Christian symbol by some stretch. As it first appears in these Egyptian texts, it's thought it may have been influenced by the ancient Egyptian symbol for eternal life, the ankh, which sometimes appears in Coptic art alongside the staurogram. Scrutiny of Egyptian sources suggests that Christianity was indeed deeply synthetic as it spread across North Africa, building on old patterns of religious behaviour rather than sweeping them away, with old festivals being rebadged as saints' days.

But just like the *chi-rho*, the staurogram also had a pre-Christian existence. It appears on a coin of Herod the Great, for instance, dating to around 40 BCE, where it stood for 'tetrarch' (Diocletian didn't invent the term). But given the potentially second-century examples on Egyptian papyri, it looks like the staurogram was already being used as a Christian symbol by the time Lactantius mentions it in relation to Constantine. There's just a single instance of the staurogram appearing on an archaeological artefact associated with Constantine – on one of his coins, minted in Antioch in 336–337 – the final year of his reign. Here, the staurogram appears next to Victory holding a cross-shaped standard, and has been interpreted as a Christian symbol (although, again, it could just be an unrelated mint mark).

Missing from all of this is the cross as a Christian symbol. This is a tricky one too, as sceptres on coins can look cross-like without meaning to. There's what looks like a tiny, equal-armed cross on a bronze coin of Constantine, minted at Ticinum in 316, and another, ankh-like cross on a coin of the 330s, from Aquileia. They could be Christian symbols. But it's not until the fifth century that more definite crosses appear on coins, sometimes in the hand of a Victory, who undergoes her own transformation into an angel.

So many symbols, so much potential syncretism; nothing is as straightforward as it first seems. What can we meaningfully draw from all of this? It's time to bring the history and archaeology together.

Reading Between the Lines

Having pored over Constantine's words, probed the iconography on his victory arch and peered at the messages stamped on his money, what can we conclude? We're left doubting whether

Constantine really did carry anything like a *chi-rho* into battle – and even if he did, we may doubt that it was meant to have symbolised Christ. The whole story of the vision and victory seems more like a literary trope. Constantine could write to bishops in terms which made him sound quite Christian, but at the same time, was having coins minted depicting *Sol Invictus*. The tiny *chi-rhos* on just a handful of his coins aren't necessarily Christian symbols at all. And there's not a shred of Christian symbolism on his triumphal arch.

There's no objective evidence that Constantine openly attacked non-Christian religious institutions – and indeed good evidence that he still supported public divination and the Imperial Cult, right until the end. After his death, he'd be deified, given the title *divus*, with his successors treated to the same honour, as late as Valentinian, who died in 375 CE. Constantine does seem to have had a personal aversion to blood sacrifice, while being suspicious of magic arts practised behind closed doors, and he may have demanded a tax on temple treasures to help fund his New Rome. He seems to have favoured Christians with some of his statutes, making special concessions for followers of this religion, but in a way that could perhaps be seen as making up for previous persecution under Diocletian, as well as potentially marking himself out as different from rivals. He appears to have used religion as a political tool, then, but stopped short of making it too polit-ically divisive – a wise move for an emperor ruling over such a large and still religiously diverse empire. Publicly, he kept his distance from the Church – there's no evidence he ever attended a service.

We're left with a confusing array of messages, trying to read between the lines. But what's fascinating from our perspective, some seventeen centuries later, is that despite a lot of missing data, we are still able to tap into a variety of information channels and see how the messaging varied between them. That in itself is fascinating. Because what Constantine was 'saying' in his coins – to perhaps the widest constituency – was not the same as what he was saying in public proclamations, and was certainly not the same as the messaging in his correspondence with Christian bishops. Constantine was representing himself in different ways to different people, in different media (at least when it came to religion; he was, on the other hand, fairly consistent when it came to projecting an image of himself as a supreme ruler).

This seems very familiar – from contemporary politics. We see the way some politicians ally themselves with particular ideologies and religions, and how they pick sides in culture wars, jumping on a bandwagon, even deliberately stirring up those culture wars to flush out 'wedge issues' – helping to define and divide themselves from rivals, and to rally support. Through time, culture wars have been staked by ambitious politicians and rulers, often using religion to rally, divide and conquer. From arguments about whether Christ really was divine, about which version of Christianity is 'orthodox' at any time, we've moved on, in the twenty-first century, to a panoply of debates about sex and gender, women's reproductive rights, climate change and vaccinations, as politicians try to rally their followers to their side. Religious divides still pertain as well, of course; even where politicians are addressing pluralistic or largely secular societies, they can use religiously-inspired rhetoric, invoking certain religious 'values', for instance.

When we look at how some politicians use culture wars, wedge issues and religion to achieve certain ends today, we may come away sceptical of the sincerity of those actors' beliefs. We ask ourselves whether their actions flow from genuine convictions – or whether they are more cynically using such ideology as a means to an end. Constantine certainly seems to have been a master of controlling the narrative, an essential skill for any diplomat or politician, then or now. We can interpret that as either cynical or clever, or perhaps – because humans are complicated creatures – a bit of both. But are we looking at someone who had a strong religious faith and acted accordingly, while ensuring that his messages would still be palatable for a predominantly non-Christian audience? Or are we looking at someone who was merely happy to be thought of as Christian, or at least, generous to Christians?

It's interesting and useful to consider Constantine's conversion (if indeed it happened) in the wider context of other fourth-century conversions. The conversion stories we know of are necessarily those of high-status Romans, belonging to the literate elite, and are hugely diverse. Even with the caveats that we are only ever reading carefully curated accounts, we can find a great range of motives and depth of beliefs. The hugely influential North African bishop and theologian Augustine of Hippo described his own conversion as a highly intense, spiritual journey in his *Confessions*. Then there's Pegasios, bishop of Ilios, who happily switched back to being a pagan priest during the rule of Julian 'the Apostate'. Importantly, even crucially, these conversions (which could be reversible, as Pegasios's story shows) didn't disrupt the lifestyles and careers of the elite. And they also involved a lot of syncretism – mixing of old and new ideas. Conversion tends to be described in such black-and-white terms, but there were clearly many shades – and many different ways of being a Christian in the fourth century; the Christian message had also been finessed by this time, too, becoming more culturally Greco-Roman.

Even if we are to accept Constantine's conversion story as more than a literary trope which highlighted his divine right to rule, we may still be left wondering about the depth of his own convictions. We have to recognise that the evidence we're looking at, whether in the form of reported speeches and laws, statuary, inscriptions or coins, was created by others. Of course, Constantine must have had some oversight, but at the same time it's very unlikely that he personally signed off the design of every statue, coin and monument. (And of course he didn't get a chance to edit the *Life of Constantine* – Eusebius wrote that after he died.) But at the same time, for the material produced during his lifetime at least, he must have been broadly happy for that public projection of his persona to be out there. And through it all, his coins – the most public and widespread of his communications – continued to convey fairly traditional, diverse and generic messages. In the end, I think it's impossible to know what Constantine himself really believed. Even with a wealth of literary and archaeological material to look at, you can dissect that and examine the entrails for signs of that truth, but it remains elusive. We can't get inside his head now, and we wouldn't even have been able to back then.

But, in fact, I want to argue that whether or not Constantine held genuine and sincere Christian beliefs – it doesn't really matter. Trying to look deep into Constantine's heart is missing the point. The question of whether Constantine really did adopt Christianity as his personal faith has dominated scholarly discussions, but it surely distracts us from the real story. In her poetically named paper, 'Framing the Sun: The Arch of Constantine and the Roman Cityscape', Elizabeth Marlowe warned against a simplistic interpretation of Constantine's 'conversion', starting with his assumed personal change of heart, and seeing everything else flowing from that. Instead, she argues that we should look at the bigger picture, and all the political interests at play; as she cautions, 'Constantine's Christianity, like his arch, is . . . [too often] divorced from the specific, local contexts for which it was created and which in turn defined its meaning.'

Whatever the quality, depth and sincerity of Constantine's personal faith, there were very real political and economic ramifications of his policies. Throughout his reign, Constantine continued to encourage broad religious tolerance – and that very much extended to Christians, who had found themselves persecuted by previous emperors. He offered the Church material support as well, granting exemptions from tax and civic service to Christian clergy (something that had never happened for religious clergy – outside Egypt, at least). He clearly saw Christian clergy as potentially useful to the state; in fact, he said just that, explaining that these exemptions meant they could 'devote themselves without interference to their own laws . . . for it seems that, rendering the greatest possible service to the deity, they most benefit the state'. This imperial support didn't come as a gift – the Church was expected to take on various functions that had previously been the preserve of the state. Constantine asked the bishop of Alexandria to take over the distribution of corn and oil to the poor in the city, while the Church in Constantinople was officially tasked with providing free funerals for the impoverished; bishops were also asked to take on legal work for the state.

There were clear political gains to be made for Christians. Whatever Constantine's own religious persuasions might have been, there were people around him who were *extremely* keen to portray him as Christian – to claim him for Christianity. The stakes were high; as historian Hartmut Ziche wrote, 'The ultimate success of the Church depended on the idea that the Christian god and his bishops had been the choice of Constantine.' On Constantine's part, he seems to have been happy to appear 'Christian enough' in his correspondence with bishops – expressing his belief in a singular God, for instance. But Eusebius certainly wanted to make sure that no one would get the impression that Constantine had been merely tolerant of Christianity, and, instead, that he had chosen and was chosen by this faith.

A coin minted after Constantine's death in 337 shows the deceased emperor wearing a veil-like shroud. On the reverse, he appears in a chariot pulled by four horses, with a hand of God poking down at the top, ready to carry him off into the heavens. It's *exactly* the same iconography that appeared on coins commemorating the death of his father, Constantius, where, as his panegyrist tells us, the hand is that of Jupiter. But on the coin showing Constantine, Eusebius assures us the hand is that of the Christian God. (Although the legend DV – *divo* – indicating that Constantine had become deified – was a concept that orthodox Christians may have found hard to swallow.) Really, what these two coins seem to be saying is 'business as usual; just another dead emperor, just another god up there'.

From the Council of Nicaea to the Cathedral of Milan

It's very easy to view the events of spring 325 from a Roman perspective – to see the Church being captured by the Roman state, and even to confer all the agency on Constantine. There's a tendency to focus on a single character, as though any person could single-handedly determine the course of history. And we, necessarily, focus on the characters we know about – the ones who appear in the written texts. Constantine becomes a single mind controlling the fate of the Roman Empire. Of course this was never the case, but we simply don't have any access to the conversations that were had between the emperor and his advisers. We only hear about decisions once they'd been made, rather than the disparate voices and discussion that must have fed into his policies. (To be fair, we often do the same with modern politicians.)

The historian Harold Drake, who has minutely dissected not only the ancient texts relating to Constantine's conversion but also the way that historians have interpreted this episode, warns of the danger in oversimplifying the political process:

'The best historians . . . have always known that they are using a kind of shorthand when they condense all the complicated processes of governmental decision making into the person of a single central character . . . The problem is that . . . it is easy for those who follow to mistake the shorthand for the complete record.'

Just as Roman government wasn't actually just one individual – however powerful he might have been – making all the decisions, the 'Church' wasn't a monolith either; it was a collection of individuals with different views, aims and agendas. But quite often, histories avoid becoming embroiled with the untidiness of all those multiple agendas, those entire, messy – and entirely messy – political ecologies. Some influential

Christians must have been actively engaging with the emperor to advance their own agendas. Bishop Ossius of Cordoba, for example, clearly had the emperor's ear – it was he who had been the driving force behind assembling the bishops in 325. More widely, those influential Christians were fighting among themselves for hegemony too, which is really what that Arian heresy and debate was all about. (People are always fighting for power in any culture war; it's important to realise that, for some, the balance of power is far more important than whatever ideological schism or debate is taking place – and they will happily co-opt the support of anyone who joins the fray imagining that it's only about ideas and beliefs.)

Consider the Nicene meeting from the point of view of the bishops. The schism over the Arian heresy was all about competing factions. But bringing in the emperor to resolve the dispute represented an important coup for the Church. It conferred an authority on the decision – even though the Council of Nicaea would not, in fact, put an end to the factional fight. But it also put the imperial stamp of authority on the Church itself; the Church was important enough to have become imperial business.

Arianism did not end that day on the shores of Lake Ascania in 325; the schism would continue to infuse and energise warring factions in the Church. But the involvement of the emperor signalled something more than just a stamp of approval for a forced moment of unity among the ranks of the bishops. It indicated, very formally, a deepening of the relationship between the Church and the Roman state. Above and beyond the favouring of one faction over another, this could have been an outcome that many bishops had been hoping for. With the most powerful and influential man in the world as an ally, and later claimed as a convert, they would be able to grow their brand – the cult would be unstoppable.

Constantine had set the ball rolling, but it would be decades before Christianity became the official religion of the Roman Empire. Over the course of the fourth century, the Church would extend its business, its influence and its authority even further. While Constantine laid the foundations, it was under Gratian and then Theodosius, towards the end of the century, that the Christian Church would emerge as a truly powerful secular institution – a complete administrative system. And the balance of power would shift, too.

Gratian would make both symbolic and real financial moves against non-Christian cults. He ended state subsidies for those cults, leaving the Church as the sole religious recipient of state funds. In 382, he ordered the Altar of Victory to be removed from the senate in Rome. There were still plenty of senators who weren't Christian, possibly even still a majority, and who appealed for the altar to be reinstated – but their pleas fell on deaf ears. The altar was a venerated antiquity, almost four centuries old; it had been set up by the first emperor of Rome, Augustus, after he defeated Marc Antony and Cleopatra's forces at the Battle of Actium, to become the single ruler of the Empire. Augustus placed a Greek statue of Victory on it, and it became the focus for senatorial prayers for the Empire, and for pledges of allegiance to new emperors. The altar may have been a pagan monument, regularly soaked in libations, but it was also steeped with the very *idea* of Empire, and its removal was very controversial.

The following year, Gratian was assassinated in Lyon, and his younger brother, the twelve-year-old Valentinian, became *augustus*. In 394, Symmachus, the urban prefect of Rome, wrote to Valentinian to ask again for the restoration of the altar. He echoed Constantine, writing that 'Everyone has his own way of life and his own way of worship' and that 'One cannot penetrate so deep a mystery by only one road'.

Symmachus was urging religious tolerance, clearly worried that Christianity was now pushing out the old cults and traditional Roman religion. And it was. Again, it's so easy to fall into the trap of that disembodied, abstract 'it'. *People* were instigating that change, with one person in particular very keen to push Christian interests at the heart of the Empire: Ambrose, the bishop of Milan. It's thought that Ambrose had leaned on Gratian to get that iconic Altar of Victory removed from the senate. And now Ambrose demanded to see the letter that Symmachus had sent Valentinian (and, in fact, he tells us that he already knew what it contained; he clearly had access to informants at court). He was very dismissive of Symmachus's plea for tolerance and his suggestion that there could be any other 'way' than Christianity. 'What you are ignorant of,' wrote Ambrose, 'we know from the word of God. And what you try to infer, we have established in truth from the very wisdom of God.' His response is quite breathtakingly arrogant, telling us Ambrose was very sure of himself and his political influence – that he had the ear of the emperor, over and above the urban prefect and those senators clinging onto the old cults.

Ambrose went as far as to lightly threaten Valentinian should the emperor bow to the demands of the non-Christians and restore the Altar: 'we bishops cannot pretend to endure this with equanimity'. He went on to say that, if Valentinian granted Symmachus's request, the emperor would be allowed to go into a church, but not to see a priest; in other words, the emperor would be effectively excommunicated. Valentinian was a teenager at the time; would Ambrose have been so bold with a more seasoned, mature emperor, we're left wondering? Rather like the case with the Arian heresy, we must just be seeing the tip of the iceberg in these accounts. We must suspect that what appears to be an argument over an altar was really, once again, evidence of different political factions jostling for power.

Six years later, with another emperor on the throne, Ambrose went ahead and imposed the sanction of excommunication on the incumbent emperor, Theodosius. The punishment followed civil unrest sparked by the imprisonment of a popular charioteer, accused of pederasty, leading to the murder of a general. Theodosius had launched a severe reprisal, wanting to impress the insurgents with a bloody example of the might of Rome – sending in troops to massacre a whole hippodrome full of spectators. After this tragic event, Ambrose wrote to the emperor to tell him that he couldn't attend mass in the cathedral at Milan – unless he were to publicly repent. Later sources would elaborate the story to make it more dramatic, suggesting that Ambrose had physically barred Theodosius from the cathedral, but in fact the letter seems to have been sufficient.

Theodosius did as he was told, donning penitential robes to ask for forgiveness. It's a fascinating episode illuminating the changing relationship between Church and state in the Roman Empire. It seems like such a crucial moment. Historians have often focused on the way that Theodosius's forced penance demonstrated the supreme power of the Church, and of its bishops, by this point in time. But think about Theodosius in all of this – on the face of it, this might look like public humiliation, like something which demeans him and lessens his status. But in fact, it does nothing of the sort – it *rescues* him. He'd been presenting himself as a merciful Christian emperor.

With popular opinion undoubtedly turning against him after that slaughter in the arena, he desperately needed a PR boost, and here was divine intervention, ready to supply just that. People may have been furious with Theodosius – the optics could hardly have been any worse – but Ambrose had arranged for him to be forgiven, by none other than God Himself. (And if in this story, Ambrose seems like a humanitarian, reacting against Theodosius's appalling massacre of innocent spectators at the games, he was markedly less compassionate in the face of another crisis. When Christians in Callicinum – now Raqqa, in Syria – burned down a synagogue, Theodosius ordered the local bishop to rebuild it with Church money. Ambrose once again threatened to bar Theodosius from taking communion until he retracted this order.)

Theodosius's public penitence is an episode very reminiscent of another king and a similar act of repentance – six centuries later. After the archbishop of Canterbury, Thomas Becket, was murdered in the cathedral in 1170, Henry II's initial response was sanguine; he even suggested that Becket had brought this disaster on himself. But he soon realised that public opinion wasn't on his side, and in fact, Becket's death place was quickly becoming a site of pilgrimage, so he 'did a Theodosius' and undertook a public act of penitence. Henry rode his horse almost all the way to Canterbury, then walked the last couple of miles, before taking off his shoes and cloak and making his way to the tomb of Becket, in the crypt of the cathedral. He spent the night there, praying – and also promised a large sum of money to the Church.

It's easy to see this as Henry being humiliated in that act of penitence, too, but like Theodosius, he gains more than he loses. Both the medieval king and the Roman emperor receive divine forgiveness. In each case, it might look like the Church is acting *against* the interests of those rulers, somehow diminishing them – but really, it's doing its job; by granting them absolution, it's legitimising their reigns and their authority. Those in high positions can do what they like and get away with it, it seems, especially if a religious lobby is prepared to support them.

Looking back at those events and political machinations over the reigns of those three late-fourth-century Roman emperors, we may well ask: who *really* wielded ultimate power? Gratian, Valentinian II and Theodosius – or the bishops, with all the community and commercial interests they represented?

Bishop Ambrose was probably less influential than his own account suggests. And in fact, it was what Theodosius had done over the decade leading up to 390 that was the real game-changer, issuing decrees that the only acceptable Christianity was the form agreed at the Council of Nicaea – and then, that pagan worship was to be banned. Gone was Constantine's vision of a religiously tolerant empire. Never before had a Roman emperor supported such an exclusive religious monopoly, throwing behind it the full coercive power of the state, effectively outlawing any alternatives, ending religious tolerance and freedom of belief. Constantine may have seen Christianity, still a minor religion in the early fourth century, as useful in various ways, while Theodosius fully committed the Empire to this one religion.

Some historians have neatly framed the Christianisation of the Roman state as a process bookended by those two important historical scenes. In 325, Constantine had appeared among the bishops in full imperial regalia – in his purple robe adorned with gold and studded with gems. He sat himself down in a resplendent gold chair in the centre of the hall of the imperial palace. In 390, in stark contrast, Theodosius appeared before the Cathedral of Milan in humble garb, ready to atone for ordering that massacre in Thessalonica. It's a bit too neat – but the story of Theodosius's penitence certainly captures the truth that, during the fourth century, Christianity and the Roman state had become increasingly enmeshed, to the extent that they ended up becoming one and the same: the Roman state was Christianised; at the same time, Christianity was Romanised. And back in 325, while the Council of Nicaea represented a pivotal moment, the process of change was already well underway – after all, the bishops were already important enough for an emperor to call them to a meeting.

Right there, in the heart of the Empire, in the centre of political power, is something that's been in front of us all the time – perhaps so close that we've overlooked it. And it's less about how Constantine presented himself to the citizens of his Empire, in public, and more about what was happening in private. It's less about the way that Constantine presented himself to recipients of his letters – flattering them and expressing common sympathy – and more about the existence of those letters *in the first place*. Although that body of correspondence may have been selectively curated by writers with their own agendas, such as Eusebius, Constantine was still writing a *lot* of letters to bishops. And although there were plenty of pagans around Constantine, among high-level statesmen and imperial advisers, Christians were also present in his trusted inner circle. They had established themselves at the heart of Empire – in its core; in the emperor's own court. Lactantius was appointed as tutor to Constantine's ill-fated son, Crispus. And Eusebius, bishop of Caesarea, wasn't just Constantine's biographer, he was right there in the heart of power. It's estimated that a tiny fraction of the population of the Roman Empire was Christian in the early fourth century – but these included some highly influential figures.

An Elite Cult

While writing this book, I constantly found myself being lured back into thinking about Christianity as a *thing* in its own right – 'How did *it* spread?', 'How did *it* take hold?' 'How did *it* achieve hegemony?' 'It' is mysteriously divorced from *people* – from the politics, the minds that encapsulated it and conveyed it. And that can perhaps lead to another intellectually unhelpful shortcut and shorthand, if we start to conceive of 'Christians' as a coherent group, with religion being the most important defining characteristic of these people – almost as if the religious persuasion of this group of people was completely separate to their traditions, their families, or their status in Roman society. And so we end up with a view of Christianity as though it was some sort of ethereal entity and not embedded in the social world; and also a very myopic view of early Christians in the Roman Empire, as if they were an entirely novel, discrete group. Their status and label as 'Christian' perhaps draws focus from other aspects of their identity – including their social standing. We've met a few powerful people close to Constantine, but what's the wider story of these Christians who came to exert so much influence on an emperor?

Although Christians made up a tiny proportion of the Roman Empire's population at large, by the mid- to late fourth century it's thought the religion may already have predominated among those in high office. Careful analysis has suggested that most senators were Christian towards the end of the century, during Gratian's reign, from 367 to 383, for instance. Emperors may not have made this religious affiliation an explicit criterion for selection to senatorial office – that would come later – but, by this time, anyone with their eye on such a position would surely have perceived that conversion to Christianity was desirable, if not essential. Roman society was all about patronage – you got on by networking, and by the later decades of the fourth century, to be Christian was becoming a distinct advantage.

Some historians have focused on the influence of emperors in the Christianisation of the Empire – notably Constantine; others have seen the change as first taking hold among the aristocracy. It's hard, practically impossible, to tease apart one from the other: the emperor held sway over the aristocracy, but he also ruled with their consent and approval, and would have absorbed influences as well as generating them.

Some aristocrats clung onto 'pagan' traditions – markers of ancient, inherited status. Others saw the way the wind was blowing and adapted; once their influential friends and associates had become Christians, they would follow. The pace of Christianisation varied across the Empire. The eastern senators of Constantinople, who were from more recently socially elevated families, and therefore more dependent on the personal favour of the emperor, appear to have led the way. Aristocrats in the western reaches of the Empire soon followed suit. Senators in Rome, on the other hand – in the original heart of the Empire – were from well-established aristocratic families, with a fierce sense of their own class, status and independence, and they took longer to convert. But by the mid-fifth century, though, paganism among the senatorial class seems to have been firmly on the way out; by this time, it had become a liability.

On the whole, the Christianisation of the elites appears to have happened in a smooth, gradual, organic fashion, taking place without upsetting the basic fabric of Roman upper-class society and governance. There were loud voices at the extremes, to be sure; some anti-Christian pagans were vociferously militating against the changing tide towards the end of the fourth century, while some fervent Christians demanded that all converts should immediately adopt a conspicuously ascetic lifestyle. But generally speaking, these were outliers, expressing extreme views. Most senators were much more moderate. They swapped a genteel sort of paganism for a genteel sort of Christianity, seamlessly preserving their place in society and their political careers, and maintaining the patriarchal social order that characterised the Empire. Whether Christian or pagan, it could be inferred that what those aristocrats really believed in was the hierarchical nature of society – with them at the top. That was simply the way things should be. Whatever their religion, however devout or holy its most prominent proponents appeared to be, this was the enduring ideology they all believed in.

As career paths in the civil service became subsumed into the Church, they maintained their status. For most fourth-century aristocrats, a switch to Christianity was much less of a radical change than might be assumed. Becoming a Christian didn't require a significant change in lifestyle. The culture and practice of the religion had also absorbed much from existing Roman secular culture – it was part of it; it didn't exist in a cultural vacuum. Leading Christian writers (themselves embedded in the aristocracy) were shaping the message of Christianity to appeal to the educated elite, actively looking for shared ideology rather than stressing the differences, and mixing in a healthy dose of familiar Platonic and Stoic Greek philosophy.

This all makes the transition to Christianity in the Roman Empire much more understandable – it was evolution, not revolution: the way that existing symbols could be blended and adopted; the way that Sol might have helped pave the way for a monotheistic faith (which itself was less singular that it might seem, with a three-in-one bargain and a load of saints available to create local connections, as we saw in Brittany); the way that Greek philosophy could be woven in (and indeed, perhaps the thing that really distinguished this particular religion was its ability to mesh with and absorb such philosophy); and the way that Christianity, by this time, just felt quite *Roman* – all helped.

By the fourth century, Christian offices, particularly epis-copal roles, had clearly become very attractive to upper-class men. The Roman state had once meted out terrible punish-ments to some Christians who'd refused to pay their respects to 'king and country' by making sacrifices to the emperor. A few centuries later, it was the pagans, followers of the old cults, who were now the ones who weren't Roman enough, while the senatorial ranks were rapidly converting.

Traditional Roman career paths saw aristocratic men ad-vancing from positions as lawyers and judges, to becoming governors, or clerks in imperial offices, and then, if they were lucky, ascending into high office, as prefects or members of the imperial court. In the late Roman Empire, there were important changes when it came to who could ascend to the senatorial class. Previous rules setting an income threshold were relaxed, making it easier for city councillors and men in military positions, including barbarians, to become senators.

Senatorial rank was inherited, so any expansion of eligibility was likely to expand, down through the generations – if fathers had more than one son.

Pagan priesthoods had run alongside these posts. Initially, some Christian priesthoods worked in the same way, but the full-time job option of bishop soon emerged. Now, rather than administrators assuming priestly roles, bishops would increasingly take on a significant administrative role within the state, assuming political authority. The proliferation of episcopal roles had a wider context, reflecting a significant change in the way the Empire itself was being run, in the late Roman period. The later third century and fourth century saw a massive expansion of Roman bureaucracy: a twenty-fold increase in administrative positions, each of which was held for only around a decade. This bureaucratic expansion seems to have been driven as much by the ambitions of the provincial ruling classes as it was by central government – as much bottom-up as it was top-down.

And as we can see so clearly in the late Roman literature, high-level secular, bureaucratic careers, military careers and religious careers were not exclusive – not in the least; instead, they were intertwined, branching off from each other, as we saw with the fifth-century careers of Sidonius, Germanus and even, we may suspect, Illtud. But even in the early fourth century, bishops were becoming a force to be reckoned with.

Examining Constantine's relationship with the Church, we find ourselves shifting focus to the bishops and the power they wielded. By the early fourth century, bishops were still very much operating alongside the secular provincial administration, but their congregations – and their influence – were growing. Not only that, but these roles had far more longevity than governorships; a governor might be in post for three years whereas a bishop could be there for thirty. The Church was also becoming a powerful instrument of communication, with weekly services where bishops and other clergy could broadcast messages. Hooking up with the Church could be seen as the late antique equivalent of owning a newspaper or an influential social media platform today. The bishops had the power to suppress or inflame social tensions; they could pacify citizens or incite riots. It's starting to look as though Constantine really had little choice – how could he have avoided engaging with these powerful figures?

But how had this Christianisation of the elites happened? Why were people in the higher echelons of Roman society turning to this new religion? The answer is often sought internally, in the pages of the Bible, in the Christian message. But, and perhaps it's the biologist in me, I need to look at the wider context; to try to understand how this 'species' of religion interacted with its environment. And there are answers to be found in something much more mundane: in the fabric of civic life; in the burgeoning, bustling cities of the Empire; in those places that became synonymous with the idea of civilisation itself.

4

THE BUSINESS OF EMPIRE

A coin of Commodus – referring to the grain fleet – showing
him as Hercules, standing on the prow of a ship and accepting
a sheaf of wheat from the goddess Isis (191–192 CE)

'What is't to us, if taxes rise or fall,
Thanks to our fortune, we pay none at all.'

CHARLES CHURCHILL, 18th-century satirist

'Such was their sense of entitlement that they
believed – and persuaded others to believe – that
a hierarchical society with them placed firmly and
unassailably at the top was the natural order of
things. Even to suggest otherwise, they implied,
was to shake the foundations of morality.'

CHRIS BRYANT, 2017 (From *How the [British]
Aristocracy Preserved Their Power*)

Civic Pride and the Urban Poor

Civilisation is taken to mean many different things. But most of the time, it is tied up with the development of cities; that's the derivation of the word, after all, from the Latin *civis*, a city dweller, giving us *civitas* – meaning 'citizenship', and eventually, in post-classical Latin, also coming to mean 'city'. (It's easy to see how this old word transmutes into Italian *città* and English *city*, especially if you consider that Romans pronounced 'v' as we'd pronounce 'w'.) Large settlements that we can reasonably call cities started to emerge as early as the Bronze Age in some places, popping up more widely in the Iron Age and really taking off in the Roman era.

Roman cities grew larger than any Hellenistic cities before them, although they were still modelled on their Greek *polis* predecessors, as self-governing population centres. And their government was in the form of a city council or *curia*, made up of local men with sufficient landholdings to qualify for the job. When a city was granted legal status under the Roman system, those elites had a lot to gain. The council could levy and spend local taxes, and individual members of the council were granted Roman citizenship, bringing its own benefits. Romanisation of the provinces may have started with legionaries' boots on the ground, but it proceeded with local elites petitioning to have their towns recognised as cities, buying into the imperial cult. As historian Peter Heather put it, 'The pressures to conform were so strong that most local agents were only ever going to make one choice.' With these powerful incentives, cities positively mushroomed and flourished across the Empire.

We see that word, 'flourish', used so often in connection with the birth of civilisation, that we hardly notice it any more.

But it suggests an inherent value judgement: that cities were beautiful, benign, gorgeous things – blossoming like flowers. They are certainly where we find the most impressive art and architecture from the ancient world – precisely because these places were where wealthy patrons gathered and demonstrated their riches, status and power.

Ancient cities were adorned with technologically astonishing feats of engineering and technically astounding, aesthetically superlative sculpture. They were enlivened with the most sophisticated drama and music that those societies produced. We see the apogee of human creativity and ingenuity on display in ancient cities. But cities were also – as indeed they are today – places of deprivation, misery, dirt and disease. The rural poor flooded into them, looking for that chance of a better life.

Rome itself was the first city in the west to swell to a population of a million inhabitants, in the second century. It was a city of stunning imperial decadence, with its impressive temples and grand palaces, its marble columns and arches – but it was also blighted by homelessness and grinding poverty.

In the fourth century, the soldier and historian Ammianus Marcellinus wrote of the people who lived 'in the crevices of the towering buildings, sleeping rough in *tabernae* or huddled in the vaults beneath the seating of theatres, circuses and amphitheatres'. Later saints' *Lives* are replete with beggars at the steps of palaces; at the city gates; at the roadside. Libanius, a teacher of rhetoric in fourth-century Antioch (modern Antakya, in Turkey), described destitute beggars in the city: some completely naked, others half naked, reaching their hands out to passers-by for a little food or money.

Urban poverty was a more pressing problem than it had ever been before. Food supply was a massive challenge in these rapidly expanding cities, which could only continue to function with a certain level of redistribution of resources. In Rome, Constantinople and other cities, citizens could claim a state handout – initially of grain, but by the fourth century, bread, pork and oil. But that wasn't enough to keep a city going – individual philanthropy was essential and expected.

Some historians – a few even writing quite recently – have suggested that the Christian Church effectively *invented* charity. It's true that Christianity enshrined an ideal of altruism, where wealthy people were expected to provide for those less fortunate. But this certainly wasn't a new idea, as is very easily demonstrated, and neither was it exclusively Christian. In the first century, Pliny the Elder wrote, 'For mortals to help mortals is divine' and his nephew, the Younger Pliny, wrote, 'It is a duty to seek out those who are in need and bring them aid.'

We can find the roots of Christian charity in the Jewish tradition (unsurprisingly, as Christianity was an offshoot of Judaism); in the Greek and Roman idea of civic euergetism, where anyone in public office was expected to fund 'good works'; and in the way in which Roman *collegia*, which were rather like guilds or clubs, operated.

The Jewish tradition had a long history of promoting charity, extending welfare to those outside a patriarchal household – the poor, landless and widowed. (This was a general expectation of good kings, too, from Egypt to Mesopotamia – as Francesca Stavrakopoulou pointed out to me.) The Book of Sirach, written by another Jesus, a Jewish scribe, in the second century BCE, and part of the Hebrew Bible, contains these words:

'Lay up thy treasure according to the commandments of the most High, and it shall bring thee more profit than gold. Shut up alms in thy storehouses: and it shall deliver thee from all afflictions. It shall fight for thee against thine enemies better than a mighty shield and strong spear. An honest man is surety for his neighbour: but he that is impudent will forsake him.'

The older Deuteronomy (part of the Torah) also promotes a charitable instinct:

'For the poor shall never cease out of the land: therefore I command thee, saying, Thou shalt open thine hand wide unto thy brother, to thy poor, and to thy needy, in thy land.'

Another concept of charity or philanthropy was embedded in the very fabric of Roman civic life. It flowed from an ancient Greek ideal of the beneficence of rulers – their *philanthropia* proving their right to rule – which grew into a general expectation that wealthier citizens would donate to those less fortunate in cities, going back to at least the third century BCE. Romans not only valued civic pride highly, there was a social contract – a very firm expectation – whereby those holding high public office, as we've seen, were expected to invest in their city, in 'good works'. This system involved gifts being exchanged for certain honours, and went right up to the emperor – whose benefaction and protection would be recognised by cultic honours – and even to the gods. Within a city, both benefactors and beneficiaries gained from this arrangement, with benefactors competing for prestige. The donors could have been motivated by civic pride or by the pursuit of honour, considered a noble virtue in itself, and most of the evidence suggests that benefactors were seeking such honour, though philosophers like Cicero and Seneca encouraged a more altruistic approach. The gifts bought the elite their continued status in society, or for the nouveaux riches, helped them gain the status they hankered after, making these donations effectively obligatory rather than voluntary. And there were sticks as well as carrots, with the very real threat of angry mobs attacking the rich if they were not beneficent enough, also acting, we can imagine, as a fairly powerful motive. Get it right, though, and the rich got enough respect to keep cities functioning in an acceptably harmonious fashion, without too much need for coercive force.

Some monetary gifts were further formalised, with the payment of liturgies becoming a legal requirement for those in high office. These could also be seen as solving a moral problem with voluntary euergetism, making it a civic duty and legal requirement rather than a gift that demanded gratitude; the same arguments about philanthropy versus welfare provided through taxation continue to this day. The city's very survival, its political stability, and the safety and well-being of its citizens, depended on this social commitment from the upper classes: their public munificence, their euergetism. And the evidence suggests that the elite were, generally, generous. When the sons of wealthy families in the provinces moved away to follow high-level administrative careers in Rome, they would spend their provincial wealth in the central city of the Empire, but also continue to send gifts back to their childhood homes, the cities where they had grown up.

The first-century Greek geographer and historian Strabo briefly mentioned how liturgies paid by the wealthy were used to provide state welfare, in a particular example on the island of Rhodes:

'[T]hey wish to take care of their multitude of poor people. Accordingly, the people are supplied with provisions and the needy are supported by the well-to-do, by a certain ancestral custom; and there are certain liturgies that supply provisions, so that at the same time the poor man receives his sustenance and the city does not run short of useful men, and in particular for the manning of the fleets.'

(STRABO, *Geogr.* 14.2.5)

There was a clear link between euergetism and the prestige and power of elite families; this link doesn't mean that charity was necessarily carried out in a cynical or self-serving way, but neither does it imply that the link between social prestige and charitable giving was severed once Christianity took over. As was the case with euergetism, the performance of public benefactions would have cast early Christian communities in a good light – they would have been contributing to civic society, and gaining social capital in a recognised, well-established way.

Just one of the ways in which benefactors could fulfil their euergetic instincts was by supporting organisations called *collegia*. Roman cities were full of *collegia*. These were voluntary membership associations, rather like guilds or clubs. They were very diverse; some were associated with particular religious cults, such as that of Mithras, others with certain professions or trades. Redistributive charitable giving was formalised in the way in which Roman *collegia* operated – they would gather in annual fees and donations and then provide help to their members by providing useful contacts, advocacy – and financial support when necessary. Some offered specific services: the 'worshippers of Diana and Antinous' at Lanuvium, just south of Rome, acted like a savings society, funding funerals for its members. Others, like the Iobacchoi in Athens, devoted to Dionysus, were more like dining clubs; many *collegia* would hold regular dinners for their members, and some also kept reserved seats in stadiums and theatres.

In the late Empire, these societies also seemed to facilitate men from more modest backgrounds rising to higher-level positions in a profession. There were links between Roman statesmen and *collegia*, with individuals in high office championing certain *collegia*, receiving honours from them, and sometimes collaborating with them to raise imperial monuments. *Collegia*, as Pliny noted, were politically important; they may not have been 'official', but as prominent manifestations of community organising, local provincial authorities took notice of them. Through organising themselves into *collegia*, individuals could wield some political power – very much in the way that trade unions operate today. And it worked both ways (as it still does today): *collegia* could throw in their support behind particular political figures, and push their own agendas through their high-level political connections (again, very similar to trade unions).

When Christian churches were first established, they were more like synagogues – unsurprisingly, given the Jewish roots of Christianity. But as the religion spread west, its institutions began to function more and more like those *collegia*, collecting funds and distributing some of that resource to members in times of need (like proto-insurance companies) and building their own monuments in cities, as a frenzy of church-building took off. While some *collegia* seem to have offered very specific services – funding funerals or dinners, for instance – others were more like department stores, providing a range of products; the Church developed along those lines, branching out into many areas of need and many different social networks. Like other *collegia*, Christian churches recruited through these social networks. Most Christian charity would have been focused on fellow Christians, but the network could grow through families and friends, with those in receipt of the Church's charity more likely to join the movement. In terms of recruitment, Christian churches had a low bar for entry – you didn't have to a be a member of a specific profession or trade; you didn't have to be the child of a Christian; and you didn't even have to be a man.

Finance was important in the operations of the early Church – it could hardly be otherwise; it would not have survived as an organisation if it hadn't been financially viable, after all. There are plenty of specific examples of links between churches and finance. Callistus, bishop of Rome in the early third century, began his career as a slave working in a bank set up by another Christian, which provided alms to widows and orphans. Callistus went on to become a deacon, rising up the ranks to become bishop. Christians in Roman cities were clearly well organised and good at this type of business. Over the third and fourth centuries, churches gradually extended their reach, accruing more and more funds from wealthy donors, and from the Roman state, with bishops assuming responsibility for disbursing these funds. And what made the churches particularly politically powerful was that they were well networked more widely across the Empire, with their bishops (their overseers) playing a key role in maintaining communication, and coordinating activity between churches in different cities. And unlike civic officials, bishops were originally chosen by their own Christian communities and so they wielded considerable popular support.

None of this should be surprising – Christianity was a product of the cultural and social milieu of Late Antiquity. It would be much more extraordinary if Christians really had come up with a completely novel concept of charity, with *no* links to longstanding cultural practices, civic institutions, social organisation and mores. Instead, it built on what was already there. As historians Mateusz Fafinski and Jakob Riemenschneider recently put it, 'The arrival of Christianity did not upend this paradigm – if anything, it offered new avenues and possibilities.'

Having said that, as Christianity spread, there were some ways in which euergetism, altruism and giving were starting to look a bit different from what had gone before. But it's very complicated to pick this apart and identify causal relationships, as we're looking at changing concepts of poverty and philanthropy that also went hand-in-hand with the rapid growth of cities. There were also other significant external factors coming into play – we're also looking back at a time when the population of the Empire was ravaged by disease.

In the second and third centuries, as plagues ripped through the Empire, and famine stalked the land, there was a rapidly expanding opportunity for any organisation that made health and welfare part of its business.

Famine, Plague and Salvation

The early Roman Empire flourished in a period of exceptional climate stability, lasting from around 100 BCE to 200 CE. There were fluctuations, of course, but generally, those centuries were warm and stable. But in the third century, as shown by the incredible record of ancient climate captured in the Greenland ice cores, as well as dendrodata (evidence from tree rings), there was significant cooling. After a long period of shrinking, the largest glacier in the Alps, the Great Aletsch glacier, began to grow again. This shift to a colder, drier climate forms the backdrop for the political turbulence of the third century, particularly in the north-western ranges of the Roman Empire. There were also between three and five volcanic eruptions, affecting global climate and impacting on food production – correlating with a historical record of political, military and financial crisis in the latter half of the third century. Egypt, a major source of grain for the Roman Empire, appears to have been less productive in the third century, perhaps due to that climatic downturn.

The Roman Empire's extensive control of resources provided resilience, but even the most resilient system will falter if food production is globally suppressed. The rapid growth of cities, which on the face of it, creates an opportunity for efficient distribution of resources, also led to people being crammed into dense housing – perfect conditions for the spread of disease. In the middle of the third century, the so-called Cyprian plague tore through populations around the Mediterranean. The fact that it's named after the bishop of Carthage, in North Africa, who lived through the epidemic and wrote about it, tells us something about how important and influential the bishops already were by this point.

Historians may be nervous about ascribing political and social changes to environmental factors, but it doesn't seem too much of a stretch to link the timing of the Cyprian plague to that volcanically induced climatic downturn. It came along at a time when systems, including food production, were already stressed, indeed perhaps *because* those systems were already strained. The biblical horsemen of the apocalypse – pestilence, conflict, famine and death – ride together through history. And they certainly did in the third century.

No fewer than twenty-three different writers documented this disease outbreak, six of whom were independent eye-witnesses, including Cyprian of Carthage. Dionysius of Alexandria, another bishop, described epidemics ravaging his city in 249 CE, causing a population crash; 'not one house' was left untouched, he wrote. His letters praised the response of Christians, who resisted the social chaos breaking out around them and stayed to bury the dead. (Whether or not there really was a difference between the way Christians and non-Christians responded to the epidemic, it's clear that this bishop wanted to project that image.)

Two texts of Cyprian's mention the plague: one is a letter to a non-Christian, imploring him not to blame Christians for the epidemic and other ills; the other was probably a sermon, urging his congregation not to 'tremble at the storms' but to stay faithful. Cyprian acknowledges that the disease attacked Christians and heathens equally, which might seem unfair, but says that the suffering was to be welcomed:

> 'This, in short, is the difference between us and others who know not God, that in misfortune they complain and murmur, while adversity does not call us away from the truth of virtue and faith, but strengthens us by its suffering.'

And anyway, even if you die, he says, that's actually a bonus:

> 'This mortality, as it is a plague to Jews and Gentiles, and enemies of Christ, so it is a departure to salvation for God's servants.'

Pontius, a deacon of Cyprian, also wrote about the horrendous mortality suffered during this outbreak of disease. The other three eyewitnesses were non-Christian writers, two of them historians from Athens. Their original texts don't survive, but they're quoted in later works. One recorded the plague lasting for fifteen years; the other mentions five thousand people dying in one day, across Rome and the cities of Greece. While it's difficult to know how reliable specific numbers are, the various sources all agree that this was a terrible epidemic, which spread quickly and carried away a huge swathe of the population.

In the surviving source thought to be a sermon, Cyprian describes in some detail the effects of the disease on the body: fever, dysentery and vomiting, loss of the extremities (possibly to gangrene), weakness, deafness and blindness. Various pathogens have been suggested as the cause, including bubonic plague, bacterial dysentery, meningitis, smallpox and a viral haemorrhagic fever (such as Lassa fever, yellow fever or Ebola); at some point, an answer may emerge from palaeogenomic studies of third-century mass burials. But what's clear from the contemporary historical records is that this disease – among all the other nasty contagions that were in regular circulation – was extraordinarily virulent and terrifying. Chilling archaeological evidence sits alongside the historical accounts. Discoveries of third-century mass graves in Rome and Egypt demonstrate a society struggling to cope with a peak in mortality that outstripped the capacity of normal burial practice.

It's long been recognised that the third century was a time of crisis – or perhaps more accurately, a whole concatenation of crises. With the climate downturn, plague, repeated military coups, rebellions and barbarian invasions across multiple borders, the Empire was dangerously unstable and in danger of fragmenting. The somewhat chaotic succession of rulers during the third century is indicative of much wider problems, including incursions across borders – the Rhine–Danube frontier in the north and the Syrian–Anatolian frontier to the east – as well as financial disruption and military leaders progressively taking over political power from traditional social elites. The Cyprian plague emerged alongside these problems; it may not have caused them on its own, but it would certainly have exacerbated them. There's a synergy between those apocalyptic horsemen.

But alongside all those perturbations – political, military, financial, pathological, societal and demographic – was a cultural transformation that saw a minor cult beginning to expand, not just as a belief system, but as a nexus of political influence and power. The expansion of Christianity is demonstrated in increasing numbers of Christian meeting places, burials and names.

It's important to keep this expansion of Christianity in context – after all, it's estimated that Christians only accounted for 1 or 2 per cent of the population of the Roman Empire by the year 300. But their number and political influence was growing through the third century. And in particular, the political power of the bishops was on the rise. Historians have looked for reasons to explain why this minority religion was gaining such traction – decades before Constantine was said to have nailed his colours to the mast, the *chi-rho* to his military standards. Some have prioritised internal factors: the attraction of the promise of life after death – especially when life was miserable and in danger of being cut short; the charisma of church leaders and martyrs; the apostolic mission and the non-hereditary joinability of the religion. As we have seen, the religion also offered a new sort of community to be part of, with a strong emphasis on charity. Any of these aspects could have made Christianity an attractive choice, *especially* during a pandemic; together, they were proving to be a winning formula. And yet external factors are crucial too, and the disease and conflict rife in the third century seemed, for some, to be the challenge for which Christianity was the solution. As sociologist Joseph Bryant put it, 'the disorder of the times [promoted] a greater receptiveness for [Christianity's] peculiar message of imminent world-destruction and alluring offer of selective deliverance from the impending doom. Promises of welfare support, spiritual empowerment, and eternal salvation . . . likewise commanded greater appeal.'

Christianity was in the right place at the right time. This crisis of the third century erupted at just the moment when this loosely organised movement was growing into a well-organised network. Locally, there were hierarchical command structures under the bishops; more widely, those bishops were maintaining communication with each other across the Empire – through both travel and letter-writing. This level of organisation meant that Christianity could deliver on its promises.

In fact, some later Christians were to remember the plague of Cyprian specifically as a turning point. Gregory Thaumaturgus, 'Gregory the Miracle Worker', was a late-third-century bishop of Neocaesarea (modern Niksar, in Turkey). A hagiography written a century later described how Gregory wanted to see everyone converted 'from idolatry to the faith which saves', and how he scoured the countryside looking for people who were still foolishly adhering to the old religion. Eventually, the entire population 'which had been in the clutch of Greek vanity' was enlightened, and the hagiography says, 'No one should doubt the means by which this change from falsehood to truth came about.' A great pestilence had swept through the city of Neocaesarea, but Gregory, calling on God's help, was able to stop its spread: 'Those who were first saved quickly spread word of his fame . . . Thus all who had been seized by the idols' deception converted to the name of Christ; some were led to the truth by illness and others held faith in Christ as a protection against the plague.' (Christians weren't alone in making a link between health and religion; in 251, the emperor Trebonianus Gallus started to mint coins depicting Apollo on the reverse, accompanied by the legend APOLL SALUTARI, 'health-bringing Apollo' or 'Apollo the Healer'; and a string of subsequent emperors followed suit.) Regardless of whether anyone really believed that Gregory stopped the plague in its tracks, that hagiography tells us something important. It may be a perspective from one corner of the Empire, but it shows that some Christians at least were making that connection between the plague of Cyprian and the spread of their faith.

But others were less sure that Christianity was the answer. In fact, the polytheist Porphyry went as far as to *blame* the rise of Christianity for the plague: for driving away the old gods, including the great healer, Asclepius. And Porphyry wasn't the only one to see Christianity as a threat. Two mid-third-century emperors, Decius and Valerian, fought battles on both military and ideological fronts. They embarked on campaigns designed to bind the citizens of the Empire together – by renovating temples and promoting the worship of traditional Roman and Greek gods. Eventually they turned to winning hearts and minds by coercion. In 249, Decius made public worship of traditional deities compulsory, in a way that meant anyone resisting would be labelled a blasphemer and a subversive. For

those who resisted, retribution was swift: some defiant bishops were executed, some imprisoned, while others fled; and
the punishments extended to ordinary Christians too. Decius
may have felt his policy was working, with reports coming in
that plenty of Christians were recanting their 'atheist' ways,
but his own days were numbered. In 251, he and his eldest son
were killed as they attempted to repel invading Goths in the
Balkans, while his younger son would fall victim to the plague.
The Christians were safe for a while, but just a few short years
later, the emperor Valerian would launch his own attacks on
Christians, forbidding them to gather, and executing resistant
Church leaders. This, too, turned out to be short-lived, however. But the Decian persecution in particular would haunt the
early Christians, bequeathing a powerful narrative of martyr-
dom on the one hand, but also the problem of how to deal with
bishops and others who had pragmatically denied their faith,
on the other.

Despite the persecutions – and perhaps even stimulated by
heroic tales of martyrs, in the long run – Christianity would
continue growing in the later third century. Some people may
well have turned to this new religion hoping that it could save
them, in this life or the next. Others may have been drawn in
through deeply moral and charitable motives, as well as wanting to find a sense of community in a time of great distress.

The Cyprian plague may not be as famous as the Antonine
Plague of the second century or the Justinianic Plague that
emerged in the sixth century – but it would have added to the
existing stresses of the third century, creating an environment
that was even more favourable to the growth of a religion that
was developing into an alternative political system, in its own
right. Whereas Edward Gibbon, in his *Decline and Fall of the*

Roman Empire, laid the blame firmly on internal factors, historians are now once again placing ancient societies in ecological context. It's a reminder of how dependent our civilisations are on the environment; we ignore ecology at our peril. But this is not an either/or question – human societies and cultures are extraordinarily complex. There will always be endogenous and exogenous factors at play (just as there are always genetic and environmental factors at work in biological development and evolution.)

What's abundantly clear is that, when it comes to understanding the rise of Christianity in the third and fourth centuries, this is not a theological question, to be resolved only by scrutinising scripture or hagiographies. The ideas contained in this religious movement had to be appealing, certainly. But this is primarily a social, political and economic question – and a very complex one, involving the destabilising influences of environmental crises as well as the way in which a new form of community, forming around one particular cult, was developing its own economic and political power within the Roman Empire.

Periods of chaos can always be exploited by those ready to spot opportunities – or by people who just happen to be in the right place at the right time. And so it could be argued that an organisation that had made charity part of its raison d'être would be set to gain when more people than ever were in need of help. Would Christianity have gained a foothold without the crisis of the third century? I think it's impossible to know.

Christianity may not have invented charity, but if it did contribute something new, it was to very effectively institutionalise it. The earliest Christians, according to Acts of the Apostles in the New Testament, had pooled all their resources, holding their possessions in common, and selling land and houses in order to give to those in need. Some biblical scholars take this to mean that these believers were creating a communist community; others that it merely acknowledges a need for alms; and some that it's an idealised account, a utopian myth. Theologian Roland Boer has suggested that it harks back to life in village communes before the urbanisation and transition to a slave economy that accompanied first the Greek and then the Roman conquest of the eastern Mediterranean. And although communism of consumption is suggested in Acts, this could not have extended to communism of production – if the rich had released their hold on that, then the pooled resources would soon run out; in order to look after the poor, and sustain the movement, the rich needed to keep making a surplus, and that would have involved, as it did throughout the Roman Empire, slave labour. But regardless of exactly how those early Christian communities organised themselves, as the religion grew, Christians would create their own administrative system. They would take the old concepts of euergetics, the insurance-like function of *collegia* and state welfare provisions and combine them, making something that had been the gift and then the duty of individual donors, and sometimes of the state, into an independent business, catering to a mass market. And Christians would succeed in making charity and welfare into an extremely profitable business indeed – spiritually and materially.

A New Deal: Your Money for Your Afterlife

The expansion of the urban poor meant new opportunities for philanthropy. The concept of euergetism was changing so that, rather than being about the well-being of the entire community, of the city very generally, at least some of that giving was focused on giving to the poor, specifically. And once the Church became involved, altruism came to represent a personally profitable business-like deal – if you were concerned about your immortal soul.

Altruistic acts bring with them an intrinsic feel-good factor – charitable giving is enjoyable for its own sake, and plenty of people in antiquity would have enjoyed that act of giving, of feeling that they were benefiting others less fortunate than themselves. But rich almsgivers could also have expected to gain social capital by their public giving, as well as that more personal satisfaction. There had always been that link between high office, philanthropy and social status in Roman (and earlier, in Greek) society. But Christianity now offered a more clearly defined deal. An almsgiver may have already expected to attract divine favour, which might translate into good fortune – but now there was also something less tangible, while extremely supernaturally, spiritually valuable: divine forgiveness.

Even this was not a completely novel idea; it would have been familiar to Jews. In the book of Daniel, a king is told that he can 'break away from [his] . . . wrongdoings by showing mercy to the poor'. So the idea that you could make up for unjust behaviour in the past, and gain divine favour by being charitable was also very much part of that earlier, Jewish tradition. In the Christian version, though, atonement meant something very important in the long term, the very long term: a better chance of life after death. Not just atonement, then, but salvation – a promise of *post-mortem* persistence. In a couple of his sermons, the fourth- to fifth-century theologian Augustine of Hippo made the transaction very explicit: a rich man could give a poor man something useful – while God could give the rich man something useful, too. (Even salvation and the promise of an afterlife weren't novel ideas; various Greco-Roman mystery religions proposed something similar, though the idea that salvation could be possible for everyone may have been novel, as Christianity was less exclusive.)

For this arrangement – the purchase of salvation through charity – to exist, both wealth and poverty are necessary. All of the benefits of altruism for the donor – political, social, psychological and spiritual – are only possible when that person is in the fortunate position of being able to donate. Philanthropy and euergetism only really work in a society where there is a sufficient and enduring gap between rich and poor.

And here, it's important to recognise that the Christian Church originally began taking hold within the Empire *before* that third-century downturn – not in a time of economic depression, but in a period that was relatively affluent, while strikingly unequal. Cities contained huge disparities between rich and poor; there was a great gulf in social experiences and expectations, and yet, remarkably, they held together. The business model of the Church – of the city, indeed – relied on there being a large enough slice of wealthy donors and patrons to support a reasonably large proportion of the population who were not only poor but effectively economically inactive. And in some ways, you could argue that the poor in society were necessary in order for the rich to feel better about themselves. A letter written by statesman, poet (and later, bishop), Paulinus of Nola, framed it in just that way:

'For, dearly beloved, the all-powerful Lord could have made all men equally rich so that no man would have need of another. But, in his infinite goodness, the merciful and pitying Lord devised a plan so that he might test your intentions in that regard. He made the one man wretched, so that he might recognise the man of mercy. He made him penniless in order to exercise the wealthy.'

(*Ep.* 34.6)

Christian charity, then, was never intended to *solve* the problem of poverty. Social inequality was absolutely necessary: the poor needed alms from the rich to survive; the rich needed the poor to save their souls. And the Church itself needed the poor as well. Poor labourers, who stayed poor, were absolutely essential to the business model. As historian Richard Finn Op has put it, the Church's income, 'which among other things supported almsgiving to the urban destitute, was drawn in part from the hard labour of the rural poor' (whether those labourers were working directly on Church estates or on other landholdings paying taxes to the Church). The Church also needed the poor at the other end of the business – it was, for their sake, after all, that the institution was to be trusted with state funds and individual donations.

So, rather than inventing charity, which it demonstrably did not, it could be argued instead that the real innovations offered by the Christian Church were: to sell redemption at a price; and to invent a new kind of poverty – or at least, a new attitude to it. This was a poverty that was somehow spiritually desirable – for the poor, and spiritually necessary for the rich, who could alleviate their guilt at possessing so much material wealth by giving some of it away. (The idea that wealth could be corrupting wasn't a new one either; the Roman historian Sallust, writing in the first century, saw the desire for money as the root of all manner of social evils; usually such views emanated from the pens of aristocrats who could afford to be so scathing.)

The literature of the Church was carefully generated and curated to justify the social inequality that the whole business model depended on. The poor were to be told that they would reap rewards in heaven. The rich were to be told that the only way they'd get to heaven was by donating to the Church. Of the surviving ninety-six sermons of Leo the Great, bishop of Rome from 440 to his death in 461, forty are focused on charity, as a way of achieving salvation. And Leo was not unusual. Many sermons that have come down to us from Late Antiquity focus on educating the rich on how to give away their resources. The patricians, in their roles as bishops and deacons, lectured their fellow elites on proper almsgiving. Preachers like Cyprian, Augustine, Pelagius and John Chrysostom certainly weren't directing their well-honed rhetoric to the poor of Rome – they were laser-focused on the well-heeled elite, the *honestiores*, whose riches needed to be directed to the Church. They also knew their audience would understand that investments should accrue interest; a small donation would be worth more in the fullness of time, in the next life even. As historian Peter Brown put it: 'With vertiginous incongruity, any Christian gift, from the smallest to the greatest, was thought to be instantly magnified out of all proportion in another world.'

This idea about the sufficiency of relatively modest donations (in comparison to the size of their assets) was convenient too. When wealthy donors took it too far, the system broke down – as with the incredibly rich Melania the Younger, who handed all of her considerable estate over to the Church; she succeeded in rendering herself piously destitute, but also created chaos for the tenants of her land. Of course, she wasn't really destitute at all – she would be sustained by the profits from her family lands, while maintaining her high social position. She was also able to liquidate land assets when the political situation looked dodgy in the west, selling up threatened estates in fifth-century Italy and sinking the proceeds into new monastic foundations – a great investment.

For the Church, the idea of asceticism could be a useful nudge for donors – again, as long it didn't go too far. Some took the messages to heart, and opted for a radical asceticism, but the Church tended to condemn them, with some even executed for their abstemious excesses. As for those inclined to separate themselves from society, the Church offered another solution, in communal monasticism, where individuals could satisfy themselves that they were following an ascetic instinct, living out the communist ideal in Acts, while remaining economically active – generating an income for the Church.

For wealthy donors wanting to relieve themselves of some of the spiritual burden of their worldly riches, the Church provided a convenient opportunity to do this at a remove, without having to meet or even see the poor, diseased and infirm. As economist Morris Silver put it:

'By acting as an intermediary, the Church, very much like a deposit bank, brought together rich donors and poor recipients without donors having to bear the economic and psychic costs of interaction, including the cost of monitoring the essential grateful prayers of the recipients. The Roman Church supplied the affluent with poor people to succor.'

But the Church did more than provide rich donors with a middle-man to pass on their largesse to the deserving poor – it actually went to great lengths to discourage direct almsgiving. Funds were to be donated to the Church and then doled out by the bishop, as he saw fit. Historians have noted that Christian preachers of Late Antiquity made 'the poor' more visible than they'd ever been before, but only really as an abstraction. The job of the preacher was to encourage the wealthy to give alms to the Church, and the bishop was a champion of the poor. But if he kept talking about the poor in an abstract way, not specifying particular groups or levels of needs, that meant he was also free to decide how those funds would be disbursed.

In contrast to the abstract mass of the poor, the great un-washed and underprivileged referred to in sermons, some hagiographies offer glimpses of individuals. Beggars are found, at the roadside or in the city, and are offered alms, adoption or employment – sometimes getting baptised as part of the deal. But even such a glimpse is really less about the plight of the poor beggars themselves, who exist as a mere cipher, and more about an opportunity for the generous bishop to demonstrate his virtue.

Just as the Church protected the rich donor from directly interacting with the poor, the poor were shielded from having to be grateful to the rich; the alms they received now came from the institution, not from a particular philanthropist. By securing funds from the state and private donors and then disbursing them, it wasn't so much the donors who received prestige and thanks for the charitable acts, but the Church. In fact, this was made quite explicit in the Bible; in Acts, God is described as an *agathourgoōn* and Jesus as a *euergetoōn*, both words meaning 'benefactor', while the apostles are also described as performing *euergesia*, benefactions or 'good works'. This language – and the expectation that a 'lord' would offer something back to his dependants, embedded not only in master–slave/servant relations but also in wider systems of patronage – would all have been very familiar to Greek-speaking Romans.

Making the Church – indeed, God, or his representative on earth, the bishop – the source of euergetism in this way was very useful for an institution growing its brand – the social capital that the elite would have gained from their acts of euergetism now accrued to the Church and its bishops. Like traditional pagan priests of old, Christian bishops had all sorts of opportunities to display their own personal status, from sponsoring public buildings and dishing out funds, to acting as judges – their charity was conspicuous, designed to be publicly recognised, and their hagiographers were keen to stress it.

But there were plenty of Christian teachings warning other donors about the danger of personal self-aggrandisement. The generosity of anyone other than the bishop was to be masked and downplayed. The Church had plenty of parables with which to warn rich donors about the spiritually corrosive position of being wealthy and impress upon them the need to get rid of chunks of money without being thanked for it. Though, of course, it's never that straightforward or tidy, and in reality there were plenty of opportunities for big donors to be publicly recognised, including having their names inscribed on various buildings and treasures, or of course going down in history with their own eulogies. This isn't to suggest that there weren't also devout Christians who were genuinely unselfish and altruistic, but simply to point out that the old euergetic deal, where funds could be exchanged for social capital, still existed. There were also plenty of opportunities for actual enrichment too, for less honourable individuals. There's plenty of evidence for embezzlement and the appropriation of Church funds. To pick an example, one fourth-century bishop was charged with melting down church plate and selling Church land for the benefit of himself and his son, as well as taking pillars and marble from Church buildings and using them in his own house.

Our old friend Ambrose, who niftily switched from being Milan's governor to its bishop in the late fourth century, also had to make his apologies for melting down the church plate. He didn't pocket the proceeds himself, however, but used them to pay the Goths to release prisoners; paying ransoms for prisoners was another of the services that the state outsourced to the Church in the fourth century. Ambrose defended his actions, arguing that it was better for a church to use its gold to help the needy; he may just have been pre-empting complaints from the rich donors whose names were probably engraved on the plate and who may have been rather disgruntled at having the public recognition of their contributions so comprehensively erased in this way.

Little by little, the Church would take over administering the redistribution of wealth that was so vital to the functioning of those large Roman cities. With at first the acquiescence, and then the positive support of the Roman state, the Church took on the business of welfare, enabling it to replace earlier charitable institutions that had existed to support the poor in some cities, further developing the idea of euergetism, and leveraging the concept that donations of worldly wealth would be paid back in heavenly riches. With such an attractive spiritual bargain to offer — as well as all the old benefits of euergetism, with the social and political capital that came with it — the Church was proving itself very good at extracting funds from the rich, while giving *just enough* of that income away. The business of the poor — so long as they stayed poor — would make the Church very, very rich indeed.

The Business of Charity

By the third century, the Church was making it its business not only to provide for its own, less fortunate members, but for the needy in cities more generally. A letter written by Cornelius, the bishop of Rome, to Fabius, the bishop of Antioch, in 251, details the numbers of people being supported in Rome, as well as the staff required to provide this service. There were 'over fifteen hundred widows and persons in distress, all of whom the grace and kindness of the Master [the bishop of Rome] nourish'. It's estimated that the Roman Church was spending between half a million to a million *sesterces* on providing for the poor each year. (It's hard to translate this into today's money, but you could have bought two loaves of bread with one *sesterce*.) And in order to supply that nourishment, with his 'grace and kindness', the bishop required the services of 'forty-six presbyters, seven deacons, seven sub-deacons, forty-two acolytes, fifty-two exorcists, readers, and janitors'. And the expanding business of welfare was creating an ever-greater need for a proliferation of ecclesiastical administrative jobs. A century later, there's a record of the Church in Antioch supporting twice the number that Cornelius lists, some three thousand widows and other needy people.

The income of the late Roman Church – upon which its welfare efforts depended – largely derived from donations, particularly of property. Even though there was no official grant from the Roman state, emperors could provide 'gifts', which were much the same thing, and extensive tax breaks helped as well. The Church was also generating its own income through its franchised operations – its monasteries. Church institutions could charge fees (always described as 'gifts') for services, but agriculture was their biggest business.

By the later fifth century, there are surviving accounts revealing some of the details of how the Church was running its
business and spending its money – and from records over ensuing centuries, it looks like there was an accepted, standardised
way of doing that. There seems to have been some distinction
between the income that churches received from their land and
the donations they received. Various letters, starting with one
written by Pope Simplicius, refer to a four-way division of this
income, or a *Quadripartum*. The recipients of these funds are laid
out in a letter from Pope Gelasius to the bishops of Lucania,
in southern Italy: 'All money received should be divided into
four portions: that is, one for the bishop and his household for
the purposes of hospitality and entertainment, a second for
the clergy, a third for the poor, and a fourth for the repair of
churches.' Sixth- and seventh-century sources from Spain refer
instead to a three-way division of funds for the bishop, the
fabric of the church and the clergy – not mentioning the poor.
And there's even some evidence that charitable efforts could
be frowned upon; among documents from the tenth Council
of Toledo in 656, historian Ian Wood discovered criticism of
a particular bishop who'd asked that the proceeds from his
bequest be given to the poor; he'd also apparently freed some
slaves and not adequately compensated the Church. In fourth-
century Syria, it seems a three-way system was also operating;
unlike the later Spanish version, this one did explicitly include
the poor, with the other two-thirds directed to the bishop's
household, and to the wider clergy.

Interestingly – and importantly – very similar arrangements
would be in place during the reign of Constantine's famously
un-Christian nephew, Julian 'the Apostate', in the mid-fourth
century. He replaced civic bishops with pagan priests, one in

each city of the Empire, and provided them with centrally disbursed resources. Records from Galatia in central Anatolia reveal that, of the thousands of measures of wheat and wine that the high priest received, four-fifths were to be charitably passed on. It was same administrative system, the same economic model, with different gods invoked – but always with that overarching dedication to the Empire itself.

Much of the historical evidence of the accounts of the Church derives from disputes where bishops were criticised by clergy for taking more than their fair share. In the late fifth/early sixth century, Pope Gregory (also known as Gregory the Great) wrote to a few bishops to remind them of their responsibility to divide up the *quarta* fairly and make sure the intended recipients did actually receive their shares. Documents from various ecclesiastical councils across the sixth and seventh centuries contain criticisms of bishops for hoarding donations and failing to divide up ecclesiastical income fairly, leaving clergy unpaid and churches falling into ruin. Building new churches and then keeping them in good repair was very expensive – as was the day-to-day running of them and the performance of the religious cult, from provisions for feasts, vellum for the production of books and expensive liturgical vessels, to the truly enormous volumes of oil needed for lighting up churches.

But all the while that these magnificent new buildings were being constructed, there was a veil of obfuscation drawn over them. In a way that harks back to those ideas about celebrity, the splendour of churches was cloaked in the rhetoric of poverty. Nowhere is this more evident than in the story of the martyrdom of St Laurence. This third-century story, recounted in gory detail by the Roman poet Prudentius, describes how the greedy prefect of Rome was effectively auditing the

wealth of the Church, and asked the deacon Laurence (effectively the treasurer) to assemble the treasure. Laurence asks
for three days to do this, promising the prefect that the nave
and colonnades will be glittering with gold and stuffed full of
coins. But when the prefect duly arrives, it turns out that the
deacon has filled the church, not with pecuniary riches, but
with a great mass of the poor and diseased, crying out for alms.
The disappointment of the prefect was fatal to Laurence, who
was literally roasted for this unusual attempt at tax evasion.
The role of the poor in the story is fascinating – their presence
represented a spiritual message, but also a distraction from the
well-hidden treasure of the Church.

It's no wonder the prefect was annoyed, because churches
were not always so coy about demonstrating and displaying
their wealth. A letter written by Paulinus of Nola describes the
setting for a funerary banquet laid on for the poor by a senator
whose wife had died, in the late fourth century. This 'poverty
party' took place in the most prestigious church in Rome, the
basilica of St Peter's, where the humble guests could enjoy
gazing in awe at the glittering architecture: the lofty ceiling,
the gilded apse, the silver altar and the bronze-canopied foun-
tain. It's not clear that Paulinus actually witnessed this event,
but in his letter he imagines it to have been a *laetum spectaculum* – a 'happy spectacle' – and much better than a show in the
arena, as Paulinus points out to his senatorial friend. Paulinus
loved a metaphor – and for him, the splendour of a church
could represent spiritual transfiguration; perhaps that was a
useful thing for wealthy churchgoers to reflect on, when they
attended church only to realise how much of their donations
must have been used to decorate the building rather than feed
the poor. (But then again, the Church also offered a more

permanent and aesthetically pleasing monument to their own euergetism.)

When it came to providing support for the poor and needy, the Church gradually took over civic and imperial systems that were already in place. Though this may never have been a conscious part of the business plan, the Church had at first positioned itself in parallel – in competition, almost – with state welfare, and then moved in to take over the whole operation. In doing so, it would build on existing institutions in cities – sometimes quite literally. In late antique Rome and other cities of the Empire, the Church institutions that were responsible for giving out poor relief were the *dioconiae* or deaconries. In many cases, these existed on the sites of the preceding *stationae annonae* – the places where the imperial grain dole, known as the *cura Annonae,* or *annona civica,* had been given out. The dole was named after the goddess Annona, whose name is related to *annus,* 'year'; she was the personification of the emperor's generosity to his subjects in providing grain – part and parcel of the Imperial Cult. In the third century, the grain dole was replaced with a handout of bread; by the fourth century, the handout included pork and oil. This ration wasn't originally for the poorest in the cities, though; it had started as an emergency measure in the days of the Roman republic, but had then become a regular fixture in imperial cities, widely distributed to registered male citizens, as a sort of universal basic income – for the eligible. By the late fourth century, though, the emperor Valentinian I would make a change that meant the grain dole was more directed more to those in need.

There's plenty of evidence of other higher-level, imperial efforts to combat hunger and poverty as well. For instance, Tiberius subsidised grain merchants in order to keep food prices down during a cost-of-living crisis in the first century, and sent aid to Asia after an earthquake. Trajan and Antoninus Pius are both recorded setting up endowments for destitute children. Towns had funds for the poor, to which the wealthy could donate. Cities also had public physicians who could be consulted without charge, and regular public dinners to help feed their citizens. The evidence also suggests that Asclepieia, the sanatoria dedicated to the healing god Asclepius, had been offering care to the whole spectrum of social classes, including the needy as well as the fee-paying well-heeled, before Christians came along; doctors may have received tax relief specifically in return for this public service. So, welfare was already institutionalised in Roman cities – there were more strategic systems in place than just individual acts of charity. The state had a duty to look after the poor, and the Church would gradually take on more and more of this responsibility – receiving funds and produce from the state and disbursing these resources to the needy.

By the fourth century, Constantine had tasked the bishop of Alexandria with disbursing corn and oil to the poor in the city, while the Church in Constantinople was officially tasked with providing free funerals for the impoverished; bishops were also being asked to take on legal work for the state. There could be fierce competition for this business; at the turn of the fifth century, John Chrysostom found his own authority in Constantinople being threatened by independent monks who'd taken it upon themselves to extract patronage from the rich and use those funds to support their own poor followers. Chrysostom recognised this move to seize political power and preached against it.

By the mid-fifth century, bishops across the Empire had taken on many civic responsibilities, including helping to distribute imperial largesse. A law passed by the emperors Valentinian and Marcian in 451 specifically mentions the churches' responsibility in this – with 'pensions (in produce) . . . given to the holy churches from the public treasury' used to 'provide for the needy'. By the early seventh century, the bishop of Rome had assumed responsibility for feeding Rome, completely replacing the civic *annona* system.

But the balance of the model was constantly shifting. One problem was the volume of deserving poor in the community. But with the Church both providing alms and making a virtue out of poverty, more people could 'choose' to be poor – or at least, rely on the safety net being provided for them. By the late fourth century, senior clerics recognised they were facing a huge challenge in this respect – and advised placing conditions on almsgiving, checking up on debtors. People who travelled to seek alms were told they'd need a letter from their bishop before they could be added to the poor rolls, making them eligible to receive benefits in another city.

Emperors and bishops also recognised the need to combat benefit fraudsters and deter scroungers; able-bodied beggars were, in modern parlance, 'economically inactive' and needed to be encouraged or forced into becoming more productive. There were even useful passages to that effect to be found in the Bible. In Paul's second letter to the Thessalonians (which some theologians doubt was actually written by Paul), the author writes, 'For even when we were with you, this we commanded you: that if any would not work, neither should he eat.'

In the late fourth century, the emperors Gratian, Valentinian and Theodosius had written to the prefect of Rome, ordering that beggars should be physically assessed, and that any found to be able-bodied could be put to work — as slaves — by the informer. Valens and Valentinian attempted various other solutions to combat voluntary poverty, including terminating tax breaks for idle monks and forcing them to become soldiers.

Much later, in 539 CE, the eastern emperor Justinian would issue a decree relating to the able-bodied unemployed, stipulating that they should be sent to look for gainful employment – in the construction industry, in bakeries, in horticulture. If they refused, they were to be expelled from Constantinople. In another decree, he urged magistrates to be firm with idlers, arguing that these strict measures were for their own good, to lift them out of misery. He also presented this rather authoritarian approach as a return to a 'praiseworthy and ancient' model of managing the labour force, one that had apparently only been recently neglected. (Writing during Justinian's reign, Procopius criticised the emperor for his public service cut-backs, which included getting rid of the grain pension traditionally given as food relief to the poor.)

The Church's own messaging had to be very delicately managed – because, while the poor were necessary on the one hand, the system simply couldn't afford for them to become too numerous. The whole business model would fail if too many people suddenly saw poverty as desirable, and wealth as undesirable, after all. Monasteries could accommodate some of those who really took the messages to heart and wanted to give up all their worldly acquisitions. They provided a home for those who'd really bought into that message of pious poverty – or who just wanted a simpler lifestyle. But while some may have been motivated by personal asceticism or a search for spiritual perfection, there were certainly more mundane considerations too. For those lower down the social ladder, monasteries offered a place to work and find food and lodgings; indeed, some may have had very little choice. They were tied to the land before the estates of the landed gentry became monasteries; they were tied to it afterwards. If they were making their own choices, women joining monasteries could have done so to avoid marriage (or remarriage and the division of estates, if they were lucky enough to own land) and childbirth (which was much more dangerous than we often acknowledge). There's also the attraction of communal life, for some, which may have been more important than any spiritual considerations. But whatever the motives for those joining such communities – and of course they would have been many and various – most of the monks and nuns in them would have been economically active, while being relieved of the burden of accumulating wealth for themselves, personally.

The monasteries themselves operated as franchised businesses of the Church. They allowed their founders and owners to manage large agricultural estates, with cheap labour and favourable tax agreements in place, generating a healthy income for the leading local representatives of the Church, as well as growing followers for the faith. Over in the western end of the Empire, the political instability of the fifth century created an opportunity for some, opening up the prospect of acquiring land (as well as losing it, like the unfortunate Paulinus of Pella). Land and agricultural production was the single most important source of wealth, and it was being divided up again and gifted to supporters of rulers, jostling with each other for power. Across the Empire, monasteries, controlling large tracts of land, would take on other administrative functions, receiving funds from rulers and doling them out, often enjoying considerable tax breaks. Aristocratic families could acquire or hang onto land by founding monasteries – and they could obtain significant tax breaks themselves by doing so. (Like cities, they would often lobby kings or emperors directly for tax exemptions.) And under the new Christian regime, such foundations also added to social prestige and increased the likelihood that men might get themselves into sought-after ecclesiastical jobs, including episcopal ones. (In the sixth century, Pope Gregory the Great complained about just this, opining that Gallic aristocrats, in particular, were founding monasteries just to get jobs in the Church.)

Sometimes, as we saw at Landévennec, there seems to have been a relatively straightforward evolution of villa-estate into monastery-estate – though it's hard to know if the same families were involved in running those establishments. It's clearer in Ireland, where entire families were encouraged to give up their land to the Church (while remaining as the managers, with heritable rights, in these 'family monasteries') and appointing their own as head of the Church. But, across Western Europe, monasteries were looking like sensible investments for landowning families – a resilient option, guaranteeing an income and careers in a time of instability. This is not to suggest that some abbots weren't devout or deeply believing in their religion and their mission. Some of them may well have been, but it's worth bearing in mind (in a way that the hagiographies tend to skate over) that their religion and mission happened to be extremely well aligned with their own naked self-interest: their own political status, economic prosperity, and the general preservation of the social elite.

The balance between the simple life and wealth generation, between poverty and riches, was one which the Church had to manage very carefully if it was to survive. It couldn't afford to run itself into the ground. People who became overly, dangerously ascetic and likely to influence too many others, swelling the numbers of the economically inactive, could find themselves branded as heretics. Asceticism was fine, even aesthetically desirable – as long as it didn't drag everyone into self-inflicted poverty, or negatively impact the revenues of the churches and the Church. It was also important for the elite – however beneficent they appeared – to also be conspicuously wealthy; prosperity was still a sign of divine favour, as it always had been.

Theologians came up with ingenious solutions, which allowed wealthy Romans to retain their status (and most of their material assets) while being just charitable *enough*. As Christianity transformed from a minor cult into a mass religion, it had to grow mass appeal. While early adherents were encouraged to give up all their worldly goods, and distance themselves from their families (a common theme in many cults), Christianity would have to become much more lenient if it were to attract more followers. Although some Christians would continue to be ferociously ascetic, most were not. The *idea* of asceticism was more important than following through. Peter Heather points out that the fourth-century Jerome of Stridon had tips for wealthy Romans wanting to live in a 'metaphorical desert', while his own 'personal "desert" consisted of living with a large library of books and scribes . . . close to the main road between Constantinople and Antioch'. Jerome stayed some three years at the monastery in Chalcis, in a 'corner of the desert' – which wasn't so remote that he couldn't get to Antioch and Constantinople to involve himself in ecclesiastical politics when necessary. The business model of the Church really wouldn't have survived long if all its members sought out real, splendid isolation.

It was also problematic if Church officials looked too money-grabbing or focused on commercial interests. Cyprian, the third-century bishop of Carthage, criticised other North African bishops who were amassing wealth through money-lending, and neglecting their congregations. The fact he complains about this lets us know that it was an acknowledged problem. In around 300 CE, the Council of Elvira in Spain stipulated that clergy should limit their business travel. These cautionary reminders were necessary precisely because clergy were drawn from the ranks of society that were most involved in business; they were certainly not the underdogs, and never had been.

In terms of who should be giving, how much and to whom, Christian commentators varied. In the first century, the apostle Paul authored letters that stand as the very first Christian literature, penned before the gospels were written. Paul prioritised Christians, writing to the Galatians, 'As we have therefore opportunity, let us do good unto all men, especially unto them who are of the household of faith.' John Chrysostom, archbishop of Constantinople at the turn of the fourth century, was more magnanimous: 'Need alone is the poor man's worthiness.' But the fourth-century bishop of Caesarea, Basil, seems to have been very targeted about his philanthropy. He's famous for giving away much of his wealth, but he still had enough (of his own and through donations) to build a large proto-hospital, called the Basilias (just so there's no doubt it was him that did it). The timing of this construction is important – it seems to have been built as a response to an egregious famine in Cappadocia around 370 CE. But it seems to have helped Basil's career prospects too, as he was elected to the episcopate in that year (reminding us that even when bishops gave up much of their wealth, as some did, there was precious social and political capital to be gained in exchange). Basil was careful to distinguish the deserving from the undeserving poor, too, writing to a fellow bishop, 'He who gives alms to beggars and the depraved, he throws the money to the dogs.'

The involvement of the Church in all this is fascinating – there are so many layers, so much going on. But if we focus on economics, the institution was doing very well for itself. Building on their *collegium*-like foundations, which had been there from the very beginning, churches became the fulfilment service for the Empire's distribution of state welfare, with state funds allocated to churches for this precise function, and private donations added to the income stream; welfare would prove to be an immensely lucrative area of business. The Church proved itself to be extremely good at capturing this sector of the economy, and the political power that came with it.

Once again, it's too easy to fall into that abstracted language and talk about 'the Church', or even 'churches', and perhaps this helps to exaggerate the changes that were happening, as well as obscure the families that were involved with this business. Yes, there may have been a new concept of poverty, as cities grew in size, and yes, there may have been a more explicit link between philanthropy and salvation once Christianity became involved. But as the churches took over more of the business of redistributing resources, a very similar social contract, commitment and expectations of the elite remained in place – and remained in place when the Empire itself crumbled in the west. Resources from the civic social elite were still being distributed, as they had been under the old practices of euergetism; it's just that the Church had taken over managing that business, and formalised it. And in turn, the civic social elite was becoming embedded in the higher echelons of the Church administration. The elites were still running things, in much the same way as they always had – just now, in a more organised fashion, under the aegis of the Church.

Very often, the spiritual attractions of converting to Christianity are pushed to the fore. The spiritual package was certainly attractive: forgiveness of sins, entry into heaven and eternal life. But these spiritual benefits could come with significant social, political and economic advantages, too. Christians joining the ranks of the episcopacy would receive funding from the state to invest in both infrastructure and salaries, growing the business of the Church – and their own social standing.

So, long before the emperor sat up and took notice of Christianity, the upper classes had seen, understood and employed its potential. Again, this should not be a surprise – Constantine was surrounded by high-ranking people who influenced him; he wasn't a lone, solitary figure, living in some sort of social void. And by the early fourth century, the bishops had acquired considerable political power, and they were organised and networked in a way that priests hadn't been before.

Our travels through fifth- and sixth-century Wales, Cornwall, Brittany and Gaul started with the sons of noble families going off to get educated, making their way into those religious careers which now dovetailed with the high-level secular administrative, legal and military pathways to leadership that their ancestors had enjoyed. We can now see this as a pattern that had developed right across the Empire, taking off in the third century, when the Church had started to look really attractive to those upper, elite echelons of Roman society.

But, in fact, the original momentum had started lower

down the social scale, if not at its lowest, going back to the very early days of the Jesus movement. It's time to rewind the clock and meet one of the most important people in the history of Christianity, whose story provides us with important clues about some of the earliest converts to this religion – who was spreading it and to whom – before it spread into the senatorial ranks.

An Itinerant Tent-Maker

The earliest writings about Christianity come from someone who never met Jesus, but became not only an enthusiastic convert but a committed evangelist. His name was Saul, though he'd later change it to Paul. His letters were copied down the centuries, and the earliest surviving copy of one of them is thought to date to the late second or early third century. Thirteen 'Pauline' epistles are included in the New Testament, of which seven are widely thought to have been written by the man himself, between the late 40s and early 60s of the first century. There are also some biographic details to be found in Acts of the Apostles – although these need to be treated with caution as it's thought that they were written some twenty to sixty years after Paul's death, and are not first-hand accounts. But from these sparse sources, it's at least possible to sketch out the events of his life – and his involvement in the early Jesus movement.

Saul (later Paul) was apparently born and grew up in Tarsus, the capital of Cilicia, which was then part of the Roman province of Syria, now within southern Turkey. There was a thriving Jewish community in Tarsus, one of many around the eastern Mediterranean whose origins can be traced back to a

Jewish diaspora that started in the sixth century BCE, after the siege of Jerusalem, when the Kingdom of Judah was conquered by the Neo-Babylonian king Nebuchadnezzar II. Saul himself was a Jew, named after the first king of Israel. Like his parents, Saul seems to have followed the particularly strict sect of Judaism known as Pharisaism, but the sources also say he was also a Roman citizen.

From his letters, we can see that he'd been educated; at least, he was knowledgeable about Greek literature, quoting Greek poets a few times, though his education would have been essentially Jewish. His parents must have been relatively wealthy – to be able to afford this level of education for their son. The young Saul is said to have continued his studies in Jerusalem, under the tutelage of an eminent rabbi named Gamaliel. Then Saul became a tent-maker, but he may also have been studying to become a rabbi as well; it was quite usual for rabbis to also follow a trade.

From what we read, he appears to have been a zealous, fairly fanatical, young man, demanding a very strict adherence to Judaism. In Jerusalem, he may have worked for the Sanhedrin, effectively the local Jewish government (continuing to operate within the Roman province of Judaea), routing out followers of a radical new Jewish sect. In Acts, he's reported as saying:

'I persecuted the followers of the Way, hounding some to death, arresting both men and women and throwing them in prison. The high priest and the whole council of elders can testify that this is so. For I received letters from them to our Jewish brothers in Damascus, authorizing me to bring the followers of the Way from there to Jerusalem, in chains, to be punished.'

This, then, is Saul as a youngish man, probably in his late twenties, and admitting to a degree of religious fanaticism that saw him hunting out heretics, killing some and handing others over to be imprisoned. The 'Way' he was describing is none other than the sect started, within Judaism, by followers of Jesus, which would eventually become known as Christianity.

Jesus himself had been executed, but he'd inspired a growing movement. It was gaining adherents in Jerusalem, and was spreading quickly around the eastern Mediterranean, perhaps initially carried by Jewish pilgrims and merchants, who would regularly travel to and from the holy city for religious festivals. But the followers of Jesus were also getting into trouble with the Jewish authorities, according to Acts, which describes how the apostles were rounded up and thrown in jail, facing a sentence of death; but Gamaliel urged restraint, and the apostles were flogged, then released – having been told to stop talking about Jesus.

But they didn't, and the movement kept growing to the point that Acts tells us the twelve men needed to engage a bigger team to look after administrative duties such as distributing food to members. One of the seven men appointed to this role was a man called Stephen, who got himself into trouble for preaching their heretical ideas at synagogues for Greek-speaking Jews in Jerusalem – including those who had come from 'Cyrene, Alexandria, Cilicia, and the province of Asia'.

According to Acts, Stephen's blasphemy provoked outrage, and he was arrested. He appeared before the Sanhedrin where he delivered a long speech about Abraham, Moses, King David and Solomon – and it all seemed to be going so well up until the point Stephen told the council of elders that they were 'stubborn . . . heathen at heart and deaf to the truth' – and that they had murdered the Messiah. He ended by proclaiming, 'Look, I see the heavens opened and the Son of Man standing in the place of honour at God's right hand!'

It was too much for the Sanhedrin. Stephen was dragged out of the city and stoned to death. Holding the coats of Stephen's attackers, watching them as they threw stones, was a certain young man by the name of Saul. The attack was just the beginning of a wider persecution, and Saul threw himself into the task of rooting out these Jewish heretics, following a movement that had only been going a few years at most.

But then Acts records that Paul underwent what seems to have been an astonishingly radical change: he switched from being a fanatical traditionalist to being a staunch supporter of the new sect – whose adherents he'd only recently been rounding up for punishment. This conversion is often presented as an astounding, even confounding, turnaround. But in some ways, perhaps it's not too surprising, given his behaviour up to this point in the story. The phenomenon of political radicals switching from one extreme to the other – from left-wing to right-wing extremism, for example – is well known. Social psychology helps us to understand why individuals might behave in this way, construing it as a choice that can enhance social status. As a Pharisee, a member of an established Jewish sect, Saul would have been a small fish in a big pond. The switch to this new breakaway sect would make him a prominent figure in a small but rapidly growing movement – one which he could help to shape. And the story Saul told about his conversion contained a familiar, dramatic trope: a divine vision.

He was making his way to Damascus in Syria, with a group of men who may have been servants or underlings of some kind. He was heading there to round up heretical followers of the Jesus movement – what else – when he experienced the original Damascene conversion, precipitated by a blinding, guilt-inducing vision of Jesus. Saul suddenly became a passionate evangelist for the Jesus movement, a few years after Jesus himself had been executed. Although he never met Jesus, Saul of Tarsus claimed that having had his vision meant that he had been personally called to become an apostle, like the original twelve who had followed and known Jesus while he was alive. The vision was helpful in explaining his sudden *volte-face*, but also to signal divine favour; Saul wanted it to be known that he had been chosen.

The Acts of the Apostles describes Saul continuing on to Damascus after his conversion, recovering his eyesight, and preaching about Jesus in Jewish synagogues. This eventually led to a death threat from other Jews, and Saul fled the city. In Galatians, Saul mentioned that he then went to Arabia before going back to Jerusalem. There, he apparently met up with a member of the Jesus movement called Barnabas, a Hellenised Jew from Cyprus, who took him to see the proponents of the movement, the apostles Peter and James (Jesus's brother). It seems these leaders of the Jesus Movement – who were said to have come from rural Galilee – were now very much city-based, having set themselves up in Jerusalem. But Saul seems to have made himself unpopular and didn't stay with them – instead it seems he returned to his home city of Tarsus. Then there's a gap of around a decade where we don't have any information on what Saul was up to.

Meanwhile, an important shift in strategy for the Jesus movement is suggested in Acts of the Apostles. Facing a threat from the Jewish authorities in Jerusalem, many followers of the Jesus movement dispersed from the city, around the eastern

Mediterranean. Some fled to Cyprus; others ended up in the capital of the Roman province of Syria, Antioch.

It's really important to remember that, this early on, the Jesus movement was very much a cult *within Judaism* – combining Jewish tradition, confused memories and end-of-the-world expectations. Its followers were still Jews – they were still worshipping at Jewish synagogues, still celebrating Jewish festivals. Converts were admitted into the community through ritual bathing – which was again something that had its roots in Jewish purification rituals. The other important ritual was a meal – bringing the community together – something shared by many ancient religions. Feasting at funerals was also a staple of Jewish, Greek and Roman cultures; for the Jesus movement, this ritual meal would assume a new meaning, becoming associated with the death of Christ. Gradually, the Jesus movement would evolve into something distinct from its 'parent' religion, though drawing on many of the same sacred texts. And it would also begin to attract non-Jews, particularly in Antioch, as described in Acts of the Apostles. Jewish followers – including the apostles Peter and James, Jesus's own brother – apparently initially disapproved. But Peter is then said to have had a dream that helps to explain why he changed his mind about the exclusivity of the movement.

According to Acts, a Roman army officer by the name of Cornelius, who is described as a 'captain of the Italian regiment' and a 'devout, God-fearing man', summoned the apostle Peter to meet him in Caesarea. Peter seems to have been unsure about whether he should go ahead and meet this non-Jewish soldier. But he had a dream in which various animals were being let down from the sky in a large sheet, and he was instructed by a disembodied voice to kill and eat them. He baulked at the suggestion, as the animals were ritually impure, but the voice insisted, 'Do not call something unclean if God has made it clean.' Peter reportedly interpreted this dream as meaning that non-Jews could be initiated into the Jesus movement. And so he agreed to meet Cornelius, ending up baptising him, and other non-Jews. This means – according to Acts – that the very first non-Jewish member of the Jesus movement to be named in the Bible was a high-ranking Roman army officer. And this was an important moment for the Jesus movement, with their chief apostle, Peter, deciding that non-Jews could now, legitimately, become members. (Again, we should reflect on the fact that Acts was written a lot later than the events it purports to describe – later than the gospels, which themselves post date Paul's letters. Acts is presenting a story which is pro-Roman and – despite the fact it's about a new Jewish sect – quite anti-Jewish).

Acts suggests that other members of the Jesus movement, who had fled to Antioch in particular after Stephen's death, had also begun to preach to non-Jews and were attracting converts. Hearing of this, the apostles sent Barnabas to Antioch. This sounds as though the apostles in Jerusalem perceived a need to stay ahead of the game, to make sure the idea didn't run away from them. Presumably it would have been important for the movement to stay connected, to send out emissaries like this, in an effort at keeping the nascent communities of the Jesus movement joined up – and to keep some funds flowing back to the hub in Jerusalem.

After preaching to non-Jewish potential converts, Barnabas is then said to have gone to Tarsus to track down Saul and bring him to Antioch too. And Acts claims, 'It was at Antioch that the believers were first called Christians.' The Jesus movement now had a name. After a year preaching in Antioch, Barnabas and Paul returned to Jerusalem, with the donations they'd collected (having apparently been told by another preacher from Jerusalem that a famine was on its way).

Saul and Barnabas then travelled together to the coast of Anatolia and on to Cyprus, preaching in the synagogues. Reaching Paphos, Acts of the Apostles says they were invited to meet the Roman governor of the island, Sergius Paulus. It looks very much like Barnabas – originally from Cyprus himself – had friends in high places, although Acts doesn't provide any more details in that vein. But it seems that, right from these very early days, the movement was focused on growing its membership through targeting affluent sponsors and community leaders; not the plebeians, but people with considerable political clout – and wealth.

Saul seems to have made an impression on Sergius. The story in Acts is that Saul blinded a 'sorcerer' in his household and that Sergius was so impressed (or perhaps scared?) that he promptly converted to Christianity. It is such a curious story. The facts are so sparse (if they are facts, indeed), leaving us wondering why on earth a Roman governor would sign up so readily to this strange new Jewish sect that was spreading out of Judaea. This Greek-speaking, Jewish, Roman citizen turns up at your house with a friend, strikes someone blind and persuades you to join their cult? What exactly was in it for this Roman governor? Did he feel threatened somehow, or have something to gain? There's clearly a lot missing from the story. But whether or not any of it happened, it's included in Acts for a reason – and surely that's all about emphasising Saul's high-status connections.

It's at this point that Acts of the Apostles switches from calling Saul 'Saul' to 'Paul'. Writing a few centuries later, St

Jerome explains this by suggesting that Saul had taken on the family name of Sergius Paulus. If that was true, this means that Saul – now Paul – was making an explicit link, affiliating himself with an elite Roman family. (In case that sounds odd, it was quite standard within the Roman system of patronage.) Another possibility is that Saul's Latin name, Paulus, derived from earlier history of patronage associated with the Roman citizenship he seems to have inherited. Either way, it seems it hadn't taken long for Christianity to reach the upper echelons of Roman society. Acts describes Barnabas and Paul continuing on their travels, with the governor Sergius's backing, as their patron, heading off to visit members of the Roman governor's family in Anatolia.

Barnabas and Paul would go on to visit several cities in Anatolia, according to Acts, focusing on preaching to non-Jews (or 'gentiles'). They returned to Antioch and met with Peter, who was visiting from Jerusalem. After this, Barnabas disappears from history, his light eclipsed by his companion. Paul, we know from Acts and his own letters, would go from city to city around the eastern Mediterranean and Aegean: to Philippi, Thessaloniki, Athens, Corinth and Ephesus. (And there's a theme developing through all of this, with the suggestion that non-Jews were more receptive to Paul's preaching than Jews; the seeds of antisemitism were being sown.)

Paul persisted with his preaching, confronting unreceptive Jewish audiences and annoying the Roman authorities. In Corinth, he found himself on trial for heresy. In May 2024, I travelled to Corinth and met up with archaeologist Socrates Koursoumis, who for many years had been curator of the wonderful open-air museum created by the archaeological excavations of the ancient city. Socrates showed me around the site, and was particularly keen to show me the rostrum (βήμα or *bēma* in Greek) of the Roman forum, which would have been used for public trials – and probably for the trial of Paul around 50 CE. According to Acts, Paul had been accused by the Jewish community of preaching heresy – saying that Jesus was the Messiah – and causing trouble. Paul was found innocent at his trial. 'The Roman administration of Corinth didn't want to get involved in a religious conflict and had no reason for convicting him,' Socrates explained.

Paul also now had competition: there were apparently several adept and charismatic Christian preachers who were attracting followers around this time. Among those preachers was the intellectually minded Apollos, who was infusing his own version of Christianity with a healthy dose of Platonism, a combination which had proved popular in Corinth. Apollos, it's been suggested, may have been mentored by the Jewish philosopher Philo of Alexandria, who sought to create a mystical synthesis of ancient Greek philosophy and Judaism; he'd written, 'Who is Plato but Moses speaking Greek?' Apollos – rather than Paul – may have been the author of the letter to the Hebrews. And there's a hint that Paul may have viewed Apollos as a competitor. When Paul wrote his first letter to 'the Corinthians' – or more accurately, to the Christians in Corinth, thought to number somewhere between 40 and 100 – he exhorted them to see themselves as united, whether they were following him, Apollos, another preacher called Cephas, or Christ. It was an early acknowledgement that schisms would be detrimental to the growth of the cult; it was also an indication that Paul, however disgruntled he might have been about the competition represented by other, potentially more eloquent, preachers, had decided it was best to team up. Still, he couldn't quite resist suggesting his superiority – or at least, his priority – to Apollos: 'I have planted, Apollos watered.'

It's quite extraordinary to read Paul's letters today – and to imagine him dictating them to his scribe. We can still read these words, which have been translated and reproduced so many times – and then shared among audiences much larger than those of any cult leader or social media influencer today. Paul's letters demonstrate his upper-class education, from the breadth of vocabulary to the philosophical terms and rhetorical style that he employs, and he also quotes from the Jewish scriptures.

The first letter to the Corinthians has been carefully preserved and passed down, and when you read it in its entirety, it seems quite astonishingly rambling and repetitive. Paul also comes across as quite anti-intellectual (in a way that seems shockingly familiar, in today's culture where it often seems that experts and scientists can be too easily brushed aside by the weight of opinion on social media). Paul keeps returning to this theme: that human wisdom is, in fact, foolishness:

> 'But God hath chosen the foolish things of the world to confound the wise . . .'
> '. . . your faith should not stand in the wisdom of men, but in the power of God.'
> 'If any man among you seemeth to be wise in this world, let him become a fool, that he may be wise. For the wisdom of this world is foolishness with God.'

Paul verbally attacked his opponents: the Jews, so wary of his heresies (which is very complicated, as he still saw himself as a Jew), and the Greeks, so learned in their philosophy, and so scathing of him. It's an interesting strategy – perhaps it's a pre-emptive strike against those who might criticise his rhetoric; he's getting his defence in early by saying that he doesn't even respect their expertise or their knowledge.

In the same letter, to the Corinthian Christians, Paul advised them to settle their disputes, not in the official law courts, but among themselves. Charles Freeman describes Paul 'developing a vision of a church as a stable and self-governing community': a society within a society. There was a Jewish model to follow here, if Christianity were to develop its own administrative and legal system – similar to the governance of the Sanhedrins, the Jewish councils, in Judaea.

After emphasising the promise of Christianity – the res-urrection of the dead – Paul returns to the very important question of funding the growing Church: the collection 'for the saints' or 'for the Lord's people'. He asks the Corinthians to do the same thing he's asked the Galatians to do: to set aside a donation on the first day of each week, so it's all ready and waiting for him when he gets to them. Then he moves swiftly on, describing his plans for future travel and promising to visit Corinth in the not-too-distant future, ending with salutations.

In his second letter to the Corinthians, Paul apologises for not making it back to see them, saying he had hoped to extend the benefit of his presence to them twice, but adversities pre-vented him from fulfilling his promise. He goes on to write about earthly tents and heavenly houses, the Christian message of reconciliation, the day of salvation (which is now), the danger of idols and of associating with unbelievers, and then he's back to the subject of finances, with a motivating tale about just how generous the Macedonian churches were, with people donating as much they were able, and then some more – and he urges the

Corinthians to follow suit. He tells them he's sending a man called Titus to collect their donation, and that they should show him 'the proof of [their] love'. Fundraising seems to have been a crucial part of his mission.

Another epistle, also thought to be an authentic letter from Paul, is addressed to the Philippians, whom he thanks for sending gifts when he was in need, adding that he was especially grateful because they were the only church who supported him in this way. And he signs off, saying, 'All God's people here send you greetings, especially those who belong to Caesar's household.' He's clearly appealing to people who think of themselves as good Roman citizens.

Paul returned to Jerusalem in around 58 CE, presumably bringing back some of the cash he'd collected from various Christian communities on his travels. Judaea at the time was troubled by increasing unrest as grumbles about nationalism and independence were growing into a roar – a roar which would erupt into a rebellion in 66, but by that time, Paul would have left the province.

Paul was apparently met with suspicion by the Christians in Jerusalem: James, the brother of Jesus, and his followers. He acceded to a purification ritual in the synagogue, but his preaching soon stirred up trouble. He was hauled up before the council of the elders, the Sanhedrin, but they were divided and didn't know what to do with him. His case was referred to the Roman court in Caesarea – and when he got there, Paul asked to be judged by the emperor himself. (This wasn't his first brush with the courts – it wasn't just in Corinth that he'd ended up in trouble; he'd been dragged before the courts in virtually every city he visited; his legal education would have stood him in good stead.) The voyage is described in the Act of the Apostles, culminating with Paul being imprisoned in Rome. He may have died in prison – although other sources suggest he might have survived to travel to Spain, then back to Rome, before he died. It seems like an odd ending to his story – unsatisfying, inconclusive, lacking resolution. But in some ways, perhaps there's more of a ring of truth to that, with such a complex character as Paul.

Paul's writings (including those misattributed to him) would go on to become massively influential (though not with immediate effect). He boiled Christianity down to a simple message, but also introduced a number of problematic views at the same time – the seeds of antisemitism, misogyny, and strict views on sex and sexuality – that would become set in stone. (We have to remember that this was a patriarchal society, a hierarchical society – so some of this is just about reinforcing middle-class norms at the time, especially when it came to the superiority of men.) Brought together as an oeuvre, his letters include spiritual guidance but also more mundane advice on how Christians should live their lives and structure their society: sex was best avoided; homosexuality was sinful; women were inferior; Jews were problematic; rational thought and wisdom were overrated.

What's really extraordinary, given his later prominence, is that Paul's immediate influence actually seems to have been very slight. His first-century mission to spread Christianity to the non-Jewish population of various cities in the eastern Mediterranean left virtually no trace, beyond his own letters. In fact, that goes for the other early missionaries too, to the extent you could even judge these missions to have failed in creating any lasting impact. (There's no archaeological trace of Paul, but that's unsurprising – there's no archaeological trace of Christianity at all, this early.) As Freeman notes, none of the early centres of Christianity – in Jerusalem, Antioch, Alexandria and Rome – were actually established by Paul. And later on, in the fourth century, when churches claimed their foundations from one early saint or another, Paul was conspicuously absent. His writings may have been viewed as too contentious and easily misinterpreted. But then, two fourth-century writers would resurrect Paul's words, polishing up his reputation and promoting his particular brand of Christianity: John Chrysostom and Augustine of Hippo. Perhaps they recognised the power of Paul's relatively simple message. Would the name of Jesus have become so well known had it not been for Paul? Would Paul's name be so well known if it were not for the golden-mouthed John or the bishop of Hippo? I don't think we'll ever know.

Paul's version of Christianity was alluringly simple. Modern politicians know the power of a slimmed-down message, a three-word slogan; and that marketing technique already existed two thousand years ago. Paul didn't say very much at all about Jesus's life and teachings. Rather conveniently – as Paul never met Jesus in person – his point of focus was not so much to be found in biographic details, but in the short, brutal, gory tale of Jesus's death – and resurrection.

Paul's Christianity drew very much on his own particular Jewish background as a Pharisee; resurrection of the dead was a core belief in Pharisaism. It was a belief that may have had a literary origin, or at least, an origin in a misinterpretation of literature, where scriptural passages originally intended as metaphors for restoration of nationhood became read literally, as describing the physical resurrection of dead bodies. No matter where it came from, the similarity between Pharisaic and Christian beliefs also reminds us that – however dramatic Paul's conversion may seem to be – he was still a Jew. He'd switched from one established Jewish tradition to a newly minted one. A new one that, perhaps allowed him to be, at last, a big fish in a small pond. But that pond could become an ocean.

And Paul's framing of Christianity was helpful – explaining how Jesus's untimely death had actually been part of the plan all along. For Paul, Jesus had most definitely been something more than just another Jewish prophet, dying an unfortunate death – he was something different, quasi-divine – though subordinate to God. Paul would also introduce a certain term that would catch on: he used the epithet *Christos*, 'the anointed one', no fewer than 270 times in his letters. Once picked up by Chrysostom and Augustine, his words would have a lasting impact – through what became the religion of the literate elite of the Empire.

Importantly, Paul had also promoted an idea that under-pinned the future success of Christianity: that it was *not just for Jews*. He opened the market up. He'd also sown the seeds of the movement as a financially viable operation – collecting donations on a regular basis and funnelling those funds back to the centre. He often ended a letter by reminding people to pay into the collection – and he'd sought out wealthy patrons right from the start.

The Middling Sort

The fourth-century Christian writers John Chrysostom and Augustine of Hippo both commented on the lowly origins of their faith, emerging as a minor cult among Jewish fishermen and tent-makers. Augustine described the faith emerging among 'plebeians, paupers, illiterates, and fishermen'. But were they overplaying it?

It's unclear how well-off the first generation of disciples had been. Several were fishermen, we're told, which seems like a humble enough occupation. But then again, we shouldn't imagine them sitting on jetties, throwing a net into the sea, hoping to catch enough for dinner. James and John appear to have worked in a family business that not only owned boats but also hired others in to help. Then there was Matthew (also called Levi), who was a tax-collector, an educated professional. They're not the social elite – but neither are they in its lowest echelons.

And as we've noted, Paul was a tent-maker, and this job wasn't perhaps as humble an occupation as it sounds. Tarsus was a famous textile-producing centre, specialising in the production of heavy cloth made from goat hair, called *cilicium* (taking its name from the region Cilicia, just as angora wool would take its name from Ankyra – modern Ankara). Tent-making was a lucrative business in the first century; tents – as well as sails and other textile products – were in great demand, furnishing everyone from wealthy travellers to the Roman military. (It could be that Saul's Roman citizenship was inherited from his father or grandfather, who had been honoured in this way after providing an act of service related to their tent-making business.) It's likely that Paul followed his father into the family business, as was the norm, and that his family were relatively affluent.

It seems that Paul continued working as he made his way around the cities of the eastern Mediterranean. Paul mentions 'labouring night and day' in one letter and 'working with our own hands' in another – which suggests that he may have been forced to undertake manual labour himself at times, rather than just managing the work of others. It could also be that Paul was dissembling here – or poetically referring to the demands of the evangelising work he was undertaking. But perhaps it's a bit of both. Some historians have suggested that he was evangelising to the professional communities that he was engaging with in the cities he visited; that the tent-making and proselytising went hand-in-hand.

In Acts, it's noted that Paul was a Roman citizen – a fairly rare privilege at the time in the eastern Mediterranean, where perhaps only one in a hundred men would have held citizenship; it was a symbol of status and wealth. Paul inherited this citizenship, so this suggests his family was important. He was far from being a plebeian.

Some historians have expressed doubt about Paul's Roman citizenship, suggesting that this claim in Acts was just invented in an attempt to legitimise Christianity. Now, it's true that Paul doesn't mention his citizenship in his epistles – but perhaps he wouldn't have been keen to parade his elite status (although on the other hand, he does boast of his noble and honourable origins). But it is certainly the case that when he was arrested in Jerusalem, he seems to have enjoyed preferential treatment, travelling under guard to Caesarea, to meet the Roman governor, Felix. Acts mentions that Felix expected Paul to offer him a bribe; the governor obviously thought Paul was a man of some financial means. And Paul then stayed with this Felix for two years, under house arrest, rather than being held in prison. Rather than being prosecuted locally by a Jewish court, it seems that Paul successfully argued that he should be tried as a Roman – as he then travelled, under guard again, to Rome, to have his case tried by Caesar. It's very unlikely Paul would have been treated like this had he not been a Roman citizen. And while in Rome, awaiting trial, Paul rented a large house, occupying a whole block or insula.

Paul was also clearly able to travel extensively around the eastern Mediterranean, with company – and this wouldn't have been cheap. He had the means to buy parchment and ink for his letters, which were most likely taken down by a scribe. Paul's letters also contain clues that he enjoyed a certain standard of life, and indeed, found it hard to imagine what life was like for those less fortunate. It would have been very hard for a poor individual, man or woman, to support themselves without a spouse. And yet Paul was advocating for single men and widowed women to *choose* to stay single. That would have been much easier for an aristocrat – it was a luxurious choice. And Paul also seemed to have been in the fortunate position of being able on occasion to refuse gifts, which itself would have been a signal of high social status. There's a strong flavour of Stoicism to some of Paul's pronouncements about wealth – that spiritual wealth outweighs material wealth; that good deeds are worth more than riches. This idea of hostility to wealth is also there in the writings of Philo of Alexandria – hailed as the most prominent Jewish thinker in Alexandria. And in fact, it's a common trope, found in many Near Eastern sources – almost all of them issuing from aristocrats. (As Plato noted, an indifference to wealth was a characteristic of those who'd inherited their fortunes.) Paul's letters are also littered with legal and accounting references, the language of business. When Paul writes to the Romans of 'storing up wrath for yourself in the day of wrath', the word often translated as 'storing' is actually *thēaurizeis*, a book-keeping term for adding debt to a ledger. He writes to the Philippians, 'Not that I desire your gifts; what I desire is that more be credited to your account.' He uses financial terms again in Colossians, when he says, 'He forgave us all our sins, having cancelled the charge of our legal indebtedness' — a loan is converted into a gift.

It's impossible to conclude that Paul was anything other than a well-educated, prosperous man, accustomed to business. He must have made significant personal, financial sacrifices in the pursuit of his evangelical work, but although some focus on his piety in this respect, there's little difference between this and traditional euergetism, where an individual's wealth could be exchanged for social capital. From early on in his career, Paul had sought to be noticed, from the work he did for the Sanhedrin, seeking out the heretics of the Jesus movement for punishment — to his pursuits within that movement. He clearly wanted to be noticed by the *right people* — he was certainly not preaching to plebeians, paupers and illiterates.

As Paul travelled from one important city to another, he'd sought the support of many people, all of them wealthy to some degree, from affluent business people to the elite, governing aristocracy. There was Sergius Paulus, the governor of Cyprus, of course, but Paul also seems to have had powerful friends in Ephesus, and in Corinth, Paul would find a convert in Erastus, a funder of public works in the city. But other supporters and patrons seem to have come from a slightly lower echelon of Roman society, the stratum that we might now refer to as middle class. In Philippi, near Thessaloniki in Macedonia, Paul enjoyed the hospitality of a woman called Lydia, having persuaded her to convert to Christianity; she was clearly a woman of some means — a 'dealer in purple cloth' no less — and she invited Paul and his companions to stay at her home. Paul also mentioned that Phoebe, deacon of the church in Cenchreae, near Corinth, 'was a patron of many, even of me myself'. And, while in Corinth, he stayed with Justus, who lived right next door to the synagogue – a prime location, right in the civic centre. He also stayed with a Greek-speaking Jewish couple (who'd left Rome after Claudius had ordered the expulsion of Jews from the city) called Aquila and Priscilla, who were also in the tent-making business. Socrates suggested to me that Paul may have planned his itinerary around different cities in order to ply his trade at well-attended, regular festivals. He may have timed his stay in Corinth to coincide with the Caesarean Games – a huge event that would have brought people flooding into the city. There would have been business opportunities with plenty of people at the festival needing tents, as well as the opportunity to communicate with people who had converged on the city from a wide area – and who could then carry the ideas preached by Paul home with them.

Some more recent historians have echoed Augustine of Hippo, suggesting that Christianity largely started to spread within the ranks of the dispossessed and disenfranchised, among people 'left behind' – people who had not enjoyed the benefits of progress. But that doesn't match up with the historical evidence, which reveals that Christianity wasn't spreading primarily within the lowest echelons of society. Early adopters were to be found, not among the rural, or even the urban, poor of the Empire – but among the urban middle and upper classes. Right from the start of his own Christian career, we can see how Paul had made it his business to reach out to well-heeled, literate members of Greco-Roman society in prominent cities of the eastern Mediterranean, and then kept in contact with them through letter-writing.

So the idea that early Christianity was the preserve of

the poor is a bit of an affectation, another manifestation of the myth of asceticism, perhaps, with a dash of Cinderella rags-to-riches romanticism. Apostles like Paul were clearly well-off and well educated, attracting support from well-off and well-educated patrons. Indeed, the cult wouldn't have got very far in the Roman world had it not been well resourced from the start; its success depended on support from rhetorically trained and financially competent urbanites. The idea spread through trade networks, into the cities of the Roman Empire, as an essentially urban phenomenon. From the cities, Christianity *then* made its way out into the countryside – not the other way round.

Having taken root in the eastern Mediterranean, and in Rome itself, Christianity was spreading to other cities in the second century. Christians were developing a more separate sense of identity – cleaving their belief system and practices from those of Judaism. And although there was never a systematic programme of persecution, the refusal of some Christians to undertake traditional, imperial religious rites was already bringing them into direct conflict with the Roman authorities, with some particularly horrific public executions of martyrs. Christian communities were appointing people to the roles of presbyters and deacons, as shown by the earliest surviving Church order, the *Didache*. By the end of the second century, Christianity had spread far and wide through the cities of the Empire, though it was still very much a minority belief, a subculture. In the city of Carthage in North Africa, there was someone who would read Paul's letters, as an adult, and convert to the religion – adding his own literary style and rhetorical flair to the movement. His writings would become enormously influential. His name was Tertullian.

We know frustratingly little about Tertullian's own life – he didn't leave many clues. He was clearly a well-educated man and may have trained in law. His lasting legacy would come not only from the fact that he wrote so eloquently, but that he was writing in Latin rather than Greek (though he clearly read Greek too); he's been called 'the first theologian of the west'. We can also understand why Christianity – as a text-based religion – would have appealed to someone like Tertullian, and he helped it to develop into an even more literary form, fairly firmly embedded in the philosophical traditions of the literate social elite.

Tertullian described persecutions against Christians and called for religious tolerance – although he also thought that the creation of martyrs had raised the profile of the faith and been somewhat helpful to its spread. Some accounts of martyr-dom were undoubtedly exaggerated, but there's no doubt that hundreds of early Christians were executed for their dogged adherence to their beliefs. However, it's important to realise that persecution was sporadic and local, rather than a contin-uous and Empire-wide phenomenon.

Tertullian rejected some philosophical ideas but brought plenty of classical Stoicism into his version of Christianity. He's famous for saying *credibile est quia ineptum est* – 'it is credible because it's absurd' – which seems to echo some of Paul's more anti-intellectual expressions, though some commentators have argued that he was a rationalist at heart. (He does bring appar-ently rational argument to bear on points of faith, certainly, but as a rhetorical device.) Tertullian was critical of the Roman Empire in some ways, but he saw no necessary conflict between it and Christianity; in fact, he advocated Christians praying for the life of the emperor and the stability of the empire:

'Without ceasing, for all our emperors we offer prayer. We pray for life prolonged; for security to the empire; for protection to the imperial house; for brave armies, a faithful senate, a virtuous people, the world at rest, whatever, as man or Cæsar, an emperor would wish . . . The Scripture says, "Pray for kings, and rulers, and powers, that all may be peace with you."'

Tertullian suggested that praying 'for the complete stability of the empire, and for Roman interests in general' was sensible in order to avoid 'a mighty shock impending over the whole earth'.

There's also something on the divine right of rulers – or rather, the fact that they must have been divinely chosen to *be* rulers: 'on valid grounds I might say Caesar is more ours than yours, for our God has appointed him.' It's ingenious – he's invoking and repurposing the ancient divine right to rule that went right back to Hellenistic ideas of kingship, and probably earlier still, and using it to argue that Christianity was more compatible with Roman-ness than some might assume. Yet Tertullian also wrote, 'Never will I call the emperor God,' then explained that this actually means he respects the emperor's position of authority even more – because only a man can be an emperor, and his role is God's gift; so it's in the emperor's interest as well to acknowledge the superiority of God. You can see why some scholars think Tertullian must have trained as a lawyer.

From Tertullian's writings, we can see that second-century Christians didn't consider their faith to be antithetical to Roman society and imperialism in general. This was important as it lowered barriers to entry if, like Tertullian (and indeed, Paul), converts saw no conflict between their *Romanitas* and their *Christianitas*. In the same way that early Christianity had been opened up to non-Jews, this argument that it was compatible with Roman-ness was also important if the religion were to broaden its appeal. It was a really important point for Tertullian to land – he had to argue this quite forcefully as it was clear, from the persecutions that had already happened, that Christians could be under threat if their religion was seen to be so un-Roman that it was effectively treasonous.

And despite the persecutions of the second century, Christians were growing in number. Tertullian celebrated this: 'We are but of yesterday,' he wrote, 'and [yet] we have filled every place among you – cities, islands, fortresses, towns, market-places, the very [military] camp, tribes, companies, palace, senate, forum – we have left nothing to you but the temples of your gods.'

There's a clear urban focus here – and Tertullian is also keen to emphasise that Christians are full participants in civic life and the local economy. But there's also an acknowledgement that some Christians were to be found within the ranks of the military, among the very forces that guaranteed the stability of the Empire – who protected its borders and who could even propel a new emperor, even someone who wasn't destined for the purple, to power. The defenders of the state were becoming – at least some of them – defenders of the faith.

Soldiers of Christ

There was another sector of Roman society that seemed warm to the idea of Christianity from early on: a group of people who loved a secretive cult; a group of people who may have lapped up the story of Constantine charging into battle with the emblem of a protector-god on his standard (or shields), propelling him to victory (whether that was true or not).

Roman soldiers appear in the Bible, asking for advice and help from Jesus and his disciples. Various non-Jews are described as becoming followers of Jesus – including that soldier in Acts, Cornelius. We've noted that Acts – and the gospels – were written decades after the events they claim to describe – but what we can draw from these inclusions is that the writers of the New Testament were not averse to Roman soldiers joining their ranks.

We get another mention of Roman soldiers who were Christian, in the 170s. Five different sources tell of a particular battle between the Roman army and treacherous barbarians known as the Quadi. The emperor Marcus Aurelius led the twelfth legion, known as *Fulminata* (lightning), to confront the Quadi in central Europe. Outnumbered and outmanoeuvred, the Roman army looked set for defeat – until the heavens opened and a rainstorm compelled the Quadi to withdraw. The soldiers seemed to have thanked divine providence for this act of deliverance. One source mentions Marcus Aurelius praying – to an unidentified deity. The non-Christian Cassius Dio wrote that an Egyptian magician had been responsible, praying to various gods, including Mercury. Two Christian writers – Tertullian and Apollinarius – mentioned Christians praying for help, their god being credited, and Marcus Aurelius duly thanking them. Historian Christopher Jones notes that the various accounts are easy to reconcile, with different soldiers in the legion praying to their various favourite gods. But it seems clear that there were at least some Christians in the legion – and, in fact, Apollinaris, bishop of Hieropolis, said it was full of them (he may have been exaggerating).

Jones also adduces some interesting archaeological evidence of Christianity in the Roman army, before Constantine's time. There are at least eight tombstones of soldiers that record the deceased as Christian – the earliest dating to 201, the tombstone of a soldier from the Legio II Parthica, from the catacombs of Domitilla. Two very early Christian churches or chapels both have military connections. One was discovered in the military fortress at Megiddo in Israel, the headquarters of the Legio II Traiana and Legio VI Ferrata, and is thought to date to the early third century. A mosaic on the floor depicts two fish, which could potentially be a symbol of Christianity. (The Greek word ΙΧΘΥC, *ichthys*, together with a pictorial version, had become a recognised cipher for Christianity by the end of the second century – as an acronym for Ἰησοῦς Χριστὸς Θεοῦ Υἱὸς Σωτήρ – 'Jesus Christ God's Son, Saviour'). On its own, the two fish might be too subtle here to be a definite indication of Christianity – and we've seen how tricky decoding messages in mosaics can be – but fortunately there's also an inscription: 'The God-loving Akeptous has offered the table to God Jesus Christ as a memorial.'

So that seems fairly conclusive.

A slightly later church, complete with a baptismal font, was found in the fortified garrison city of Dura-Europos in Syria. This church only survived because it was deliberately filled with earth to strengthen the walls of the city against Persian attack in the mid-third century. The city fell, and was destroyed – but the buried church survived to tell the tale. On its walls were graffitied names of soldiers that also appear in the military quarter of the town.

The literary sources – so few and far between – can be hard to interpret but there's certainly evidence that there were

Roman soldiers who followed Christianity in the second and third centuries. Sextus Julius Africanus was the Christian author of several works of history, and from these we also find out a bit about the man himself: he was an officer in the Roman army who went on to become a diplomat. He doesn't seem to have seen any conflict between the religion he followed and his military career.

Tertullian's later work has often been quoted to demonstrate that early Roman Christians were pacifists. But earlier in his life, he doesn't seem to have any problem with soldiers being Christian (in fact his father may have been a centurion, later writers suggested), mentioning their presence in military bases and clearly stating that, among the places Christians had 'filled', were fortresses and military camps. It was later on that he became much less enamoured of the Roman state, and its military, and whether or not Tertullian approved, it's clear that there were still Christians in the Roman military at this time.

Origen, a hugely prolific author, writing just a little later, into the third century, has also been interpreted in this way. He wrote his discourse 'Against Celsus' – from which tract we learn about Celsus's own antipathy towards Christianity. We discover that Celsus had criticised Christians for not signing up to the military; Origen, on the other hand, argued that the Christians provided an even better service by staying home to pray for victory. (Note that he didn't think the imperial use of military force was wrong in itself.) Both Tertullian and Origen lived in relatively peaceful parts of the Empire (Carthage and Alexandria, respectively); perhaps they could afford to be pacifist. (Once Christianity developed into the official state religion in the late fourth century, pacifism would be less talked about; the Empire had to be able to wield military might to protect its interests, after all.) Clement of Alexandria, another late-second, early-third century Christian commentator, had no such qualms and saw soldiering as simply another profession.

Although Tertullian and Origen may have been relatively insulated from military strife, the third century was a time of great turmoil for the Empire, as we have seen, with fighting breaking out on every front. Most of the Roman military was stationed around the periphery, guarding the frontiers. There were battles with foreign forces, civil wars and military coups. Christians, still relative newcomers on the block, could find themselves a targeted minority in these unsettled times. From time to time in the third century, resentment against Christians in the Empire would explode into full-blown persecution, often sparked when a particular individual refused to publicly avow loyalty to the Empire and its emperor. Worshipping the emperor was an important ceremonial act of allegiance; refusing to sacrifice to the emperor could be seen as a very definite mark of resistance and disloyalty. Persecutions against Christians went back to the reign of Nero in the first century, and flared up at various times through the centuries, but sporadically; there wasn't a continuous or Empire-wide persecution of Christians.

From 285, Diocletian embarked on a policy of zero tolerance with his army: if soldiers refused to worship Roman gods, they'd be ejected from the army, sometimes in a fatal way. Scores of military martyrs entered the annals of history at this time. And so it's clear from this record of persecution that there were Christians in the Roman army in the third century – and while they may have got themselves into trouble by refusing to sacrifice to the emperor, they obviously hadn't considered a military career to be incompatible with their religion.

There are a couple of notable examples of Christian army officers who fell foul of the Roman authorities during the persecutions carried out under the Tetrarchy. One was Aurelius Gaius, a cavalry officer whose comprehensive biography, including various military manoeuvres in Germany, Scythia and Pannonia, was inscribed on his wife's tombstone. The epitaph finishes:

> 'I have erected this stele with the fruits of my own
> labours as a memorial till the Resurrection.'

According to tradition, the widely venerated St George (of Lydda, modern Lod, in Israel) was a Praetorian guard during the reign of Diocletian – and one of those martyred during the purging of Christians from the military in 303 CE. (The myth about him killing a dragon emerged many centuries later.) Another Roman officer, Julius Eugenius, hung on in the army for a few years after the edict of persecution unleashed by the emperor Maximinus Daia in 306. And then, around 315, Eugenius became bishop of Laodicaea, swapping his military office for an ecclesiastical one.

Modern writers portraying Roman Christians as uniformly pacifist are, as Christopher Jones put it, 'reaching back for a mythical past that never existed'. And the God that was said to have sponsored Constantine's victory certainly wasn't a pacific deity. He was like a new version of Mars – sponsoring warriors, ensuring victories. You can see why he would have appealed to the military. As Christianity became more intertwined with Rome, Christ himself became moulded into a Roman leader – a Roman deity – with martial connotations.

It seems likely that there were still a significant (though still relatively small) number of Christians in the army by the time of Constantine. While the persecutions had been designed to purge the army of Christians, there are some stories of Christian soldiers who managed to keep their religion quiet up to a point when it was revealed; there must have been others who managed to keep it secret at this time. And at the same time, Constantine's biographers were making the case for the compatibility of Christianity, Empire and war.

Even if Constantine never put a Christian symbol on his shields or standards, the stories about the Battle of Milvian Bridge were written by churchmen. They were happy to write about their God guaranteeing the success of this usurper-emperor – as he tore through the old empire, slaughtering the other emperors who had stood in the way of his total domination. Eusebius would draw on Old Testament texts to explain the emperor's victories, harking back to Pharaoh's forces being overwhelmed in the Red Sea; a suitably watery analogy for the fate of Maxentius and his troops in the Tiber. Christians had reinterpreted Hebrew scriptures as prophesying the coming of Christ; now Eusebius turned to them to find support for the idea of a Roman emperor rising to power through bloody victories on the battlefield. And indeed, he even suggested that Constantine's conversion to Christianity was a rational choice – explicitly linked to a belief that this God would be more likely to propel him to military victory. (This seems quite an extraordinary claim to us today – while Eusebius was claiming Constantine for Christianity, he was also suggesting that the emperor's raw ambition was his prime motive; in fact this just lays bare the way that the political, the secular and the religious were completely intertwined in the ancient world – in a way that can surprise us today.)

Later in the fourth century, in 380, Theodosius I would make Christianity the official religion of the state – including its army. As barbarian recruits joined up, they would also be joining the faith. And that faith was by now quite explicitly linked to warfare. Ambrose, bishop of Milan, wrote in the 370s that 'The army is not led by military eagles or the flight of birds but by your name, Lord Jesus, and your worship.' (And if we think those martial connotations are very much ancient history, reflect on one of the leaked comments about a US bombing mission into Yemen in 2025, where vice-president JD Vance said, 'I will say a prayer for victory.')

Moving into the fifth century, by which time, higher-status individuals were seeking out ecclesiastical jobs, there seemed to have been an open door between high-ranking military positions and roles in the Church. We saw just that with Germanus of Auxerre, the military *dux* of Gaul, turned warrior-bishop – and the seventh-century Northumbrian saint, Cuthbert, who served in the military before joining the ranks of the Church. That backstory of noble birth and military service is something that characterises many other early ecclesiastical figures of note.

But in the earlier third and fourth centuries, a foothold in the military would have given Christianity a chance to spread right across the Empire, as troops were moved around and redeployed. That was a well-trodden path, following the dissemination of other cults such as Mithraism – which also originally came from the eastern reaches of the Empire and quickly spread, after becoming popular in Rome, to its most westerly parts.

And what's interesting about Mithras and the army is that the inscriptions that testify to the popularity of this cult also show us that followers came from a specific stratum in the army. They weren't to be found among the lowly legionaries, but among higher level 'career soldiers' – the officers: centurions, lancers and praetorian guards. It's been suggested that the Mithras cult was operating like a club for ambitious military men, very much along the lines of those widespread Roman societies, the *collegia*.

And it seems that Christianity was doing the same – appealing to those higher-ranking officers of the Roman army of the third century, like Aurelius Gaius and Julius Eugenius. And at the same time, it was finding converts among other professions, too.

A Professional Calling

Our story, our trail of investigation, started with a monastery in South Wales – perhaps the first monastery in Britain, even – and that moment when we noticed that the monastic curriculum looked a *lot* like elite Roman education, with the scriptures bolted on. A literary education had always been a marker of high status and a prerequisite for Roman high office; the Church would preserve that system, that transmission of literary culture to the elite; its schools developed out of that very Roman, socially divisive, educational tradition. For Christianity to flourish in the Empire, it had to absorb and promote that elite culture – and that would also involve bringing classical philosophy, the bedrock of Roman education, together with Christian teaching (just as at Illtud's monastery). This wasn't easy at first, and many fourth-century writers considered the grammarians' teachings to be antithetical to Christianity; by the fifth century, this tension had been resolved, with the grammarians adding the scriptures to their curricula. (And the grammarians would give these texts the same treatment they'd always applied to the classical canon – examining different ways of reading a passage to extract moral teaching from it; finding creative solutions to apparent contradictions and spiritually unhelpful stories.)

Eventually the Church would take over the business of education; before that, clerics would have trained at the same private schools, with the same tutors (grammarians and then rhetoricians) as any other young men hoping to pursue professional careers. Then monastic schools emerged alongside those other providers, eventually replacing them. (And in these monasteries, there was a very clear link back to the sort of communal living that would have characterised urban schools of rhetoric – and philosophical sects like Pythagoreans and Essenes, who also held common property; now the students were also monks.) In the sixth century, monastic schools existed right across what had been the old Roman Empire – from Illtud's school in the west to the School of Nisibis in Syria.

The origins of Christianity in that elitist social system are clear to see – once the veil is lifted. And as the third century wore on into the fourth and fifth, many professional careers that were once secular (even though there was always a religious dimension to affairs of the Roman state), together with the training that underpinned them, were brought into the orbit of Christianity.

Most of the early Church leaders, and even quite a few fifth-century bishops, as we've seen, did something else before they were ordained as clergy. They were judges, generals and governors before they joined the Church. In the biographies, the hagiographies, we can see quite clearly how those older Roman professions begat those religious careers. Eminent rhetoricians too – men like Augustine of Hippo and John Chrysostom – found themselves welcomed into ecclesiastical careers; they had very useful skills, having been trained in the art of communication and persuasion. They could mould their own careers, too, with the culture of their privileged backgrounds, their education and their prior professions, infusing the institution of the Church.

But it wasn't just those higher-level professional careers that were becoming Christianised. They draw the eye, perhaps because more ink was spent on them, and history always focuses on the fortunes of the elite. The aristocracy had influence, and were definitely well represented among the upper echelons of the Church, as it seamlessly replaced (or took over) secular administrative positions in the Roman state in the third and fourth centuries. Clerics were also drawn from the middling ranks: from other professions, among the doctors, lawyers and artisans of small towns as well as the larger cities. And in fact, the transformation had really started with this stratum of Roman society.

In the first half of the third century, the Church went from being run by volunteers to being well on the way to becoming a professional organisation with very well-paid jobs (although it would still be a while before the highest echelons of Roman society considered ecclesiastical careers a favourable prospect). As the religion spread and became more organised, it began to exert more control over who could be admitted to the ranks of priests. It wasn't acceptable for someone just to *decide* to become a preacher – a calling wasn't enough – there had to be serious gatekeeping to make sure the right sort of people entered the profession. The professionalisation of the clergy happened in the third century, and went hand-in-hand with the Church's gradual takeover of secular state administration and its provision of welfare. At this time, it seems few bishops came from truly aristocratic stock (before episcopal roles were added in to the *cursus honorum,* from the fourth into the fifth centuries). The process of Christianisation was well underway in the middling ranks of Roman society; this isn't to say that more lowly people weren't attracted to Christianity, but simply that they weren't *driving* its growth. The leading proponents of the religion, the people who would bring their own influence into it and promulgate its spread, were relatively privileged, well-off and literate.

It could be quite reasonably argued that it was not the elites, in fact, who were drawing everyone else into their social and cultural gravitational field — but those middle classes. And then, eventually, the elite had little choice, other than to engage. In this view, the Christianisation of Roman society wasn't bottom-up or top-down, but started in the middle.

Tax officials may have unwittingly (or wittingly) facilitated the Christianisation of middle-class careers. A study of clerics in late antique Italy and Greece found that a large proportion had been physicians. Before the shift, doctors had already enjoyed tax-free status — and would continue to do so within the Church. The public purse wasn't short-changed by physicians assuming clerical positions, and the individuals in question didn't need to worry about a hefty tax bill suddenly coming their way. The salary for a cleric was also similar to that of a doctor. The transition could be quite seamless, then, and this direct importation of medical training into the Church, in the person of the physicians themselves, goes a long way to helping to explain how this religious institution so quickly moved into the business of founding and running hospitals, adding that business to its rapidly expanding portfolio.

It might seem strange to us today that such apparently mundane and secular jobs were being transformed into more explicitly religious roles, but there was much less separation between the sacred and the profane in ancient society; doctors had previously taken oaths to Apollo, Asclepius and Hygeia, for instance; the state itself was always a religious as well as a political institution. So it was not so much the religious aspects of the roles that changed, but the involvement of a more formal structure and institution governing those roles.

A training in law and rhetoric was also conducive to finding a job in the Church as it expanded its operations, as we've already seen at the higher levels. But people with skills as clerks and notaries were also useful. Legally trained clerics could defend the Church when it tangled with the Roman courts, as well as making great preachers. When the Church developed its own property portfolio, it would require the services of its own attorneys, while those who had trained as notaries were well suited to ecclesiastical record-keeping. Legally trained clerics may have been even more influential than physicians in shaping the ethics and operations of the Church.

Roles in the Church were attractive for all these professionals; entering the clergy came with considerable economic benefits, with the Church arranging wages to attract suitable candidates. Clerics – and their families – were also granted favourable tax breaks. They were also exempt from other sorts of compulsory service, and even tradesmen more loosely affiliated with the Church could enjoy tax breaks.

Tax exemptions and harmonisation of salaries meant that there was no financial bump to be suffered when a professional man entered the Church, and as a bonus, his prospects suddenly improved. While a priest in a major see would receive an equivalent wage to a physician or professor, the Church offered new opportunities for progression and promotion, and its higher-level earners were absolutely raking it in. In the sixth century, for instance, the bishop of Ravenna earned a salary equivalent to about half that of a praetorian prefect – the highest-paid job in the Empire. There are plenty of accounts of bishops being offered bribes for ordinations – unsurprisingly as ordination brought with it the chance of upward social mobility and tidy financial rewards. The benefits went both ways – the Church as an institution reaped all the educational investment that wealthy families had poured into their sons – all that human capital.

In terms of training clerics, to begin with, there was no need for anything specific. The schools that trained those intending to be lawyers and doctors now trained those who would become lawyers and doctors and *then* clerics. The system of private schools was enough, it seems, for a while – until monasteries, such as Illtud's, started to take on that role as well. Christianity remained – right at its core, at its heart – a literary tradition; a product of Roman literary culture.

Historians of this period of history have been highlighting this reality – the transformation of Roman professional, middle-class careers into ecclesiastical ones – for decades, but it still seems to have been pushed into the shadows somewhat. Rather like celebrities cloaking themselves in pious asceticism, it seems that its representatives and apologists have preferred that we think of the Church as a grassroots movement – as a challenge to the *status quo* rather than quite such an obvious extension of it. And yet the Church was cloaked in the culture of the educated classes – quite literally in some ways. Just as generals-turned-bishops might continue to wear military-style cloaks, ecclesiastical vestments hinted at the original professional backgrounds of those middle-class citizens who entered into clerical careers: the tunic or *pallium* was the standard dress of lawyers, doctors and teachers (with higher ecclesiastic ranks adding a dash of purple to indicate their status, as was already the fashion in Roman society). Belts worn by military and civic leaders also became adopted as part of clerical dress. Other features of the professions were also adopted, including an ecclesiastical re-creation of the *collegium*-style system of patronage, which allowed some social climbing for some less well-educated men (although it would still remain practically impossible for anyone illiterate to be ordained).

And professional language would also be picked up by the Church. With plenty of clerics joining from the ranks of professors, physicians and lawyers, it's perhaps not surprising that terminology employed by the guilds or *collegia*, Roman municipal government, and indeed the Roman military, found its way into the organisation of the Church. Just as *basilicae* became churches, and *baptisteria* became baptisteries, the various social divisions in the Church and the titles of office-holders borrowed from secular Roman life. In general society, there were *plebs* (ordinary people) and *curiales* (wealthier men with property – and therefore civic responsibility, sitting on the town council or *curia*); the Church had an *ordo laicus* (laity) and an *ordo clericus* (clerical order; clergy). Even the term *ordo* was a borrowed term, originally meaning 'order', 'rank' or 'class'.

More broadly, the organisation of the Church – and the terminology it used – was all based on Roman and Greek antecedents. Even the term *ecclesia*, used for church or

congregation, comes from the Greek, *ekklēsia*: an assembly –
exactly the term used for the political assembly that governed
a Greek polis. An *episcopos* was an overseer before he was a
Christian bishop – 'bishop' being a straightforward corruption
of the Greek word *episkopos*. (The earliest bishops, of small
Christian communities in the first century, were little more
than treasurers or book-keepers, but they became increasingly
powerful and networked, becoming, as Harold Drake put
it, 'the glue that held the movement together'.) A *dioecesis* or
diocese was a Roman district run by a secular governor, a sub-
division of the prefecture, embracing a few provinces – before
it became the term used for a bishop's territory. A vicar was a
vicarius, a prefect's deputy, before the word became used for a
religious representative.

The historian Leif Vaage has pointed out that the early
Christians were already adopting the language of empire in
a very purposeful way in the scriptures. They used the word
kyrios for Jesus, a word that meant 'lord' or 'master'; he was
also described as *soter* – saviour – using the same word used
as an epithet for many Greek gods and Hellenistic rulers.
Members of their movement would be admitted to a divine *ba-
sileia* or kingdom; the word for gospel, *euaggelion*, was the same
word used by the emperor Augustus just a few decades earlier
for his religio-political propaganda – proclaiming a new age of
peace following his victories. (Some historians have suggested
that Christianity was challenging the imperial propaganda by
making this explicit link, but it could also be seen as supporting it – with the *pax Augusta* on earth reinforced by a divine
pax Christi. Similarly, although there are passages in the New
Testament that can be read as anti-imperial, they often describe
one empire being replaced by another, and the Romans were

used to fairly rapid turnover at the top.) Even Jesus's ascension to heaven, following his resurrection, is described in a similar way to the apotheosis of emperors, being borne up to heaven on their deaths, even down to the confirmation from eyewitnesses.

Culturally, linguistically, Christianity can be seen as a product of empire – employing conventional Roman rhetoric and borrowing familiar terms that related to a well-ordered patriarchal household, to slave–master and client–patron relations, to the language of empire itself.

The expansion of the Church into all these areas of professional endeavour, all these businesses, is quite phenomenal. Very soon, it was *everywhere*. And there I go again, talking about 'the Church' as if it were a monolithic entity – with ambitions and agency. It is an abstraction, an idea – but a very powerful one indeed, one with the potential to transform society. Ultimately, we are looking at individuals making choices, but in the process creating something much bigger – a huge sociological, economic, political, religious entity. In that respect, the 'Church' is very much like the 'State', an idea that becomes pervasive and powerful, and which has a real, physical presence and impact in the world, through the agency of humans.

It's interesting to consider what was going on from different perspectives as the Church extended its reach into and over the professions of the Roman Empire. If, for a moment, we allow ourselves to think in terms of abstractions, the Church was set to grow very powerful as it mopped up the professions and expanded its business. But we could also see the Church as something the middle classes came up with – a huge *collegium* that helped to protect their jobs, prospects and income. And when you look at it like that, they'd invented something that would keep them safe even when the Roman Empire itself crumbled; something that would preserve the elements of civilisation that they valued. And yet it seems unlikely that anyone in the third or fourth centuries was thinking in those terms, or this systematically; these are outcomes that we can only see with the benefit of hindsight.

On the ground, at the time, those already on the inside seem to have recognised and grasped opportunities to grow the business of the Church, arranging things to attract more people from different sectors. On the outside, middle-class professionals might have joined because they saw an opportunity for better job security, better pay, better prospects, better networking; or simply because everyone else was doing it – so, why not?

Many of the individuals involved in the expanding work of the Church may have believed deeply in what they were doing, of course. Roman aristocrats and businessmen had always been very good at persuading themselves, and others, that civilisation depended on them – as much as it also depended on the rich staying rich and the poor staying poor. Among the Christian clergy, there was a strong belief that they were simply the right people for the job.

As Norman Underwood put it:

'Like the bureaucrats and politicians managing the emerging nation-states of early modern and Victorian Europe, early Christian bishops imagined themselves the rightful caretakers of their citizenries, and they found technologies of power to funnel resources into their novel and expansive visions of increasing "care" . . .'

The motives of those converting and spreading the word in those early centuries, as well as joining the Church as clerics, would have been many and various. We read a lot about piety and depth of faith – enthusiastic converts would have been motivated to write in this way, and monks would have been more likely to copy their works. Some may well have been very pious and deeply religious, but it can't be denied that joining the Church was developing into an attractive proposition in many other ways. This is not to denigrate the Church or those within it – but simply to point out that they were both worldly.

At the very least, newly appointed clerics wouldn't have had to sacrifice anything in the way of status or lifestyle. Even if individuals believed, deep within themselves, that they were joining the Church because they believed in the doctrine, because they had real concerns about their immortal souls, or because they believed in the work the Church carried out as an institution, this choice would also have aligned with their own self-interest; the interests of their families and class; and the interests of their businesses. (And after all, some centuries later, plenty of their descendants of these elite families would switch over to another ideology as Islam rose to prominence in the east.) It would be foolish to claim that everyone involved was primarily acting piously or selflessly, just as it would be silly to claim that absolutely everyone was really only in it for themselves. Evidence abounds of abuses of power, corruption and self-interest in the early Church – just as there had always been. It's impossible to know how many were truly devout and how many were simply acting expediently – and, rather like the question of Constantine's own convictions, it doesn't really matter in the long term anyway. (Although, as Peter Heather comments, the speed of conversion suggests a certain degree of pragmatism at play for most.)

If we frame this history by just focusing on the major players as learned, pious, religious leaders – we miss so much. That may be how their own hagiographers wrote about them, turning them into saints just as emperors were turned into gods; their authority emphasised after death because it validated the authority of those who claimed to be rightful successors. But history shouldn't just be about repeating the claims of the hagiographers. And of course the very reason we know about these individuals is because of the political power they wielded: because they were intimately and inextricably involved with the systems of power. (And it's not surprising – this is how the Roman model of administration and power had always worked: governors were also priests; the emperor himself was *pontifex maximus*.)

A huge swathe of the business of empire was being swept up into the Church, in the fourth and fifth centuries, with hundreds of thousands of what had been secular jobs becoming transformed into more explicitly religious ones. It's just as absurd to claim that business interests and self-interest were never on the minds of salaried churchmen or lay affiliates, in the same way it would be absurd to claim that people running commercial enterprises today are only ever motivated by greed and selfishness. People are diverse and complicated. But the pursuit of economic security – for individuals and their families, which often goes hand-in-hand with social standing – is a broadly ubiquitous feature of human societies. It would be much more surprising if the Church *wasn't* worldly in this way.

It was Constantine who granted similar benefits to Christian clergy as were already enjoyed by other professions like professors and physicians – giving them equivalent tax relief, making it possible for those clerical roles to be full-time jobs. Then – not particularly surprisingly – there was a rush on those jobs, which Constantine doesn't seem to have anticipated; fifteen years later he would find himself in the rather awkward position of having to revoke some of that fiscal relief.

Constantine's vision seems to have been that the Church would take on the business of the poor, while the wealthier members of society, the *curiales*, would continue in their secular administrative jobs in the city councils. But the Church proceeded to greedily swallow up that level of administration too.

Subsequent emperors would have to put actual bans in place to stop too many members of some professions migrating over to the Church; Valentinian prohibited bakers from taking holy orders, while Arcadius put the same restriction onto dyers. (In fact, even before the Church took on such a significant administrative role, emperors had been trying to stem the exodus of ambitious men from city *curiae* into the burgeoning bureaucratic roles of the later Empire – to no avail.) At the other end of the pile, slaves and tenants were banned from escaping their proper role in society by becoming monks. There's evidence that bishops found it hard to find enough suitable people to fill clerical positions once those bans were in place, especially as clerics needed to be literate, and only some 5–20 per cent of the population could read.

But, aside from those professional groups – the doctors, lawyers and professors – there was another group among the middling sort, among whom literacy was widespread, and who also tended not to have regular commitments in the town *curiae*, preventing them from taking on a clerical role: merchants.

Christianity had always had a close relationship with commerce. Back in the third century, a fragment of a business letter about a certain sale of goods mentions the bishop of Alexandria in such a way that implies he was operating as a banker, helping to fund Christian businesses. The Church operated like a big *collegium*, a membership club for Christians, as we've seen; some *collegia* were associated with specific trades and industries (and cults), and also functioned like trade associations, insurance companies and banks for their members, as well.

From very early on, Christians had not been averse to commercial enterprise; in fact, the evidence suggests that it was *particularly* among the urban business-classes – merchants, traders, shopkeepers and bankers – that the Christian movement first took hold. Clerics had run businesses 'on the side' going right back as far as Paul of Tarsus, making and selling his tents. Early Christians were doctors, lawyers and rhetoricians – but also businessmen and entrepreneurs. (We get an insight into just how widespread business interests were among clerics from edicts attempting to rein them in. A meeting of the Council of Elvira in southern Spain around the year 300 issued guidance that 'Bishops, presbyters, and deacons are not to abandon their territories for commercial reasons': the need for such guidance to be issued suggests that enough clerics were doing just that.)

And just as physicians would bring the business of treating disease and running hospitals into the Church, so the merchants would bring their business – their commercial interests and experience. The Church may have started with the business of the poor but its portfolio was growing larger and larger – hand-in-hand with the expansion of its property portfolio, donated by converts – as the Church took on the business of agriculture and food security.

And of course there was an important link between these two major arms of the Church's business: agriculture and welfare. The Church was responsible for feeding the poor on one hand, and for generating that food supply on the other. Keeping Rome, Constantinople and the other burgeoning cities of the Empire supplied with food was very, very big business indeed. And in the eastern end of the Empire, much of that food came from North Africa, from the fertile Nile Valley, channelled through the granaries and port of Alexandria.

The Breadbasket of Rome

Ancient Alexandria was a hugely important port city, lying on the north-western edge of the Nile Delta. The river, flowing into Lake Mareotis, linked the port city to fertile lands along the Nile Valley for more than 1,000 kilometres. Vessels could travel north to south by letting the prevailing winds fill their sails; from south to north – laden with grain – using the current of the river. Egypt was the breadbasket of Rome, and emperors made significant investments to ensure its productivity; under Augustus, the Roman army would be tasked with maintaining irrigation and navigational canals across the Nile Delta. In the year 102 CE, Dio Chrysostom visited Alexandria and waxed lyrical about the port:

> '. . . not only have you a monopoly of the shipping of the entire Mediterranean by reason of the beauty of your harbours, the magnitude of your fleet, and the abundance and marketing of the products of every land, but also the outer waters that lie beyond are in your grasp, both the Red Sea and the Indian Ocean, whose name was rarely heard in former days. The result is that the trade . . . of the whole world is yours.'

And of all that trade passing through the port of Alexandria, the largest export was surely grain. Every year during the early imperial period, thousands of tons of grain would be shipped from Egypt, leaving Alexandria, heading for other Mediterranean destinations, including Constantinople, which grew to a population of half a million in the fourth century. And that population was mainly Greek-speaking, with a significant proportion of Hellenistic Jews – possibly the largest population of Jews in any city outside Jerusalem. Alexandria was also a famous centre of learning, and Christianity spread within the well-educated elite of the city.

Christianity spread rapidly in Egypt – from a significant but minor religion at the start of the fourth to the majority religion by the beginning of the fifth century. The expansion of clergy and monasteries is well documented in Egyptian papyri. Fifth-century leases show how churches acquired more and more land in a patchwork fashion, as people donated their property – and they would lease that land to tenant farmers. Rent could be paid in cash or in kind, often in grain. Grain could also be gifted to churches, along with a great range of other goods, including milk, cheese, fruits, honey, meat, wool, furniture and textiles, animals and even slaves. Some gifts would come from the emperor himself, with evidence of regular grain subsidies – *annonae* – being paid to churches out of local taxes, in Naples, Antioch and Alexandria. But mostly, gifts to churches were voluntary (though strongly encouraged).

Piece by piece, the Church massively expanded its ownership of land along the Nile, parcelled up and run by a great proliferation of monasteries. Another way the Church acquired land was from landowners who were struggling to pay taxes. By donating their land, the proprietors avoided tax – and could continue to farm as tenants. Property was also left to the Church in wills.

In fact, the Church was getting into property, into agricultural land, in a big way – right across the Empire; the Church obtained a significant proportion of its income from the land it owned. As the donations and bequests rolled in, with the elites trading in their worldly goods for a ticket to heaven, the Church found itself in receipt not just of pecuniary resources, but of land – the biggest business of all in the Roman world. (Over in the west, in Ireland, it's thought that rural landowners may have driven conversion, as entire families handed their land – and the peasants who farmed it – to the Church, establishing tax-exempt monasteries which they still headed up. It's, if not a bottom-up model of conversion, a 'middle-up' one.) The Christian Church would grow to become the single biggest landowner in Europe in the Middle Ages – but we're getting ahead of ourselves. Even in Roman times, it was controlling a significant chunk of agricultural land, assuming a very significant role in food supply and security.

Roman temples had never really been in the business of owning large tracts of agricultural land in the way that the Christian Church quickly developed, although this model did hark back to the older temple societies of ancient Egypt and the Levant. Donations to most Roman temples seem to have taken the form of valuable treasure, the temples acting in some ways as banks. Alongside land ownership, another big change under Christianity was the emergence of full-time, paid priesthoods – which went hand-in-hand with the expanding property portfolio of the Church, and its ability to fund those roles, which included significant administrative duties.

In the early centuries, the Church focused on growing its

membership; once it had achieved its monopoly, it focused on boosting its revenues, through operating franchises, such as monasteries, and general acquisition and accumulation – through donations and bequests, and payments for the increasing number of services it provided, on an increasingly exclusive basis.

The Church rapidly and effectively scooped up a large portion of the business of the Empire – in welfare and redistribution of funds, in all the professional services it was operating too, and as a major landowner, effectively operating an enormous agricultural business. And in Egypt, that business was booming.

As well as controlling grain production, the Church had a hand in transport. A papyrus from the late fourth century refers to the captain of a Nile boat that belonged to the Alexandrian Church. Another refers to a *nauton ekklesias* – a church boat. One priest in fourth-century Oxyrhynchus on the Nile worked on his own ships on his days off, while the son of the local bishop was also a ship-owner. By the end of the sixth century, more comprehensive records show the patriarchate of Alexandria in possession of its own fleet of at least thirteen seagoing ships.

In terms of how much of its agricultural produce churches might be expected to hand over, this seems to have varied a lot. Some institutions may have been able to secure exemptions. But in Egypt, it seems that a normal rate of taxation would have been around 10–40 per cent of the land's grain yield.

Running these agricultural businesses required a huge investment in human resources. As well as full-time clergy, there were jobs for agricultural managers, clerks and secretaries. In Egypt, one bishop employed a whole host of farm workers, craftspeople and builders, messengers and delivery agents.

The Alexandrian bishops were formidably powerful – because they were formidably wealthy. And the source of their wealth – and political heft – was that Egyptian grain. It fed the populations of Rome and Byzantium; it fed the army. And as historian Michael Hollerich put it, 'No more fatal allegation could be made against a bishop than that he was meddling with the grain supply, and Alexandria's fractious Christians were not reluctant to use such an effective polemical weapon.'

A papyrus letter dating to the late third century contains an important clue. It was written by a Christian in Rome, to a Christian community in the Arsinoite Nome – the modern Fayum basin, south-west of Cairo. It mentions Maximus, bishop of Alexandria, and his clergy. And it seems to refer to the imperial grain export – with the implication that the cost of shipping even then was being handled by the Alexandrian Church. At the very least, it reveals that the Alexandrian bishop was running something like a deposit bank for Christian entrepreneurs.

More links between the bishops and the grain business emerge later, in the fourth century. In 335, the Alexandrian bishop Athanasius claimed he'd been exiled after Eusebius of Caesarea accused him of threatening an interruption to grain exports. In order for this accusation to have been possible, the Alexandrian episcopate must have had significant control over grain production and export by this time – and this is just seven years after the Council of Nicaea.

In 338, Athanasius would be in trouble again, this time for selling the portion of grain reserved for the poor for his own gain. And somehow, control of this foodstuff – of grain, of bread, and particularly in relation to poor relief – seems to have played a role in the ongoing rumbling of the Arian heresy.

When the Arian bishop George seized power in 357, he was said to have stolen the 'loaves of orphans'. So the fight over Arianism wasn't just about a nuance of theology; it was about who got to profit from that – immensely profitable – Egyptian grain business. (It may be just as instructive to look at the economic milieu of culture wars today.) With potentially such high stakes, no wonder the Alexandrian bishops wanted to meet with Constantine and thrash it out; no wonder Constantine thought it so very important to meet with them.

Most of the literature on the Arian heresy focuses on the esoteric nuances of the theological debate – not on the economic importance of Alexandria and the crucial supply of Egyptian grain to Constantinople and the Roman army in the east. It may not be intentional, but this framing does feel like we're being directed to look *here*, not *there*. Pondering the nature of divinity draws our attention away from the more worldly aspects of the Church. It was concerned with theology and spiritual matters, of course, but it was also very big business.

Living in a Material World

We've come so far from the Vale of Glamorgan and that question about why Illtud was founding a monastery there, as we started to notice a link between the Church and the ruling powers. We've travelled to Brittany, where local leaders were sanctified, and further into fifth-century Gaul, where governors and generals were slipping comfortably into episcopal roles. We've seen how the middle classes were early adopters, and how the ecclesiastical system maintained and preserved the status of the ruling elite; how public buildings became Christian – from basilicas to baptisteries; how *Romanitas*

333

became *Christianitas* and survived the fragmentation of the western Empire.

And then we saw how a man remembered for being the first Christian emperor may not have been as devout a believer as his principal biographer claimed. We've had to admit we'll never know what he actually believed in his heart of hearts – at the same time realising that this question of the depth of Constantine's faith draws us away from the bigger picture. Whatever he actually believed, he engaged with the senior leaders of the Church in a way that his predecessors simply had not done. And we've seen how much those leaders had to gain if they could claim him – and his Empire, indeed – for their Church.

And then, peel away the religious overlay and what you're left with is a huge, sophisticated system of interconnected businesses: welfare, health, legal, agribusiness, shipping, education – fingers in many pies. And while the Church claimed to be acting in the public interest, its members consistently behaved in ways that advanced the interests of the institution (and those involved in it), including extending its business interests, maintaining its monopoly and accumulating vast quantities of land and wealth. By gaining imperial favour, Church leaders would also be protecting their own business interests.

Once you notice it, the religious nature of this business *almost* seems like a distraction – a veil draped over it. But it's important – essential, fundamental – to the brand. All those businesses could have been independent enterprises, but the powerful ideology of the Church was used to bring them together to create a behemoth. Some will baulk at this approach – lifting the veil. And yet you can't explain what was happening in Europe in the third, fourth and fifth centuries without peeking underneath – and when you do, what emerges into the light is a different (though in so many ways, very familiar) story from the one we're usually sold.

An apparent reluctance to discuss or recognise the economic dimension to this history seems to be a relatively recent affectation – if still centuries old. If it's considered at all uncouth to notice or comment on the wealth of the Church, previous generations had no such qualms. When Daniel, bishop of Winchester, wrote to his friend, the missionary Boniface, in the eighth century, he told him to be sure to mention just how prosperous Christian communities were compared with pagan ones. Prosperity was something to be proud of – a mark of God's favour (and the general effectiveness of the Christian way of managing business). Prosperity was demonstrated and celebrated. The glittering churches, gilded Bibles and purple-clad bishops make even more sense from this medieval perspective.

Having reached this point in my investigative journey, the picture is crystallising. There's something like a Damascene moment as the veil falls away. Whatever the rhetoric, whatever spiritual messages were being adduced, the entity as a whole is looking very much like Roman business, Roman society as usual. The eternal truth is not theological; gods come and go, temples rise and fall – but business is always business. People always need feeding and homing; products need to be produced; shipments need to be shipped; accounts need to be filed and taxes need to be collected; business interests need protecting and armies need to be paid.

Church historians have written plenty about the work the institution was carrying out, but perhaps with less focus on the financial side of that business. Reams have been written on ecclesiastical law, and how that supported religious doctrine, providing a legal background to spiritual guidance. But what has received less attention is that the Church also made a *massive* profit through its legal services. By the Middle Ages, payment of fines was a major source of revenue for the Church. There were spiritual sanctions for those who failed to cough up – and these were backed up with very real, temporal sanctions. Clerics who didn't pay their taxes to the papacy could be excommunicated – curbing their trading, strangling their business interests and damaging their own revenues. The related punishment of interdict could be applied to entire towns or even regions, effectively imposing trading sanctions on them. And yet, excommunication is often discussed as though it were only a spiritual threat – the very real economic implications receiving much less attention.

In their 1996 book, *Sacred Trust*, Ekelund and Tollison undertook an economic analysis of the medieval Church, arguing that this economic perspective offered a valuable insight. They applied rational choice theory to explain the behaviour of individuals and examined the operation of the Church as an organisation. They modelled it as a multidivisional firm, exploring how it controlled franchises and came to operate a monopoly. Monasteries, for example, operated as franchised businesses of the Church, governed by urban bishops. They fulfilled a couple of important functions: advertising the Church (and its promise of salvation) and undertaking agribusiness. As Ekelund and Tollison put it, 'In the corporate structure of Christendom the medieval monastery operated as a (downstream) franchised firm, receiving quality assurance and name-brand recognition from the Church of Rome in return for certain payments (upstream).' And yet – how often do we hear of monasteries described in this way? They are often presented as primarily (or even solely) centres of faith and centres of learning. They were both these things, but – at the same time – could be extremely lucrative businesses.

And yet this approach – scrutinising the economics of the Church, approaching the history of this organisation as an economist might approach any other – touched a nerve. In 2024, almost thirty years after Ekelund and Tollison's book was published, the debate got rather heated. The ecclesiastical historian David d'Avray penned a damning review. He didn't much like the way they analysed the Church as though it were an economic firm, and his criticism of the economists' approach was rudely dismissive; he wrote that 'specialists in the field of medieval and ecclesiastical history regard [their] argument as something of a joke'.

Political scientist Anthony Gill rode to the defence of Ekelund and Tollison; to him, the idea of the Church as an economic firm wasn't just a metaphor, it was literally true – so this sort of economic analysis is powerful and can provide real causal explanations. While d'Avray accused Ekelund and Tollison of ignoring or misinterpreting historians, Gill suggested that d'Avray was himself guilty of oversimplifying and misunderstanding economics.

D'Avray had baulked at the idea that the Church was motivated by money or primarily profit-driven. Comparing the Church to universities today, he opined that some greater good is always the motive, and that making a profit is just a means to an end. For universities, that greater good lies in a belief in the inherent value of teaching and research.

But this kind of interpretation, while giving university academics a pious free pass, also casts entrepreneurs in a dim light – it implies that business people are *only* motivated by profit, and therefore any suggestion that clerics (or indeed academics) are entrepreneurial is to suggest that they are also *only* motivated by money. Gill is keen to point out that some entrepreneurs are driven by a desire to 'do good'. As he puts it, 'Those who create businesses that eventually become firms are often driven by the desire for status or to provide a creative solution to an unmet need they see in society.' And even if Church leaders were primarily motivated by beneficence, they couldn't have done their work if their finances weren't viable. Being commercially sound doesn't mean an organisation (or a person) is *only* motivated by money. Many clerics may have been acting primarily from a position of faith, and of genuine belief in the Church as a force for good in society, but it can't be argued that this didn't also fit well with their own economic self-interest, and that of the institution. Organisations cannot survive without an income. The very persistence of the Church is testament to its economic efficiency; it's evolutionary – organisations that succeed and persist are those which maximise profits. Belief is certainly part of the puzzle – the Church wouldn't have worked if ordinary Christians didn't believe that bishops derived authority from God, for instance – but it's not the whole answer.

In the end, it's very difficult to argue that the Church *wasn't* a firm. (And it's not a new idea. As Adam Smith wrote in the *Wealth of Nations*, albeit focusing on the eighteenth-century Church, 'The clergy of every established church constitute a great incorporation' – and he discussed the finances of the Church in this light.) What we're seeing in those crucial centuries around the middle of the first millennium is the emergence of a huge and powerful corporation. And indeed, Anthony Gill went as far as to describe the Church as the world's *first firm*.

In fact, it went beyond that, becoming a system of government too (and so perhaps we could even draw an analogy there to corporations like the East India Company, so many centuries later, and many more recent examples, gaining extraordinary power in geopolitics today).

Another of d'Avray's criticisms of *Sacred Trust* was that the Church wasn't a centralised monolith. But actually Ekelund and Tollison embraced that, in the way that they modelled the medieval Church as nearest in structure to a multidivisional (M-form) firm. But still, the organisation did involve a funnelling of money up through a hierarchy of divisions, even if that flow could be somewhat sporadic and inconsistent. The Church would also engage in a top-down control of brand and message – *trying* to be monolithic as it attempted to weed out those troublesome heretics. (Perhaps it's best to view the Church as a collection of disparate parts but with monolithic tendencies, or at least aspirations.)

A focus on the agents of change, on the *people* who were actually converting to Christianity, perhaps removes us from the criticism of d'Avray's, that you can't construe or even model the Church as a firm. And Ekelund and Tollison also sought to understand the Church at the level of individuals.

In so many discussions around Church and state, the perspective is so wide and distant that commentators necessarily end up dealing with such abstract notions as 'Church' and 'state'. While it's always useful to draw out to view the bigger picture, we have to remember that those abstractions are just useful symbols, at this level of resolution. They have meaning – but no real agency. Even monarchs are imbued with a degree of agency that they wouldn't – as individuals – have enacted on their own. The real actors here – the 'selfish genes', as it were, are not the 'Church' or the state as monolithic abstractions, nor even the monarch as a sole agent – but *people* in the upper echelons of society, interacting in a coherent, collaborative and competitive network. When we look at individuals, we can more clearly see the operation of rational choice and the way that late-Roman upper-class men seamlessly segued into ecclesiastical positions from high-level military and secular, administrative roles. Those are well-documented facts that are impossible to deny. We've also seen how the religion was adopted by people who were members of the middle classes, the *plebs media* – the people who ran the businesses, processed the accounts, treated the sick and managed the disbursement of welfare. Some of them were more elite – members of the noble families that had effectively ruled Europe under the aegis of the Roman Empire, and would continue to rule it afterwards. The emperor, the kings, were just the tip of a very large iceberg. And in a very real way, they were actually replaceable – while the whole system of local provincial government was not.

The sociologist Rodney Stark argued that, after the Edict of Milan, when Christians were included in that extension of religious tolerance, they could be roughly divided into those pursuing the faith for self-interest and financial gain (the 'Church of Power') and those pursuing the ideology for more spiritual reasons (the 'Church of Piety'). Those falling into the latter camp could find a home – perhaps as ascetics, in a remote place – but would inevitably end up threatening the financial viability and institutional unity of the Church if they dragged too many followers with them. The Church could accommodate and support such individuals as long as they didn't impact the business model of the 'Church of Power' too negatively, and actually, having a few people like this – a few charismatic 'influencers' – could even be good for the brand. Monasteries weren't only franchises in a financial sense; they could also be places where truly pious individuals could be contained without ruining everything for the wealthy, powerful end of the Church. But there was tension; as Gill put it, 'theological challenges were property rights disputes: arguments over who had the ability to define the spiritual product.)

The Church (there I go again, talking in abstractions) needed to do three things, which can be defined as: financial management, relationships with political power, and brand management (which is where the theology comes in). All three were linked: there was a deep theological need to maintain control of the brand, but there was an economic and a political imperative as well.

We've seen how creative the Church was in its ways of raising revenue, from garnering state grants to performing certain (paid) duties through to receiving individual donations and bequests, and running agricultural businesses. These funds tended to accrue at a local or regional level, but a portion of that revenue needed to come back to the centre, as an effective taxation, so there had to be incentives and sanctions in place to ensure that this happened. As for relationships with power, and brand management, what better example of both of these than the Council of Nicaea.

The meeting was, as Anthony Gill put it, 'the initial salvo in creating a centralized "firm" – a collective organization with many units designed to produce a specified product and exercise quality control over it'. After 325, Christianity was no longer a loose grassroots movement with a diversity of approaches and beliefs – you had to conform to a centrally agreed paradigm.

There is no doubt that the Council of Nicaea marked a significant move towards the Church becoming more central-ised, with better connections between its regional bases – and enmeshed with the Roman state. It set a precedent, being the first of a long series of ecumenical councils – called by emper-ors – in the late Roman period. Emperors had to ensure the unity of the brand which increasingly conferred legitimacy on *them*, and they called Church leaders to court to bash out their debates, while usually having prior views about which faction would 'win' and gain imperial support. (That support was economically important; the losing faction would see their leaders exiled, their landholdings seized and their supporters fined.) Viewed through a wider lens, with the worldly side of the Church in mind, the schisms can be seen as, principally, ar-guments about authority and brand management, not theology. And in a way that might remind us of the Arian heresy that was the impetus for this religion colliding, colluding, combining with the Roman Empire – if the Church wasn't *essentially* a firm, it was certainly very *similar* to one.

5

RULER OF ALL

'The imperial state and its inner workings . . .
played a decisive role in the Christian takeover of
the Roman world. Without them, the victory of
Christianity is inconceivable.'

PETER HEATHER, 2022

The Colour of Power

When he appeared at the Palace of Nicaea to meet the assembled bishops, Constantine was enveloped in imperial regalia – in purple robes encrusted with gold and jewels. He was definitely dressed to impress. According to Eusebius, Constantine ended his speech to the bishops by calling himself their 'fellow servant'. Four centuries earlier, Augustus had presented himself at the senate as 'one among equals', even apparently greeting every senator by name, but everyone knew it was all a show; as classicist Mary Beard puts it, 'it was more a pageant of power than a recognition of citizenly equality.' Constantine's appeal to equality in Nicaea is reminiscent of the myth of asceticism – and we're also seeing Constantine seeking to establish himself as a colleague of the bishops, in the way that Augustus had positioned himself as a colleague of the senators.

And yet Constantine's demeanour and his sumptuous clothing suggests he didn't consider himself to be among equals, any more than Augustus had with the senate. Perhaps even more than the gold and gems, it was the deep, rich colour of Constantine's robes that positively oozed with imperial power. Purple – specifically Tyrian purple – had been the colour of ultimate power for centuries. Derived from certain sea snails, which secrete a bromine compound from their mucous glands, this purple dye was extremely expensive to produce. It had been the ultimate status symbol for the Phoenicians, the Greeks and then the Romans. And sumptuary laws in the fourth century meant that only the emperor was permitted to wear it.

In 2023, an excavation at a monumental set of Roman baths in Carlisle, northern England, turned up an innocuous-looking muddy lump that, when broken open, was found to contain a shockingly vivid violet colour. I saw it with my own eyes, and knowing that the emperor Septimius Severus had stayed in Carlisle in the early third century, I couldn't help wondering if there could be an imperial connection. A year later, tests on the vividly purple substance, including infrared spectroscopy, revealed that it contained bromine, a tell-tale sign of marine origin; it seemed this was indeed Tyrian purple. Mixed with beeswax, the purple was surely as bright as it had been when it was brought to Carlisle, eighteen centuries ago.

In praise speeches and in his *Vita Constantini*, or *Life of Constantine*, Eusebius uses the standard word *halourgos* (ἁλουργός) to describe the purple robes of emperors. The etymology of the word is intriguing – it literally means 'salt-work'. This may be linked to the manufacturing process; Pliny the Elder described how the dye was produced, by soaking parts of sea snails in warm brine. The way that the ancient Greeks employed this term, usually in relation to textiles, makes it clear that they were referring to this colour, this purple dye made from molluscs, and not simply salt production.

Before he wrote his *Life of Constantine*, Eusebius had penned two praise speeches or 'panegyrics' in which he'd described Constantine's use of the colour purple. One describes how Constantine had donned a purple garment after the death after the death of his father in York: 'straightaway the soldiers threw the purple over you despite your tears, taking more account of the public advantage than your feelings, for it was not right to mourn any longer a ruler who had been consecrated as a god.) It seems the army was encouraging him to assume this potent imperial symbol, despite the fact that he wasn't next-in-line under the system of the tetrarchy – but Constantine doesn't seem to have needed much persuading. Both panegyrics refer to Maxentius, portrayed as a usurper, improperly wearing purple. In Eusebius's eyes, and, perhaps, those of the army, only Constantine could legitimately wear this iconic colour.

Two decades later, as he walked into that hall in the old palace of Licinius, resplendent in imperial purple, Constantine was consciously presenting himself as emperor – and also, it could be argued, as the reimagined *pontifex maximus*. Roman emperors had always taken that title – as the 'chief priest' of the Empire; Roman state and religion had never been separate. Christianity had emerged as a separate cult – drawing a definite distinction between allegiance to God and allegiance to Roman rulers; as Jesus is described in the gospels as saying: 'Render unto Caesar the things that are Caesar's, and unto God the things that are God's.' But just as Constantine had been propelled to power as a usurper, endorsed by the army, he was now endorsing a usurping religion. This minor religion was not only being embraced by Constantine himself, who was calling himself a 'fellow servant' of the bishops (while appearing in imperial purple), Christianity was being drawn into the Roman state – the things that were God's were also to become Caesar's.

Christianity would end up adopting the colour of power for itself, draping it over not only its priests but its sacred scriptures. A letter written by the Roman theologian Jerome to a noblewoman called Eustochium, in the later fourth century, refers to the sumptuousness of some Bibles, whose 'parchments are dyed purple, gold is melted for lettering, manuscripts are decked with jewels: and Christ lies at their door naked and dying'. The books of the Church had become clothed in the imperial symbols of power: gold and purple. Jerome didn't approve. But the bishops, too, were clothing themselves in the same finery.

Thessaloniki, the ancient capital of Macedonia, lying at the north-west corner of the Aegean, became a regional capital under the tetrarchs and the seat of Galerius, who built himself a magnificent palace, a triumphal arch and a mausoleum. All of these archaeologically important structures can be seen in the modern city, and the mausoleum, known as the Rotunda, is especially impressive. It's a stunning pink-brick building, just over 24 metres in diameter, with walls 6 metres thick, and it has survived several earthquakes, though its dome bears the scars. When Galerius died in 311, he was buried, not in Thessaloniki, but in Gamzigrad, modern Zaječar, in Serbia. The Rotunda stood empty, but some time between the fourth and sixth centuries – the exact date is debated – it was converted into a church. The whole of its dome, on the inside, was decorated with rich golden mosaics, only fragments of which remain today. There was once a figure of Christ in the centre, but he is long gone. The bottom of the middle register is ringed by just the feet of what were probably angels. Below that are eight panels, depicting buildings, with saints standing in front of them, hands raised in prayer. These holy men include bishops, soldiers, physicians – we know because written beside each is their name, profession, and the month in which they were meant be worshipped: 'Onesiphoros, soldier, August'; 'Damianos, physician, September'; 'Philippos, bishop, October'. Some can be identified, linked up with other historical evidence; most were eastern Christian martyrs from the time of Diocletian. The depictions, particularly the style of the faces, belong to a Greco-Roman portrait tradition; they are very similar to earlier, pagan funerary portraits, like those painted onto wooden coffin lids in the Fayum area of Ptolemaic Egypt. (The Fayum portraits survived due to a quirk of climate; it's assumed this sort of portraiture was spread widely around the Mediterranean but did not survive elsewhere.)

The saints in the Rotunda are dressed in white and purple tunics and cloaks. The imperial connotations were impossible to ignore. The connections may have been literal in some cases – perhaps the soldier saints Eukarpion and Leon were members of the imperial guard. But everyone has some purple on their dress, even Philemon, the flute-player. They still shine today, these mosaic portraits; each saint set against a background of glittering gold.

The Church had taken on the trappings of empire: its most magnificent buildings, adorning them with precious metals and gems; books and bishops were decorated, wearing the time-honoured colour of power. The Church was investing in its image, providing that *laetum spectaculum*, that 'happy spectacle' – the imperial purple, gold and jewels reinforcing its ultimate authority and its access to other-worldly wealth. As Eva Perón would put it so piquantly, so many centuries later, 'The poor like to see me beautiful.'

Arriving into that hall in the palace at Nicaea, glowing with jewels, decked out in imperial purple, bringing imperial judgement and favour to bear, in the company of those troublesome priests, Constantine stepped into a new era. It's an extraordinary moment that echoes down the ages.

Schism and Brand

As it grew in power, wealth and influence, the Church would become much less tolerant of other religions and cults, and of any dissent or disagreement within its ranks. The medieval Church would jealously guard its monopoly and its control of the theological marketplace. Any competitors – emerging inside or outside – would be branded as heretics and removed as swiftly as possible. The wealth of those heretical competitors would be seized. The Church often appealed to secular monarchs to help in squashing heretics, in which case the proceeds could be divided between them. The medieval Church would even launch into military action in an attempt to preserve its religious monopoly, most notably the crusades, against followers of Christianity's major competitor, Islam.

But, in fact, the Church was jealously guarding its monopoly much earlier, even as it built it. It needed to control its USP: its doctrine, its interpretation of scripture. Any dissenters were potential competitors and needed to be eliminated – through excommunication (the concept of which also existed in Judaism) and, if necessary, violence and death.

Which brings us back to the Council of Nicaea – convened, on the face of it, to settle a heresy. For Constantine, schism and heresy diminished the political power of the Church – but it also had serious economic implications. This particular disagreement had broken out more than six hundred miles away in Alexandria – that economically vital port city. In the early fourth century, Christianity was not the force to be reckoned with that it would become – and yet it was clearly politically significant enough for an emperor to get involved in this dispute. At this point, we need to dig into the background and context a bit more to find out why.

Although some historians have claimed that around 10 per cent of the population of the Empire may have been Christian by this time, this is surely a wild overestimate. Most of the

Empire's population was rural, and Christianity was very much an urban phenomenon at this time. A more likely estimate, extrapolating from the few records that exist, places the proportion at around 1–2 per cent. Most of these Christians were based in cities – but even within major cities, the proportion of Christians would have been less than 10 per cent.

It's thought that around a third of the 1,800 towns and cities of the Empire had a bishop by the year 300 CE. But these bishops were not evenly distributed. Records from councils, including that of Nicaea, show that most of these bishoprics were concentrated in four areas: North Africa (200–250), Egypt (70–100), Asia Minor (around 100) and Syria-Palestine (75 bishops). Italy, Gaul and Spain each had less than thirty, while Britain had only between three and six. But although their flocks may have been relatively small, some bishops enjoyed considerable influence, particularly in North Africa. They'd assumed prominent roles in society, exerting considerable control over the local population, helping to keep the peace (or break it), as well as wielding wider political and economic power.

As early as 312, Constantine may have realised how politically useful the Christian Church could be (or at least, he and his biographers claimed that to be the case, retrospectively). But the emperor also seems to have been keenly aware that internal debates could weaken its appeal and its power. Prior to 325, Constantine had already intervened to facilitate swift settlements of internal disagreements and schisms within the Church, strategically funding priests to help to resolve such issues. But the debates continued to bubble up and rage on.

In the 320s, in a suburb of Alexandria, a priest called Arius had caused more than a bit of a stir by preaching an unorthodox version of Christianity, suggesting that Jesus Christ was separate and inferior – distinct in personhood and subordinate in divine nature to God the Father. Plenty of priests initially thought Arius's ideas acceptable, and supported him – including Constantine's biographer, Eusebius of Caesarea – and another Eusebius, the bishop of Nicomedia. But the powerful bishop of Alexandria, Alexander, was not at all so well disposed to Arius, seeing him as threatening his own position, and exiled him. What looks, on the face of it, to be a theological dispute, and is often treated as such, without looking at the wider context, was intensely political – with potentially serious economic ramifications.

Whole books have been written about the Arian heresy; a sea of ink has been spilled. The theological debate revolved around the question of whether God the Father was something separate from the Son, and had existed before the Son, or whether the two of them were one and the same thing, sharing the same 'substance', and had both existed forever. The debate shone a light on a cognitive dissonance at the heart of the religion. God was meant to be unique and immutable, but if he was duplicated in his Son, then he wasn't unique any more. If the Son was created *from* him, then God must have lost something in the process – he must have changed; he must be mutable. The Arian heresy essentially emerged from the untidiness of the scriptures: the inconsistencies that were baked into them, which even clever grammarians struggled to resolve. In particular, there was a tension between the portrait of Jesus emerging from the synoptic gospels, where he seemed quite human, and his depiction in the Gospel of John, where he's much more at one with God. The Arian heresy represented a challenge to unity, an admission that the scriptures could be read in different ways, and was even a threat to the monotheistic nature of Christianity itself.

Earlier clerics had advised Christian leaders not to debate points of theology in public. It was thought that the best course of action was to introduce followers to the less controversial aspects of Christianity first, and keep the more esoteric bones of contention for discussion only among well-versed scholars – to avoid the risk of sowing seeds of confusion.

Bishops were keen for people not to think about such theological dilemmas too hard – probably including themselves, for their own sanity. Eusebius of Caesarea, in his *Demonstratio Evangelica*, which he penned before the Council of Nicaea was convened, was at pains to stress that the exact way in which the Son came into being was beyond human comprehension. It's a neat answer to a reasonable question – don't try to use reason. Eusebius was keen to avoid any materialising theories; these divine entities were not physical bodies, at least not in any way that humans could understand. Riffing off John's gospel, Eusebius suggested a metaphor might help, for understanding how Jesus had come into being:

'Who shall explain his generation . . . if anyone ventures to go further and compare what is totally inconceivable with visible and corporeal examples, perhaps he might say that the Son came forth from the unborn nature and indescribable substance of the Father like some fragrance and ray of light.'

It's hardly a satisfying explanation, but then – as Eusebius may have told us, with a wave of his hand – you're not *meant* to understand it. It's that combination of mysticism and dogma that would come to characterise Christianity as a faith: it's beyond understanding, but it must still be accepted as an explanation. The Arian heresy exposed a sort of polytheism battling to escape the straitjacket of Christian monotheism; it awkwardly revealed some of the cracks in the story. The historian of religion Francesca Stavrakopoulou has explored in detail how the God in Christianity emerged out of earlier Jewish mythology, and even more ancient Levantine religious myths, becoming less corporeal, more ethereal and mystical over time. Tracing the history of this religion is fascinating; this deity started off as one god among many, ending up as a single deity as the rest of the pantheon was gradually pruned and relegated around him, as city states in the Levant battled it out for supremacy – but that's a much more ancient story. Nevertheless, the ghost of polytheism still haunted this apparently monotheistic religion.

The question at the heart of the Arian heresy seems extremely esoteric, and yet it had the potential not only to highlight a problematic intellectual fault line in the Christian thesis – but to divide people into factions. Such issues would emerge time and time again throughout history; Christian scripture and interpretation involved so many contradictions and ambiguities: God as man, Christ as peace-lover or soldier, prosperity as a symbol of God's favour while wealth was sinful. Its flexibility and ability to mean many things to different people may have underpinned Christianity's success as a mass movement, but also created fertile ground for schisms.

It's easy to be drawn into the theology of the Arian heresy, to focus on that – just like the culture wars of today. But a wider perspective means we see the real meaning of these polarised debates much more clearly. Today, we are alert to the fact that many culture wars are manufactured, or at least fuelled, by politicking forces and cunning politicians who see these debates as a useful way of winning followers and votes.

Back in the 1990s, historian Christopher Haas was arguing

that the wider context of the Arian heresy had been ignored. He remarked on a floodtide of scholarly work on Arius's theology – with a peculiar blind spot when it came to the bigger picture. 'Intellectual history', he wrote, 'seldom takes place in a vacuum. Alexandria in the early fourth century was probably the second-largest city in the Roman Empire, and served as the commercial entrepôt for the entire eastern Mediterranean. Tightly organised communities of Jews, pagans and Christians jostled one another in their ongoing competition for socio-cultural hegemony within this cosmopolitan urban milieu.'

Alexandria seems to have been a city where tensions were always bubbling just under the surface – and often erupting. Back in the first century, the prominent Jewish writer and diplomat Philo of Alexandria had described the 'mob which, out of its restlessness and love of an unquiet and disorderly life, was always filling every place with tumult and confusion, and who, because of their habitual idleness and laziness, were full of treachery and revolutionary plans'. Later on, in the fifth century, the historian Socrates Scholasticus would describe how the support of the mob propelled Cyril to power, when he became bishop in 412 – against the wishes of the Roman governor. (Cyril was later implicated in the mob violence that led to the murder of the prominent pagan philosopher and teacher Hypatia.) Scholasticus wrote, 'The Alexandrians are more delighted with a riot than any other people; and if they can find a pretext, they will break out into the most intolerable excesses. Then it is scarcely possible to check their impetuosity until there has been much bloodshed.'

Haas examined how, in the 320s, the Arian heresy was also creating a divide in this notoriously volatile city, with Arius on one side and the bishop of Alexandria, Alexander, on the other. There were supporters, influential ones, on both sides. Alexander had gathered up allies among leading bishops in Syria and Palestine. Arius had found support in Eusebius, the bishop of Nicomedia (just down the road from Nicaea) and a very influential presence in Constantine's court. Arius himself was just a lowly presbyter of a minor parish church at a place called Baucalis, or Boukolou, on the outskirts of Alexandria, an area on the shores of Lake Mareotis. The name of the area comes from the Greek word for 'cowherd'; in the fourth century, it seems to have been a place where cattle grazed, perhaps the location of a cattle market too, as well as being the site of a necropolis. It was a notoriously rough spot, where travellers were sometimes attacked. The area also seemed to draw people who were attracted to asceticism; in the middle of the fourth century, there were plenty of hermits reported to be living among the tombs of the necropolis. Arius fitted in here; he was preaching an ascetic version of Christianity and had plenty of followers – enough that he seems to have been recognised as a threat to the authority of the bishop. (Arius wasn't the only one, either – Bishop Alexander would excommunicate at least five presbyters and another five deacons over the course of his career.)

These tensions could easily spill over into real unrest and violence in such a city. If the Arian heresy were to have erupted into a full-blown riot in Alexandria, that would have threatened the stability of the episcopate – potentially affecting the grain supply to the eastern Empire, and to Constantinople in particular. As we've seen, the wealth that the Church was protecting wasn't just spiritual and theological, it was very much material; man cannot live by bread alone, but bread is a pretty fundamental human need. It's possible the schism that erupted in Alexandria threatened to tear its granaries apart. The supply of wheat to Constantinople was at risk. Constantine's ability to feed his citizens, and his army, could be threatened. When Bishop Alexander sought imperial support, it was in both his and Constantine's interest to resolve the matter speedily.

Even after the Council of Nicaea, the Arian debate rumbled on, developing into that tension between the Homoean (philosophically related to the Arian) and Nicene versions of Christianity that we saw troubling Ulfilas the Goth and his contemporaries – and it was always about politically opposed factions. The urban elite of Alexandria seemed agile at shifting their support, depending on which version of Christianity, which particular faction, appeared to be gaining the upper hand. But factional violence could occasionally break out, just as it did between supporters of different chariot teams in Roman cities. Such violence reveals the political power of these polarised debates – pitting two sides against each other. Monks were involved in these clashes, supporting one political urban faction, or one bishop's diocese, against another. Throughout the fourth, fifth and sixth centuries, there are plenty of examples of monastic involvement in civil unrest, from the destruction of the temple of Serapis in Alexandria in 391, to outbreaks of violence in Antioch and Jerusalem, to the Nika riots in Constantinople in 531. Back in the early fourth century, the Arian heresy could easily have kicked off a riot in Alexandria. At this period in history, the way that emperors usually dealt with such riots was not to get personally involved in a debate, but to punish whole cities after the event. In Alexandria, at this time, the scale of the wider political and economic repercussions must have been on Constantine's mind when he decided to break with tradition and wade in *before* violence broke out.

In fact, it wasn't the first time that Constantine had got involved in infighting within the Church. Back in 312, he'd sent funds to favoured bishops in North Africa in an attempt to crush a schism, taking advice from Bishop Ossius of Cordoba, in Spain. He had tried imposing sanctions too, but hadn't been particularly successful. That particular episode was hot on the heels of Constantine deposing Maxentius and taking Rome; it looked like a new emperor was in the ascendancy – an emperor who could be an ally of Christianity, for the first time, and bishops were quick to stake their claim. On Constantine's side, the support of that minor but still politically powerful constituency was there for the asking. In the east, his co-emperor Licinius had avoided getting involved with rivalries between bishops, operating an aloof policy of toleration when it came to the different versions of Christianity being weaponised by rival factions. But Constantine waded in – and would do again in 325; this time, in an even more personal way.

And of course it wasn't the case that Constantine simply decided to step into the debate of his own accord. It's important to remember the wider context surrounding the Arian heresy – Constantine would have been seriously lobbied by the various factions fighting for his patronage. As Peter Heather wrote in *Christendom*:

'Taxation aside, the main intrusion by the imperial centre into these localities came when regional grandees sought central assistance (directly from emperors if they were influential enough . . .) to win or protect some kind of advantage over their local rivals.'

357

So there's nothing really unusual happening here – we're looking at the sort of lobbying that was incredibly common; it's just that, in this case, the 'regional grandee' was a bishop. And of course, with Constantine's grant of privileged tax status to clergy, there were real monetary gains to be made too, with rival Christian factions in a city fighting for their chosen bishop and that golden ticket of imperial patronage and tax exemptions.

The Arian heresy had come to a head in 321, when Bishop Alexander had confronted Arius, and then, with the support of nearly a hundred North African bishops, excommunicated the presbyter. Arius retreated to Palestine, where he somehow persuaded Eusebius of Caesarea to join his existing ally, Eusebius of Nicomedia, and convened his own council in Bithynia, seeking to gain wider support from other bishops. Licinius, who was at this point still Constantine's co-emperor in the east, responded to this factionalism by banning further church meetings.

But Licinius had his own problems, of course – not least his co-emperor's determination to be the sole ruler. In 324 he was thrashed in Thrace by Constantine, deposed and exiled – to be executed the following year. Meanwhile, the factions in the eastern Church remained. And an even more profound political dimension to the Arian schism was now laid bare, marking a deep political divide between Bishop Alexander and his cohort, who were close to Constantine, and those bishops, like Eusebius of Nicomedia, who had been favoured by Licinius. Having been supported by the ex-emperor who'd ended up on the losing side, in a fatal way, was a dangerous position to be in.

Constantine maintained Licinius's ban on church councils, while dispatching his trusted envoy, Ossius of Cordoba, to Alexandria to sort things out. Ossius carried with him a letter from the emperor himself, urging an end to the infighting, asking the clerics to put aside their differences and 'heal the body of the Church'. This plea failed, and it seems that Ossius then planned to convene a meeting of bishops to iron out the problem, in Ankyra (modern Ankara).

But then the meeting was moved to Nicaea. Constantine wrote to the bishops to tell them that the venue had changed, to make it easier for western bishops to attend (few did), because Nicaea had a better climate, and because – perhaps the real reason – the new venue was easier for him to get to, from his own palace at Nicomedia. There would surely also be the consideration that the original venue, Ankyra, was politically problematic as the local bishop there was a fierce opponent of Arianism; Nicomedia was also potentially problematic as its bishop, Eusebius, supported Arius. Constantine may have wanted a more neutral location.

Nicaea had long been an important royal seat and administrative centre in Bithynia, in north-western Anatolia, vying with nearby Nicomedia to be capital of the region. It had been under Roman control since 72 BCE, and Constantine's recently dispatched rival, Licinius, had kept a splendid palace in the lakeside city; it was this palace that would be the venue for the ecclesiastical council.

Constantine put the call out to some three thousand bishops and religious leaders; around two hundred and fifty actually turned up in the spring of 325, for what would be a month-long meeting. Although the gathering was badged as the first 'worldwide' or *ecumenical* gathering of Church leaders, most of the bishops came from the eastern Empire. Only around six came from the western end of the Empire, including one from Britain. The Council of Nicaea was described by three bishops who were actually present at it: Eusebius of Caesarea, whose account we examined earlier and who seems to have written up his notes or recollections shortly afterwards; Athanasius, whose surviving text was written up to a quarter-century after the event; and Eustathius, whose report dates from some time in between.

The Council of Nicaea represented a high-level branding meeting for the Church. Its purpose was to define the brand – in the face of that bitter disagreement among senior leaders – and thus to establish trust with followers and build loyalty. Constantine wanted the senior leaders in the Church to formally agree on the central tenets of the religion – the core values of the brand – and put an end to the politically divisive schism.

The crucial debate that needed to be settled was the Arian heresy – the nature of Jesus's divinity – but there was another issue on the agenda: the timing of Easter, the most important event in the Christian calendar. An intolerable situation had arisen where different branches of the Church were celebrating the festival at different times. Here again, there was a clear need for consistency and standardisation.

Ossius seems to have led the discussions, with Constantine to preside over the final deliberations and a resolution to the disagreement. The bishops started by levelling accusations at each other and informing on their colleagues. The knives were out. Constantine refused to get into the details of those accusations and counter-accusations and melodramatically burned them without reading them. He wanted unity, and would rather burn documents than people, as historians have noted. He also had little patience with the theological issues, at least as Eusebius reported it, claiming that Constantine had said the matter was 'small and utterly trivial' and 'unworthy of so much controversy'.

At the start of the conference, Arius had already been at a disadvantage, with only around twenty bishops supporting his version of Christianity. After a month of debate, his supporters had dwindled to just two. The assembled bishops ended up by throwing out the Arian heresy, agreeing instead on a concept where God the Father and God the Son were consubstantial and co-eternal. In the end, the form of words that eventually became the 'Nicene Creed' (finally published by another council, in Constantinople, in 381) covered quite a few bases, capturing some scriptural language from the Gospel of John; Jesus Christ being described as the 'God from God, Light from Light, true God from true God, begotten, not made'. It seems a huge fudge, saying Christ could somehow be 'begotten' but 'not made' – and yet it seemed to do the job. Constantine appeared happy with it, but suggested an addition that it seems he'd previously agreed with Ossius: to include the Greek word *homoousios* – meaning 'of the same essence or substance'. This was an unusual suggestion – a word taken from Greek philosophy, not Christian scripture. It was also a directly anti-Arian inclusion. It wasn't enough to say what 'the Church' believed in; they also had to agree on what they *didn't* believe – to crush the heresy. And so they went on to decide that certain statements, such as 'once he was not' or 'of another essence' were anathemas – and couldn't be applied to Jesus. Most of the original Arian sympathisers were persuaded to sign the document. Arius himself and his two North African supporters refused to sign it – and were exiled. (Although Eusebius of Nicomedia signed the document, his support of Arianism was enough to see him exiled some months later.)

Ossius tried to get another doctrine signed off by the council – a stipulation that married priests should refrain from
sex with their wives. It was an unpopular suggestion and not
agreed. But the date of Easter was sorted out – with a decision
to separate it from the Jewish festival of Passover. This was
important because it signalled a firm separation of Christianity
from its Jewish roots. The church's hierarchy was also further
formalised at the meeting, with the leading authority of the
bishops of Alexandria, Rome and Antioch, over each of their
wider regions, also confirmed. Constantine rewarded the
compliant bishops in reaching their conclusion by agreeing an
annual grant to churches to provide for poor women including
widows and clerics, and they all celebrated the resolution of
the heresy by attending a great feast.

Despite his original sympathy with Arianism, Eusebius of
Caesarea hung on as bishop, having expediently signed up
to the agreement at Nicaea. But he wasn't done. In 326, he
moved against his main rival, Eustathius of Antioch, bringing
his orthodoxy into question. Conveniently, a prostitute also
turned up to claim that her baby was the illegitimate child of
Eustathius. He couldn't survive this scandal and was banished
to Thrace. In an incredible turnaround, the Arians were in the
ascendancy again. Constantine invited Arius himself to meet
him at Nicomedia; by the end of the year, the head heretic
himself was back in the fold (though Alexander resisted his
reinstatement). The other excommunicated and exiled bishops,
including Eusebius of Nicomedia, were welcomed back into
the Church. (His association with Licinius forgiven if not forgotten, it would be Eusebius of Nicomedia who would baptise
Constantine on his deathbed.)

After Alexander of Alexandria died in 328, his deacon

Athanasius was consecrated as bishop – and Constantine now demanded that the new bishop accept Arius back into the Church. Athanasius was staunchly resistant – and became embroiled in strife in Alexandria, which saw him exiled to Gaul. Arius was invited to Constantinople, with the promise of being readmitted into the Church, but he fell ill – and was then found dead in a latrine. Some suspected foul play (but this also has the whiff of an urban myth, propagated by his detractors – associating his death with excrement).

And so, however much Constantine might have hoped to lay the matter to rest in 325, the schisming and scheming, the factionalism and infighting, would continue. Historian Robert M. Grant closed his 1975 essay 'Religion and Politics at the Council of Nicaea' with these words:

> 'The story of Nicaea is like most church history, early and late. It is the story of men who tried to achieve final solutions and total victory over their opponents and then saw their work crumble. Perhaps we can learn from Nicaea the advisability of pursuing less absolute goals in less totalitarian ways.'

The Council of Nicaea represents an important, perhaps even pivotal, moment in history; not because of the resolution of a fairly esoteric and ethereal theological question (in fact, it wasn't resolved and neither were the factions united, as time would tell), but because of the agreement that there should be one 'official' version of Christianity – and that local variation would no longer be tolerated. The Church was turning into something much more organised, more linked-up – and from now on, ecumenical councils would be an important way in which the Church maintained its unified identity and brand.

As we've seen, the Church was selling all sorts of things, from legal services to Egyptian grain, but also eternal life, community and social status. Internal schisms threatened its market dominance. So the Council of Nicaea – and other ecumenical councils after that – were essential to ensuring that everyone was on brand. But perhaps even more important than all of that, at this particular gathering of bishops, was the presence of Constantine.

We can only see this clearly with the benefit of hindsight because we know what was coming. A seismic power shift at the heart of the Roman Empire, rippling out from that moment, in 325, when Constantine invited the bishops to the palace in Nicaea. The fourth century is such a crucial period in the history of Christianity. It was a minor cult at the start of that century, with only 1–2 per cent of the Roman Empire likely to have been Christian. But by the end of the century, it would be the official religion of the Empire and its successor states in the west, with the majority of the population baptised into the faith. But in fact, Constantine didn't start that ripple; as we've seen, Christianity was already spreading within the elite networks of the Empire, the networks that sustained the Roman state. But it seems very unlikely that Christianity would have grown so rapidly over that century had an emperor not involved himself with it – so visibly and publicly.

Why did he – and later emperors – embrace Christianity? Historians have suggested three main reasons: because they believed in the religion; because the Church had become powerful and they needed its support; because the Church also needed the state to survive.

The first reason is tricky; hard to assess, even. As we've seen with Constantine, it's impossible to know if he really was a believer, as he projected different messages, different images to different sections of the population – and because his biographer, Eusebius, had a huge vested interest in claiming him for the Church. And, as I've also argued, it doesn't really matter – it's the outcome that's historically important: the fusion of the imperial cult and the business of the Empire with Christianity and the business of the Church. Combining the last two reasons, the Church and state became mutually interdependent.

The Church had already become economically (and therefore politically) powerful by the fourth century – as we've seen so compellingly with the involvement of the Alexandrian patriarchate in the Egyptian grain business, in the business of feeding the Empire. Constantine couldn't actually afford to ignore it. If he'd failed to feed Constantinople; if he'd failed to feed his army – he surely wouldn't have lasted long. There would have been other pressures too; the Church had so thoroughly embedded itself in the business of Empire even more widely by that time.

And there were other useful functions of a strong, organised state religion too: its leviathan-like potential to suppress outbursts of violence in cities (or indeed, to instigate them, as happened so often in Alexandria) and the possibility of efficient mass communication (forgive the pun): the Church could help to broadcast specific imperial messages, as well as act as a general public relations agency for the Empire – as it would keep doing for any monarch it favoured, down the centuries. Of course, support wasn't guaranteed – the Church could also disseminate its own messages that were antagonistic to the state, as popes and emperors vied with each other for power. But the holy alliance of monarchy, state and Church was there right from the moment Constantine set foot in the great hall of the palace at Nicaea.

The Fall and Rise of an Empire

I started this journey wondering how Christianity had spread to the point where it turned up in a valley in South Wales, thousands of miles from its birthplace. I wanted to find out how it had become so successful.

For many historians, looking for the reason behind the spread of Christianity, often framed as its 'triumph', the answer is to be found in its theology, its ideas and its promises. But I think there's a problem with this thesis – because those ideas were not unique. They flowed from Christianity's Jewish roots, with a dose of Greek philosophy mixed in. The idea that good deeds might be rewarded with divine favour was not new, as we've seen. In classical antiquity, heroes could expect a glorious afterlife; Pharisaic Judaism and Mithraism also contained ideas about salvation. Christianity's only upgrade in this area was that it perhaps went further by opening up that offer to all its members, regardless of ethnicity, status or parentage. Christianity offered a personal and experiential relationship with God – but so did other Greco-Roman mystery cults. Christianity was neither better at providing an explanation for plagues (as some have argued), nor did it offer a better survival rate. It offered no more hope for the future than other competing religions and worldviews.

A longstanding explanation for those searching for the reason behind this religion's success has been to suggest that imperial Roman society had sunk into a spiritual malaise, with Christianity coming along at just the right time, as an antidote. And yet the opposite seems to be true: the Empire was alive with diverse cults. Some historians and sociologists have suggested that Christians were simply more dedicated and devoted than other cultists, but there's no good evidence to support such an assertion – and it just rehearses old tropes about the innate superiority of Christianity that have always been part of the self-narrative, and still form part of more critical approaches, ever since Edward Gibbon's *The History of the Decline and Fall of the Roman Empire*.

And yet Christianity *did* succeed, in a spectacular way, in this crowded arena of competing ideas. The secret to its success must have rested in part on its package of ideas, even though none were entirely novel or unique. But beyond the ideas contained in Christian scripture, there were some great marketing techniques, whether or not these were employed knowingly at the time. Some have suggested an important difference existed between Christianity and other Roman cults, in that it – like Judaism – was exclusive: you could not (or at least, *should not*) be a Christian and worship other gods. That exclusivity may not have been perfect and ubiquitous (there's plenty of evidence for syncretism early on), but it was an ideal: Christianity discouraged its followers from shopping around. And perhaps that meant it could build and maintain brand loyalty in a way that other cults were perhaps failing to do, or at least, failing to do so as successfully – over time. (It's really important to recognise that huge or absolute differences are not necessary – all that's required is a slight competitive edge, for a brand to achieve dominance over time.)

But if we just look at this question in terms of the ideas that Christianity represented, and even at how it marketed itself, we miss something extremely important: its business-like worldliness. This is the aspect I have concentrated on in this investigative journey – exploring the wider political and economic milieu; looking at the 'species' in its environmental context. And so my investigation reveals only a part of the picture too, but I forgive myself that focus because it also seemed to me to be a less widely discussed perspective – something that was definitely there in the academic literature, but perhaps missing from the wider discourse. I'm sure that apologist historians (including some who claim not to be Christian, but seem to be suffering some kind of Stockholm syndrome) and theologians, and lots of other people who want to believe that organised religion is about something other than money or power, will be queuing up to shoot me down on this. But nothing I'm saying here has not been said before. It's there in the histories; it's there in the coins and the marble arches and the Roman baths turned into baptisteries. And yet, somehow, it seems to be considered uncouth to point it out; to be so blunt.

It's been a twisting, turning journey – picking up crumbs of evidence, feeling our way from the valley in Wales to the landscape of Brittany, littered with saints, to the bishops in Gaul, making friends with new Visigothic rulers, all the way to the row in Alexandria that brought Constantine to convene the meeting in the palace at Nicaea. This is not, and was never intended to be, a comprehensive overview or survey of Christianity in the Roman Empire, but I hope that it's been an interesting excursion, illuminated with fascinating fragments of text and intriguing archaeological artefacts.

Questioning the *who*, *how* and *why* proved most informative along the way, helping to reveal the real agents of change, the real movers and shakers. When it comes to *who*: Constantine cottoned onto something that had been percolating upwards from the lower echelons of Roman society – but not the lowest. Christianity wasn't a grassroots movement – or at least, not for long – it was very much led by the middle classes and the elites.

We've seen, in the west, how the Roman Empire fragmented but its structures, its wealthier citizens and its elite families, its ways of doing things, all stayed in place — under the aegis of Christianity.

With emperors coming and going, barbarians seizing power in the west, and the political landscape of the fourth century looking decidedly unstable, the families who effectively ran the economy — from the middling sort, the merchants, lawyers and doctors, to the social elites — had hit upon an elegant solution. It may have crept up on them, almost inadvertently, but it worked. They'd found a way to protect their interests and to keep everything running, no matter who was, officially, in charge, whether that was a usurping Roman emperor or a new Visigothic king.

Roman society had always been patriarchal; the fusion of that social model with the religious framework of Christianity ensured that the sons of the elite still had careers to look forward to when the Empire lost control of its western provinces. And the status that had always come with holding high civic office was now offered by roles within the Church. If anything, it seems that the elites at the western end of the Empire may have been particularly early adopters of Christianity. In many ways, this was probably a similar process to that of Romanisation of the provinces in the first place; provincial elites bought into the imperial cult because they could see the advantages that were on offer. Now Christianity carried with it a stamp of imperial authority; an idea of what it *meant* to be civilised and Roman — even as the Empire itself was fragmenting.

This simplifies a very complex series of events, combining so many individual motives and intents into an overarching theme — but it summarises the large-scale effects of the change.

Christianisation may never have been carried out with such forethought, but the general outcome was that businesses were protected, and families with commercial interests were partly insulated from the negative impacts of political instability and regime change.

That was the *who*; as for the *how*, the success of Christianity derived from the fact that it superimposed itself on the life-blood of the Empire – it was the business model of the Empire. As Christianity spread, it was an ideology that not only became identified with the *idea* of the Roman Empire, but was en-meshed with the practicalities of the Empire, too. Perhaps our perspective, from the relatively secularised twenty-first century, is unhelpful here. We might expect religion to be an ethereal, spiritual thing, but it has always been much more worldly; we might expect more separation between Church and state – but organised religion, business and government have *always* been intertwined. And we can't hope to understand how one religion achieved hegemony across such a large swathe of the globe, as Christianity did, if we ignore that worldly, real, very human angle.

The *why* is perhaps trickier, but reaching the end of the journey, we can see that the success of Christianity, as an or-ganised religion, depended on its worldliness and its inherent Roman-ness. Its business model grew wider and wider; it was enormously acquisitive, mopping up more and more of the business of Empire, becoming enmeshed with existing civic so-ciety, elite literary education, health, welfare and the economy of the Empire, ultimately taking over the public cults, too, as the religion of state and city. And this is when the exclusivity of Christianity really came into play – when it became a state religion, effectively fusing with the state. It was culturally extremely well fitted to this function, too – 'pre-adapted', to borrow a biological term – with its scriptures laden with imperial terms, tropes and themes. The Roman Empire was then shaped by the Church – shifting from being broadly tolerant, permitting a multiplicity of cults, as long as they were practised in a way that didn't threaten imperial hegemony, to pushing a single, state-sanctioned religious monopoly.

The Roman Empire would become so comprehensively captured by the Christian Church that, eventually, the Church would be the way it lived on. In a very real way, the Empire *became* the Church. Although perhaps it's more accurate to say that they became each other, growing and merging together: the Christianisation of the Empire was just as much the Romanisation of Christianity, as Peter Heather points out. The Church would become more Roman than Roman. We've seen that this idea was already there, in Tertullian's prayer:

'We [Christians] pray for life prolonged; for security to the empire; for protection to the imperial house; for brave armies, a faithful senate, a virtuous people, the world at rest, whatever, as man or Caesar, an emperor would wish.'

Looking back over the journey, over the evidence we've collected, it's certainly possible to see the process of change in Late Antiquity into the early Middle Ages as a powerful state with bolted-on religious aspects morphing into a powerful religion with bolted-on state functions. The business of the Empire was comprehensively taken over, in a piecemeal fashion, until the Church was more powerful than the Empire – as an economic system and network that could survive the carving up of territory into smaller polities.

In many ways, the Church that remained, as the Roman Empire shrank and fragmented, looks very much like an absolutely massive, networked Roman *collegium*: a member organisation, with an insurance-like function, distributing resources to individuals in need, and with active business interests (including welfare) that effectively made it the world's first multinational corporation. With its chief executive first as the Roman emperor and later the pope; its archiepiscopal board of directors; its franchises – all those episcopal dioceses and monasteries – the Church would prove to be a more successful business than the Empire itself. As early as the fifth century, some churchmen appeared to be grasping the potential of the Church as an independent, supranational organisation – that's effectively what Augustine of Hippo was describing in his *City of God*, even though it was written at a time when the Roman emperor was still the ultimate religious authority.

Did it all get out of hand? The economic model forged by the Church would be *immensely* successful. By the year 900 CE, the medieval Church would own a third of all agricultural land in Europe, making it the largest single landowner, while the construction of churches and associated buildings represented the largest capital investment that was taking place anywhere. The annual income of the Church outstripped that of any individual kingdom or larger polity, excepting that of the Byzantine Empire (with which it was virtually synonymous, in the east, anyway).

The worldly aspects of the Church are undeniable. Wealth and power go hand-in-hand, and the Church had both in abundance. Some historians of Christianity have blamed Constantine for ruining Christianity. They've claimed that this was when the rot set in – when the pure, altruistic, pacifist and anarchist nature of early Christianity became tainted with impurity, self-interest, violence and power. It may be a somewhat appealing hypothesis, but this concept of the 'fall of the Church' doesn't match with the evidence; it doesn't reflect what Christianity already was – who Christians *were*, and what they were doing – before Constantine noticed them. And once again it draws us into thinking in abstractions, rather than looking at all the different motives that existed for choices and behaviours – accepting that people are nothing if not diverse. And yet, while we may not agree with the suggestion that the Roman state ruined the Church, it makes sense to see the process as the Roman state being Christianised, while Christianity was Romanised – fused with the imperial cult.

Eusebius anticipated this, writing in 336. He saw how the imperial cult wouldn't so much go extinct as evolve into something new, something compatible with Christianity. There was only God now, so the emperor couldn't be one as well. But his power could be seen as God-given and, as a single monarch ruling on earth, his reign reflected the rule of God over the whole world. As Eusebius put it:

'Thus outfitted in the likeness of the Kingdom of Heaven, he pilots affairs below with an upward gaze to steer by the archetypal form. He grows strong in his model of monarchic rule which the Ruler of All has given to the race of man alone of those on earth.'

It was very clever of Eusebius. Let's not forget that Constantine had brutally, ruthlessly cleared out the other emperors of the Tetrarchy to get back to a position where one emperor would be left standing, ruling the whole Empire. But that was divinely sanctioned. And the emperor wasn't competing with God, but emulating him. Constantine paved the way for the evolution of the Empire, its fall and rise. But it would be an empire that didn't need an emperor; any monarch would do. This new empire would survive the political fragmentation of the old Roman world. In this view, the western Empire never fell.

And from then on, it was bishops supporting kings supporting bishops . . . all the way down.

POSTSCRIPT

In 1907, archaeologists were excavating on the acropolis, the high city, of Sparta. Digging among the remains of the temple to Athena Chalkioikos (Athena of the bronze house), they found the remains of many terracotta and bronze bells. Few were ever seen by the public; the remains have lain hidden in the archives of Sparta Museum. Recent research in those storerooms has uncovered 102 terracotta bells and 34 bronze bells, some just fragments, others complete. Most are very small, ranging from 2 to 8 centimetres tall. Some carry votive inscriptions to Athena. They're thought to date to between the fifth and fourth centuries BCE.

It's a huge haul of bells, but they're not unique. Ancient bells have been found all over Greece, across the mainland and the islands, though usually just one or two at a time. Some are from houses, others from sanctuaries or graves. The earliest ones come from Cyprus and Samos, dating to around 700 BCE. They seem to have spread there from the Near East, and may have started out as horse bells.

Placed as votive offerings in the temple of Athena, who as well as being Chalkioikos was Poliachos, protector of the city, the bells may have some resonance with her cult and festival, which involved chariot- and horse-racing. But they may have been used as handbells too – there are classical Greek images showing bells used in this way. Literature tells us that bells were used in Greek and Roman cities to indicate the opening of baths and markets, and as signals by town guards, and as doorbells.

Athena Chalkioikos may have been worshipped as a patron of bronze-workers – and weaponry. The sound of the bronze bells could have represented that side of her, as a goddess not only of war but of the means to enact it. There could be a more generic aspect to the bells, with the suggestion that bells may have been worn by sacrificial animals, but there's only a single image related to this idea: a pig with a bell around its neck from a house in Delos. There's much more evidence of bells being used in cultic music, especially associated with the party god Dionysus. And there's an association between 'beating bronze' and purification rituals, including during lunar eclipses and funerals. The Ancient Greek historian Diodorus Siculus wrote that the funeral carriage and coffin of Alexander the Great were adorned with bells. Roman sources also refer to the apotropaic power of the sound of bronze – warding off evil. Bells are also thought to have been used during liturgies, including as part of the imperial cult.

Some three hundred Roman bells have been found in Britain, with a concentration in the south-east, and in rural sites as well as forts and cities. Some would undoubtedly have had mundane functions, announcing the opening and closing of public baths, or been worn by animals. Some are from graves; a few from other ritual sites, such as Coventina's well on Hadrian's Wall. At Segontium – modern Caernarvon in North Wales – archaeologists discovered fragments of what appeared an iron bell-stand. Iron bells have been found at two other Mithraeums, in Belgium and eastern France. It's thought that the bells were rung at key moments during the narration of the Mithras myth, at meetings of this cult that was so loved by the military.

An ancient sound – a Roman sound – echoing down to us through the ages.

PPS

A final note from Anthony Gill:

'. . . As a scholar who early on has used economic theory and public choice insights to analyze religion and other non-traditional topics in the field and who has faced continual skepticism in that endeavor, I would like to end with one final observation of this ongoing debate. The study of economics is frequently viewed as the study of commercial interests and "money-making". Such actions, while necessary for human survival, are portrayed as being more "carnal" than the loftier pursuits of beauty, educational edification, and spiritual enlightenment.

Where these things come into play, it is argued, economics has little to offer. Religion, perhaps the loftiest of pursuits, falls outside the realm of "mere economics". But all loftier pursuits require material support and organization, not to mention the less tangible qualities of human effort and ingenuity. Humans pursue the lofty pursuits of beauty, enlightenment, and spirituality and all humans are subject to making essential trade-offs in a world of scarcity. And when humans try to cooperate towards greater ends, including the glorification of God and the spread of the Good News, they subject themselves to the same economic forces that limit other pursuits. Accepting this does not diminish the beauty or moral importance of any particular organization, but it only reminds us that all of our choices and activities, whether they be mundane or edifying, are connected by a unified logic to which public choice has much to contribute.'

SELECTED REFERENCES

Abdy R (2016) From page to coin: origins and development of Christian designs on Roman coinage. In: *Historia Mundi. Le Medaglie e le Monete Raccontano la Storia, l'Arte, la Cultura dell'Uomo: 5*. Città del Vaticano.

Allen JR (1893) Iolo Morganwg's readings of the inscriptions on the crosses at Llantwit Major. *Archaeologia Cambrensis* 10: 326–331.

Andacht F (2010) Reflections on iconic celebrity: . . .such stuff as dreams are made on. In: *Intersémiotique des arts*. Constantini M (ed) L'Harmattan.

Ausonius, Paulinus Pellaeus (c. 310–395) *Volume II: Books 18–20. Paulinus Pellaeus: Eucharisticus*. Evelyn-White HG (tr) Loeb Classical Library 115. Harvard University Press (1921).

Barnes TD (1990) The consecration of Ulfila. *Journal of Theological Studies* 41: 541–545.

Becker SO, Pfaff S (2023) Church, state, and historical political economy. In: *The Oxford Handbook of Historical Political Economy*. Jenkins JA, Rubin J (eds) Oxford University Press.

Bhola RK (2015) *A Man of Visions: A New Examination of the*

Vision(s) of Constantine (Panegyric VI, Lactantius' De mortibus persecutorum, and Eusebius' De vita Constantini). PhD thesis. University of Ottawa.

Blair J *et al.* (2023) Shakenoak revisited: post-Roman occupation and burial at a Cotswold-edge villa in the light of new evidence and approaches. *Archaeological Journal* 180: 35–81. DOI: 10.1080/00665983.2023.2267891

Boer R (2011) The fate of Christian communism. *Minnesota Review* 77: 111–130.

Briggman A (2011) Revisiting Irenaeus' philosophical acumen. *Vigiliae Christianae* 65: 115–124.

Brøns C, Droß-Krüpe K (2018) The colour purple? Reconsidering the Greek word halourgos (ἀλουργ#ς) and its relation to ancient textiles. *Textile History* 49: 22–43. DOI: 10.1080/00404969.2018.1438237

Bryant C (2017) How the aristocracy preserved their power. *The Guardian*, 7 September. https://www.theguardian.com/news/2017/sep/07/how-the-aristocracy-preserved-their-power

Bryant JM (2023) Decius & Valerian, Novatian & Cyprian: persecution and schism in the making of a Catholic Christianity, part I. *Athens Journal of History* 9: 125–158.

Burgess RW (1992) From Gallia Romana to Gallia Gothica: the view from Spain. In: *Fifth-Century Gaul: a Crisis of Identity?* Drinkwater J & Elton H (eds) Cambridge University Press.

Burrell B (2004) Nikaia: Koinon of Bithynia. In: *Neokoroi: Greek Cities and Roman Emperors.* Burrell B (ed) Cincinnati Classical Studies New Series Volume IX. Brill.

Bykov AA (2015) The origin of Christian charity. *Procedia – Social and Behavioral Sciences* 166: 609–615.

Calomino D (2023) Greek festival culture and 'political' games at Nikaia in Bithynia. In: *The Material Dynamics of Festivals in the Graeco-Roman East.* Newby Z (ed) Oxford University Press.

Campbell E *et al.* (2023) A new chronology for the Welsh hillfort of Dinas Powys. *Antiquity* 97: 1548–1563.

Caner D (2018) Not a hospital but a leprosarium. *Dumbarton Oaks Papers* 72: 25–48.

Cohick L (1998) Melito of Sardis's 'PERI PASCHA' and its 'Israel'. *Harvard Theological Review* 91: 351–372.

Clark V (2009) *Constantine the Great: The Coins Speak.* MA thesis. Middle Tennessee State University.

Curran J (1996) Constantine and the ancient cults of Rome: the legal evidence. *Greece & Rome* 43: 68–80.

Cusack C (1998) *The Rise of Christianity in Northern Europe, 300–1000.* Cassell.

D'Avray D (2024) The medieval church as an economic firm? *Public Choice* 201: 1–20.

Delaine J (1988) Recent research on Roman baths. *Journal of Roman Archaeology* 1: 11–32.

Demolder K (2024) How self-denial become the must-have trend of 2024. RTÉ online, 8 August. https://www.rte. ie/lifestyle/living/2024/0808/1463999-kate-demolder-how-self-denial-become-the-must-have-trend/

Dierkens A, Périn P (1997). Death and burial in Gaul and Germania, 4th–8th century. In: *The Transformation of the Roman World, AD 400–900.* Webster L, Brown M (eds) University of California Press.

Doble GH (1997) *The Saints of Cornwall.* Llanerch Publishers.

Drake HA (2000) *Constantine and the Bishops: The Politics of Intolerance.* Johns Hopkins University Press.

Drinkwater J (1992) The Bacaudae of fifth-century Gaul.
In: *Fifth-Century Gaul: a Crisis of Identity?* Drinkwater J &
Elton H (eds) Cambridge University Press.

Eckardt H, Williams S (2018) The sound of magic? Bells in
Roman Britain. *Britannia* 49: 179–210.

Edwards N (2020) Early medieval carved stones in
Wales. Comisiwn Brenhinol Henebion Cymru/
Royal Commission on the Ancient and Historical
Monuments of Wales. https://rcahmw.gov.uk/
early-medieval-carved-stones-in-wales-by-professor-
nancy-edwards-chair-of-the-commissioners-rcahmw/

Ekelund RB, Hébert RF, Tollison RD, Anderson GM,
Davidson AB (1996) *Sacred Trust: The Medieval Church as an
Economic Firm.* Oxford University Press.

Elliott TG (1990) The language of Constantine's propaganda.
Transactions of the American Philological Association 120:
349–353.

Elliott TG (1991) Eusebian frauds in the 'Vita Constantini'.
Phoenix 45: 162–171.

Elton H (1992) Defence in fifth-century Gaul. In:
Fifth-Century Gaul: a Crisis of Identity? Drinkwater J &
Elton H (eds) Cambridge University Press.

Elton H (2007) Warfare and the military. In: *The Cambridge
Companion to the Age of Constantine.* Lenski N (ed)
Cambridge University Press.

Eusebius Pamphilius (c. 290–300) *Church History.* In: *A Select
Library of Nicene and Post-Nicene Fathers of the Christian
Church, Vol II.* Schaff P (ed) Christian Literature Co.
(1887).

Eusebius Pamphilius (1887) *Life of Constantine.* In: *A Select
Library of Nicene and Post-Nicene Fathers of the Christian*

Church, Vol II. Schaff P (ed) Christian Literature Co. (1887).

Evenepoel W (1998–1999) Ambrose vs. Symmachus: Christians and pagans in AD 384. *Ancient Society* 29: 283–306.

Fanning S (1992) Emperors and empires in fifth-century Gaul. In: *Fifth-Century Gaul: a Crisis of Identity?* Drinkwater J & Elton H (eds) Cambridge University Press.

Fernandez S (2020) Who convened the first council of Nicaea: Constantine or Ossius? *Journal of Theological Studies* 71: 196–211.

Finn R (2006) Portraying the poor: descriptions of poverty in Christian texts from the late Roman empire. In: *Poverty in the Roman World.* Atkins M, Osborne R (eds) Cambridge University Press.

Flechner R (2017) Conversion to Christianity in early medieval Ireland. In: *Companion to the Church in Early Medieval Ireland.*

Flower R (2012) Visions of Constantine. *Journal of Roman Studies* 102: 287–305.

Frye D (1991) Bishops as pawns in early fifth-century Gaul. *Journal of Ecclesiastical History* 42: 349–360.

Gill A (2024) Of principals, agents, and transaction costs: a response to d'Avray. *Public Choice* 201: 39–51.

Goffart W (1982) Old and new in Merovingian taxation. *Past & Present* 96: 3–21.

Goldberg EJ (1995) The fall of the Roman Empire revisited: Sidonius Apollinaris and his crisis of identity. *Essays in History* 37. Corcoran Department of History at the University of Virginia.

Grant RM (1975) Religion and politics at the Council at Nicaea. *Journal of Religion* 55: 1–12.

Green C (2017) The fifth- to sixth-century British church in the forum at Lincoln: a brief discussion. https://www.caitlingreen.org/2017/12/fifth-to-sixth-century-british-church-lincoln.html

Grigg L (2006) Throwing parties for the poor: poverty and splendour in the late antique church. In: *Poverty in the Roman World*. Atkins M, Osborne R (eds) Cambridge University Press.

Guy B (ed) (2019) *Vita Sancti Samsonis (Liber Landavensis)*. Seintiau. https://saints.wales/wp-content/uploads/VSSamsonis.pdf

Haas C (1993) The Arians of Alexandria. *Vigiliae Christianae* 47: 234–245.

Hahn DE (1963) Roman nobility and the three major priesthoods, 218–167 BC. *Transactions and Proceedings of the American Philological Association* 94: 73–85.

Halsall G (1992) The origins of *Reihengraberzivilisation*: forty years on. In: *Fifth-Century Gaul: A Crisis of Identity?* Drinkwater J & Elton H (eds) Cambridge University Press.

Halsall G (2010) *Cemeteries and Society in Merovingian Gaul: Selected Studies in History and Archaeology, 1992–2009*. Brill's Series on the Early Middle Ages Volume 18. Brill.

Harper K (2015) Pandemics and passages to late antiquity: rethinking the plague of c.249–270 described by Cyprian. *Journal of Roman Archaeology* 28: 223–260.

Harries J (1992) Sidonius Apollinaris, Rome and the barbarians: a climate of treason? In: *Fifth-Century Gaul: a Crisis of Identity?* Drinkwater J & Elton H (eds) Cambridge University Press.

Hawes AB (1913) Charities and philanthropies in the Roman Empire. *Classical Weekly* 6: 178–181.

Hays CM (2019) The early Church, the Roman state and ancient civil society: whose responsibility are the poor? In: *Poverty in the Early Church and Today: A Conversation.* Walton S, Swithinbank H (eds) T&T Clark.

Heather P (1992) The emergence of the Visigothic kingdom. In: *Fifth-Century Gaul: A Crisis of Identity?* Drinkwater J & Elton H (eds) Cambridge University Press.

Hecht K, MacArthur D, Savage M, Friedman S (2020) Social mobility at the top: how elites in the UK are pulling away. Posted in: LSE British and Irish Politics and Policy blog, 22 January.

Hébert RF (2024) Loose language or stylized facts? D'Avray on Ekelund and Tollison. *Public Choice* 201: 21–26.

Hollerich MJ (1982) The Alexandrian bishops and the grain trade: ecclesiastical commerce in late Roman Egypt. *Journal of the Economic and Social History of the Orient* 25: 187–207.

Josephus, Flavius (c. 75) *The War of the Jews. Vol III. Books 5–7.* Whiston W (ed), London (1737).

Khalil E (2010) The sea, the river and the lake: all the waterways lead to Alexandria. *Bollettino di Archeologia* 1: 33–48.

Kiilerich B (2007) Picturing ideal beauty: the saints in the Rotunda at Thessaloniki. *An Tard* 15: 321–336.

Knight JK (2005) From villa to monastery: Llandough in context. *Medieval Archaeology* 49: 93–107.

Lactantius (c. 240–c. 320) *De Mortibus Persecutorum.* Creed JL (ed) Clarendon Press (1984).

Lenski N (2008) Evoking the pagan past: *Instinctu divinitatis* and Constantine's capture of Rome. *Journal of Late Antiquity* 1: 204–257.

Lenski N (2015) Constantine and the Tyche of Constantinople. In: *Contested Monarchy: Integrating the Roman Empire in the Fourth Century AD*. Wienand J (ed) Oxford University Press.

Lewis PE (2003) The origin of the chi-rho monogram as a Christian symbol. *Journal of the Numismatic Association of Australia*. 14: 19–31.

Litovchenko E *et al.* (2019) Sidonius Appolinaris as a flexible thinking person of fifth-century Gaul. *Journal of Research in Applied Linguistics* 10 (special issue): 366–373.

Maréchal S (2015) *Lauacrum*: just another word for baths? How the terminology of baths may have reflected changes in bathing habits. *Revue belge de philologie et d'histoire* 93: 139–177.

Marlowe E (2006) Framing the sun: the arch of Constantine and the Roman cityscape. *Art Bulletin* 88: 223–242.

Marcellinus, Ammianus (c.380–400) *History, Volume III: Books 27–31. Excerpta Valesiana*. Rolfe JC (tr). Loeb Classical Library 331. Harvard University Press (1939).

Martínez Jiménez J (2024) Civic commitment in the post-Roman west: the Visigothic case study. In: *City, Citizen, Citizenship, 400–1500: A Comparative Approach*. Rose E, Flierman R, de Bruin-van de Beek M (eds). Palgrave Macmillan.

Mathisen RW (2002) The Christianization of the late Roman senatorial order: circumstances and scholarship. *International Journal of the Classical Tradition* 9: 257–278.

Malone CW (2022) Constantine and Christianity in the Roman imperial army. In: *The Roman Empire*. Dillon M, Matthew C (eds) Pen & Sword Books.

McCormick M *et al.* (2012) Climate change during and after the Roman Empire: reconstructing the past from scientific and historical evidence. *Journal of Interdisciplinary History* 43: 169–220.

McGovern JB (1904) Concerning the 'chi-rho' monogram. *The Antiquary* 40: 5–9.

Migne JP (1858) The life of Gregory the Wonderworker. In: *Patrologia Graecae* Vol 44.

Morris P (2020) *Llanilltud: The Story of a Celtic Christian Community.* Y Lolfa.

Muhlberger S (1992) Looking back from mid century: the Gallic Chronicler of 452 and the crisis of Honorius' reign. In: *Fifth-Century Gaul: a Crisis of Identity?* Drinkwater J & Elton H (eds) Cambridge University Press.

Murphy K (2021) The archaeology of the medieval towns of southwest Wales: Tenby. Dyfed Archaeological Trust Report No. 2021–38.

Newton M (2016) *Text: Vita Sancti Samsonis.* Adapted from: *The Life of St Samson of Dol.* Taylor T. Society for Promoting Christian Knowledge (1925).

Niehoff MR (2013) A Jewish critique of Christianity from second century Alexandria: revisiting the Jew mentioned in *Contra Celsum. Journal of Early Christian Studies* 21: 151–175.

Nixon CEV (1992) Relations between Visigoths and Romans in fifth-century Gaul. In: *Fifth-Century Gaul: a Crisis of Identity?* Drinkwater J & Elton H (eds) Cambridge University Press.

Nuffelen PV (2011) Eusebius of Caesarea and the concept of paganism. In: *The Archaeology of Late Antique Paganism.* Lavan L, Mulryan M (eds) Brill.

Omissi A (2018) Tyranny and betrayal: Constantine, Maximian, Maxentius, and Licinius. In: *Emperors and*

Usurpers in the Later Roman Empire: Civil War, Panegyric, and the Construction of Legitimacy. Oxford University Press.

Origen (c. 248) *Contra Celsum*. In: *Ante-Nicene Fathers*, Vol. 4. Crombie F (tr). Roberts A, Donaldson J, Coxe AC (eds). Christian Literature Publishing Co. (1885).

Osborne R (2006) Introduction: Roman poverty in context. In: *Poverty in the Roman World*. Atkins M, Osborne R (eds) Cambridge University Press.

Percival J (1992) The fifth-century villa: new life or death postponed? In: *Fifth-Century Gaul: A Crisis of Identity?* Drinkwater J & Elton H (eds) Cambridge University Press.

Rasimus T (2012) Revisiting the *ICHTHYS*: a suggestion concerning the original christological fish symbolism. *Nag Hammadi and Manichaean Studies* 76: 327–348.

Reid J (2023) *The Eagle and the Bear: A New History of Roman Scotland*. Birlinn.

RIB 4. Dedication to Mithras and the Invincible Sun. https:// romaninscriptionsofbritain.org/inscriptions/4

Rivet ALF (1969) *The Roman Villa in Britain*. Routledge & Kegan Paul.

Rose CB (2021) Reconsidering the frieze on the Arch of Constantine. *Journal of Roman Archaeology* 34: 175–210.

Salter AW (2024) Rationally revealing religion: in defense of Ekelund and Tollison on method. *Public Choice* 201: 27–38.

Sánchez-Ostiz Á (2018) 'Under this sign you shall be the ruler!' Eusebius, the chi-rho letters and the arch of Constantine. In: *Beginning and End: From Ammianus Marcellinus to Eusebius of Cesarea*. Sánchez-Ostiz Á (ed) Universidad de Huelva.

Scott E (2018) Three burials at Norton Disney — and the end of Roman villas in Britain. Eleanor Scott Archaeology blog, 31 January. eleanorscottarchaeology.com/els-archaeology-blog/2018/1/29/three-burials-at-norton-disney-and-the-end-of-roman-villas-in-britain

Serfas A (2002) *Church Finances from Constantine to Justinian 312–565 CE.* PhD thesis. Stanford University.

Sessa K (2019) The new environmental fall of Rome: a methodological consideration. *Journal of Late Antiquity* 12: 211–255.

Setzer CJ (1994) *Jewish Responses to Early Christians.* Fortress Press.

Sheridan JJ (1966) The altar of Victory — paganism's last battle. *L'Antiquité Classique* 35: 186–206.

Sidonius (c. 430–490) *Letters of Gaius Sollius Apollinaris Sidonius.* Anderson WB (tr). Loeb Classical Library 296. Harvard University Press (1936).

Silver M (2014) The business model of the early Christian Church and its implications for labour force participation in the Roman Empire. *Marburger Beiträge zur Antiken Handels-, Wirtschafts-und Sozialgeschichte* 32: 71–116.

Sivan H (1992) The dedicatory presentation in Late Antiquity: the example of Ausonius. *Illinois Classical Studies* 17: 83–101.

Smith A (1776) *An Inquiry into the Nature and Causes of the Wealth of Nations.* Oxford World's Classics. Oxford University Press (2008).

Smith D (1997) The religion of Constantius I. *Greek, Roman and Byzantine Studies* 38: 187–208.

Stead GC (1973) 'Eusebius' and the Council of Nicaea. *Journal of Theological Studies* 24: 85–100.

Stegemann E, Stegemann W (1999) *Jesus Movement: A Social History of the First Century.* Fortress Press.

Steuernagel D (2020) Roman baths as locations of religious practice. In: *Urban Religion in Late Antiquity.* Lätzer-Lazar A, Urciuoli ER (eds) De Gruyter.

Stevens P (2010) For whom the bell tolls: the monastic site at Clonfad 3, Co. Westmeath. In: *Creative Minds: Production, Manufacturing and Invention – Proceedings of a Public Seminar on Archaeological Discoveries on National Road Schemes.* Stanley MS, Danaher ED, Eogan JE (eds) National Roads Authority.

Stoll O (2022) The cult of Mithras and the Roman Imperial Army. In: *The Roman Empire.* Dillon M, Matthew C (eds) Pen & Sword Books.

Strabo (c. 17–23 CE). *Geography* Volume VI: Books 13–14. Jones HL (tr). Loeb Classical Library 223. Harvard University Press (1929).

Teall JL (1959) The grain supply of the Byzantine Empire, 330–1025. *Dumbarton Oaks Papers* 13: 87–139.

Teitler HC (1992) Un-Roman activities in late antique Gaul: the cases of Arvandus and Seronatus. In: *Fifth-Century Gaul: A Crisis of Identity?* Drinkwater J & Elton H (eds) Cambridge University Press.

Theuws F (2009) Grave goods, ethnicity, and the rhetoric of burial rites in Late Antique Northern Gaul. In: *Ethnic Constructs in Antiquity: The Role of Power and Tradition.* Dennis T & Roymans N (eds) Amsterdam University Press.

Touber J (2016) Patristic scholarship and religious contention, 1678–1716: the rediscovery and publication of Lactantius's 'De Mortibus Persecutorum,' with special focus on Gijsbert Cuper (1644–1716). *Church History and Religious Culture* 96: 266–303.

Underwood NR (2018) *The Professionalization of the Clergy in Late Antiquity.* PhD thesis. University of California, Berkeley.

Underwood NR (2020) Labouring for God. In: *Capital, Investment, and Innovation in the Roman World.* Erdkamp P, Verboven K, Zuiderhoek A (eds) Oxford University Press.

Unger DJ, Dillon DJ (1992) *St Irenaeus of Lyons Against the Heresies.* Newman Press.

Van Dam R (1992) *Leadership and Community in Late Antique Gaul.* University of California Press.

Vargas MM (2016) *Causes of the Jewish Diaspora Revolt in Alexandria: Regional Uprisings from the Margins of Greco-Roman Society.* MA thesis. University of North Texas.

Vermaseren MJ (1955) The new Mithraic temple in London. *Numen* 2: 139–145.

Villing A (2002) For whom did the bell toll in ancient Greece? Archaic and Classical Greek bells at Sparta and beyond. *Annual of the British School at Athens* 97: 223–295.

Visser J (2014) Sidonius Apollinaris, Ep. II.2: the man and his villa. *Journal for Late Antique Religion and Culture* 8: 26–45.

Wade-Evans AW (ed) (1944) *Vitae Sanctorum Britanniae et Genealogiae.* University of Wales Press.

Warner R (1991) The earliest history of Ireland. In: *The Illustrated Archaeology of Ireland.* Ryan M (ed) Country House.

Welch JW (2011) How rich was Paul? . . .And why it matters. In: *Bountiful Harvest: Essays in Honor of S. Kent Brown.* Skinner AC, Davis DM, Griffin C (eds) Brigham Young University.

Willmott HB, Daubney A (2020) Of saints, sows or smiths? Copper-brazed iron handbells in Early Medieval England. *Archaeological Journal* 177: 336–355.

Wood IN (1992) Continuity or calamity: the constraints of literary models. In: *Fifth-Century Gaul: A Crisis of Identity?* Drinkwater J & Elton H (eds) Cambridge University Press.

Wood IN (2022) The distribution and redistribution of Church wealth in early medieval Europe. In: *The Christian Economy in the Early Medieval West: Towards a Temple Society.* Wood IN (ed) Punctum Books.

Young, F (1977) Christian attitudes to finance in the first four centuries. *Epworth Review* 4.3: 78–86.

Ziche H (2022) Misremembering Constantine in Eusebius and Zosimus. In: *Making and Unmaking Ancient Memory.* De Marre M, Bhola RK (eds) Routledge.

ACKNOWLEDGEMENTS

Writing a book that brings together ideas from history, archaeology and economics has been a huge challenge, and I'll be eternally grateful to all those colleagues who have so kindly and generously shared their expertise and insights with me, and especially to those who carefully read and commented on drafts. It's important to say that any errors which persist in these pages are all mine.

A huge thank you, then, to Socrates Koursoumis, archaeologist in the Hellenic Ministry of Culture in Greece, who showed me the wonders of ancient Corinth; Tim Young, geo-archaeologist at the University of Cardiff, who shared his new findings at Llantwit Major with me, as well as sharing insights on relationships between monasteries, kingdoms, Samson and Illtud; Catherine Nixey, historian and author; David Gwynn, Reader in Ancient and Late Antique History at Royal Holloway, University of London; Philip Burton, Reader in Latin and Early Christian Studies at the University of Birmingham; and Francesca Stavrakopoulou, historian of religion at Exeter University. And I am particularly indebted to John Hines, of the University of Cardiff. Thank you all so much.

I must also thank my fabulous literary agent Luigi Bonomi,

and all the fantastic team at Simon & Schuster, but especially my amazing editor, Kat Ailes. And my family – my children who get to hear all about the latest chapter on our dog walks, and my husband, who is always a great sounding board and cooks the best prawn patia to boot.

INDEX

Britain/Britannia — *continued*
  Germanus in 117–20
  mosaics in 213–14
  monastery, earliest in 2–8, 10, 12, 71,
      78–9, 94, 106, 314
  Roman army invades (43 CE) 79
  Roman army withdraws from (410
      CE) 3, 48, 91, 105–6, 117, 215
  Roman bells in 1, 3–5, 23, 26, 72,
      375–7
  Roman coups originate in 108,
      171–2
  Roman villas in 89, 90, 91–3, 95–6,
      151, 213–14
  See also individual nation name
Brittany xii, 7, 81, 84, 106
  Armorica 30, 47, 48, 54, 57–8, 60,
      64–5, 107, 108, 119
  early archaeological traces of
      Christianity in 71–5, 80
  origins of 45–57, 107
  ruin of 57–66, 90
  saints in 8–10, 12, 14, 16, 17–31, 34,
      74–5, 80, 237, 281, 333, 368
Bronze Age 78, 80, 242
brooches 50, 60, 61–2, 67
Brown, Peter 263
Bryant, Chris 217
Bryant, Joseph 255
Budoc, Bishop of Dol 75, 76
Burdigalam 113, 114, 115
Burgundians 106, 108, 109, 120–21,
    127, 130
burials xi, 18
  Anglo-Saxon graves 67, 80, 92
  Brittany and 71–3
  cemeteries xi, 67, 68, 69, 71, 79, 80,
      92–5
  female 61
  'Germanic' 60–64
  graves *see* graves
  mass burials 253
  orientation of graves 66, 68–9
  parish churches and 151–2
  'rituals of termination' 80
  Roman 151

saints and 69
villa sites 80, 91–5, 151
weapons appearing in 60, 66
Byzantium 193, 195, 332, 372

Cadfan, King 55
Cadoc, Saint 11, 34
Cadog, Saint 27
Caecilianus, Bishop of Carthage 191
Caerleon 79
Caermead 79–80, 94
caesares (deputy emperors) 166, 168, 171,
    172, 173, 177, 189, 200, 299–300,
    305, 346
Caesarean Games 302
Caldey Island 12, 30, 43
Caledonia 171
Callicinum 231
Callistus, Bishop of Rome 249
Cappadocia 99, 279–80
Caracalla, Emperor 143, 154
Caradoc, Saint 4
Carausius 108
Cardiff University 2
Carlisle 344–5
Carthage 112–13, 191, 251, 252, 279,
    303, 309
Carus, Emperor 166
Cassius Dio 160, 307
Castor 195
cathedrals 5, 20, 149, 150, 154, 230,
    231, 233
Catholicism 17, 105, 123, 133; 'catholic',
    term 104, 121
celebrity 34, 35, 36–7, 39, 43–4, 270,
    319
celibacy 9
Celts/Celtic 73, 81
  crosses 6
  insular or Celtic Church 3, 6, 21,
      28–9, 31, 33, 45, 50, 55
  languages 18–19, 26, 56, 94
  term 18, 45–6
cemeteries xi, 67, 68, 69, 71, 79, 80,
    92–5
Cephas 291